W9-BCZ-147

Revolutionary Afghanistan

A Reappraisal

Beverley Male

ST. MARTIN'S PRESS NEW YORK

Wingate College Library

©Beverley Male 1982

All rights reserved. For information, write:
St. Martin's Press, Inc., 175 Fifth Avenue, New York, NY 10010
Printed in Great Britain
First published in the United States of America in 1982

Library of Congress Cataloging in Publication Data

Male, Beverley.
    Revolutionary Afghanistan.

    Bibliography: p. 216.
    1. Afghanistan – Politics and government – 1973-.
I. Title
DS371.2.M34 1982   958'.1044   81-14443
ISBN 0-312-67997-1   AACR2

089220

CONTENTS

Preface

PREFACE

The idea for this book arose from a visit to Kabul in March 1979 when it became immediately obvious that what was happening in Afghanistan bore little relation to reports appearing in the Western media. Further research subsequently reinforced that impression. Much of the material on which the book is based was collected in the course of my 1979 field trip which took me to India, Pakistan and the United Kingdom as well as Afghanistan and during a follow-up trip to India and Pakistan from December 1980 to January 1981. Unfortunately by then times had changed and on this second occasion the Afghan government refused me a visa.

Texts of speeches and statements by Afghan leaders and other Afghan government documents have for the most part been taken from the *Kabul Times*, since these are in effect the official version. I have however taken the liberty where necessary of adjusting the syntax of the Afghan translator.

The problem of transliteration is inescapable, and at the risk of offending the purists I have chosen what appears to be the simplest spelling of Afghan names and have tried to be consistent. Where I have failed, I beg the reader's indulgence and plead in defence that not even the *Kabul Times* achieved complete consistency in this respect.

Writing about contemporary politics is always a little like assembling a jigsaw puzzle knowing that some of the pieces are missing. Revolutionary Afghanistan is no exception. While it is important to acknowledge the gaps it seems worthwhile to attempt to put together the pieces available in the hope that a more accurate picture may emerge than many others so far presented. As new pieces are discovered they can be placed in position. Although responsibility for assembling this particular jigsaw and hence for the overall picture must ultimately and inevitably be my own, I should like to express my gratitude to those who helped me fill some of the gaps.

My thanks must go first of all to the many people in India, Pakistan and Afghanistan, and in Australia who talked to me freely, frankly and at length about the people and events in Afghanistan with which many of them had been intimately connected. To name them all would be to create severe embarrassment for some; to name only a few would be unjust to the others. But they will know who I mean. Some of them will probably disagree with what I have written but I hope they will not feel that they have been misrepresented.

I should also like to thank Dr Richard Lawless of the Documentation Section of the Centre for the Middle East and Islamic Studies at the University of Durham for placing the facilities of the Section at my disposal; Professor Brian Beddie, who once described Afghanistan as a contagious disease, but who nevertheless gave generous support to the project; Mrs Shirley Mason, who patiently typed and re-typed the manuscript, and who was an unfailing source of encouragement throughout; those many good friends who bore stoically with my obsession, gave me unstinting and kindly assistance and (happily) are still talking to me; and last but by no means least, my parents Mary and Bruce Male to whom I owe a debt of gratitude beyond words.

I heard they brought him wounded;
My heart started pounding in fear,
What if the wound is on his back?

(Anonymous Pashtun couplet)

The leader of the People's Democratic Party of Afghanistan always said the object of the struggle should not be death because this emanates from adventurism and egoism. The struggle should aim at rescuing the people from oppressive exploitation. And this struggle calls for gallantry, resistance and patience. Therefore, one should live to struggle . . .

(Hafizullah Amin, 21 February 1979)

IN SEARCH OF HAFIZULLAH AMIN

When Soviet tanks rumbled across the Afghan border and down through the Hindu Kush in December 1979 the Western world was shaken from its post-Christmas torpor. Why had the Russians made such a dramatic and potentially dangerous move? For some the answer was simple: they thought the Soviets were heading for the oil fields and warm waters of the Persian Gulf. The fact that if this was so the Russians were going the long way around and doing it the hard way was an inconvenience swiftly dismissed by the protagonists of the expansionist school.

Others saw the Soviet move as essentially defensive, although they were divided over precisely what it was the USSR was defending itself against. Two such schools of thought argued that the Soviet objective was to prevent the imminent overthrow of a neighbouring communist government but they differed over the nature of the threat confronting that government. One group believed it came from an invincible Islamic tide, already sweeping Iran and Pakistan, intolerant of the alien, atheist, Marxist philosophy represented by the People's Democratic Party of Afghanistan, and with serious implications for the security of the Soviet Central Asian republics to the north. The other, discounting the political importance of Islam, claimed that the Afghan government had too narrow a base of support and had alienated even this by its harsh measures. It was losing its grip, not before an Islamic rebellion, but in the face of mounting internal chaos. In either case, the overthrow of the Afghan government would have serious consequences for the USSR.

These two theories proved convenient for both the right and the left. For the right, the imminent collapse of the PDPA government before an overwhelming Islamic uprising was important, for a socialist revolution must not be allowed to appear successful. For the left, the myth that the government was no longer in control of a situation which threatened the survival of the PDPA regime is essential, because it saves the necessity of explaining the destruction by the Soviet Union of a perfectly competent socialist government.

A third school of thought argued that, as a result of the instability in Iran and the seizure of the American hostages in Tehran the USSR perceived the international environment as suddenly more menacing. It therefore moved to replace a government in Afghanistan which, even though it was socialist, Moscow could not control and regarded as

Wingate College Library

potentially hostile, with one more amenable to Soviet tutelage.

At the centre of this controversy was one man, Hafizullah Amin, the Afghan President destroyed by the Soviet intervention. Seldom has any revolution been so widely misrepresented as that which began in Afghanistan in April 1978, or any revolutionary leader so viciously slandered as Hafizullah Amin. For the most part Amin has been condemned with scant regard for the evidence by his enemies across the ideological spectrum. They claim that he was at once so cunning and powerful that no one could outmanoeuvre him, and so weak and unpopular that he was about to be overthrown. The fact remains that Amin commanded immense personal loyalty among members of the PDPA and the armed forces. When he was finally overthrown, it was not by any internal Afghan opposition, but by four thousand specially trained Soviet airborne troops, backed by three divisions of the Soviet army. Despite the claims of Babrak Karmal, the new Soviet-backed Afghan president, that Amin had lost the support of the Revolutionary Council, Karmal was able to retain only four of Amin's ministers, while three of the former president's closest supporters, including one who had been involved in the early stages of the April 1978 uprising, were executed in June 1980.[1]

For the persistent misrepresentation of events in Afghanistan the Western media bears special, but by no means sole, responsibility.

Afghanistan has traditionally been recognised as a difficult country from which to report and about which to collect information, but the problem was compounded, after the 1978 Revolution, by journalists who arrived with preconceived ideas which they never questioned. Those who bothered to interview President Taraki or his Foreign Minister Hafizullah Amin seldom reported these interviews (the texts of which were usually published in the *Kabul Times* or broadcast over Kabul Radio) in any depth. Despite the frequently hostile and ignorant questions, Taraki and Amin patiently tried to explain what their revolution was about. Consistently they requested that Western journalists report accurately and honestly what they had been told, what they had seen. They might as well have saved their breath. The stories were written long before the journalists set foot in Kabul. One American journalist who went to Kabul in the wake of the April Revolution did not wait for President Taraki's first press conference on 6 May despite the uncertainty in the West regarding the aims of the new leadership. 'I had all the atmosphere I needed, and I figured I could get the rest from the wire-services', he said.[2] A *New York Times* report gave more column inches to an unidentified student malcontent than it did to the Afghan

Foreign Minister, with whom the journalist had recently had a long interview, and even then, he managed to quote Amin out of context.[3]

In contrast, press conferences given by leaders of the Afghan counter-revolution in Pakistan were reported sympathetically and uncritically, their extravagant claims taken at face value. Propaganda was one of their principal and most effective weapons, and the journalists who swallowed the line and wrote up the stories became the *de facto* allies of the counter-revolution.

The problem of misleading reporting grew worse as the power struggle within the Afghan leadership developed through the summer of 1979. Most writers failed even to attempt to discover the issues involved, remaining content to take the easy way out and explain the conflict in terms of personalities. The chief victim of this apparently deliberate campaign of slander was Hafizullah Amin, whose central role in the People's Democratic Party and in the Afghan government, though widely recognised, has been widely misunderstood.

In the wake of the Soviet invasion of December 1979, in the course of which Amin was overthrown and probably killed, the Soviet and Afghan propaganda machines have joined the Western media in an all-out attempt to discredit him. Evidence which contradicts conventional wisdom has often been ignored, and if reported at all, is not allowed to interfere with well established myths.

Consider the widely accepted image of Amin as a ruthless executioner, destroying any who opposed him – a man whose actions, it is often suggested, bordered on genocide. Let us look at the record. There can be little doubt, in the light of the subsequent activities of Babrak Karmal and his associates, that there was more than a grain of truth in the allegations made by Taraki and Amin in September 1978 that Karmal and the Parchamites, along with certain senior army officers, were plotting against them. Yet Babrak Karmal, Anahita Ratebzada, Nur Ahmad Nur, Abdul Wakil and Mahmoud Baryalai were merely posted abroad as ambassadors. When the full extent of their activities was discovered they were recalled. Instead of returning to Afghanistan they vanished. There was some speculation in the Western press that they had been killed. Several others were arrested and imprisoned, including the Defence Minister, Abdul Qadir, the Planning Minister, Sultan Ali Kishtmand, the Public Works Minister, Mohammad Rafie and the Chief of the General Staff Lieutenant-General Shahpur. Again there was wide speculation that they had been summarily executed. However, in October 1979, after he emerged victorious from the power struggle with Taraki, Amin as President *commuted the death sentences passed on*

Qadir and Kishtmand and reduced the prison sentence awarded Rafie.
The only prominent member of that conspiracy who presumably was
executed was Lieutenant-General Shahpur. Was this action of Amin's
that of a ruthless killer? Compare it with the record of Babrak Karmal
since he became President!

Consistently, people believed to have been executed at Amin's behest
have reappeared in Babrak Karmal's Revolutionary Council, or among
the ranks of rebel leaders in Peshawar, yet no admission has ever been
made that earlier assessments of Amin might have been mistaken.

But what, people will ask, became of the 17,000 prisoners in Puli
Charki prison in Kabul, who 'vanished' during Taraki's and Amin's rule?
Surely this proves that Amin was a mass murderer?

Even if the figure of 17,000 deaths *was* correct, it would not be a
particularly large figure in the context of the bitter counter-revolutionary
campaign being waged by the remnants of the *ancien regime* whose own
record of violence, before and after the April Revolution, is well documented. And it is not clear that Hafizullah Amin would bear the sole
responsibility. But where did this figure of 17,000 come from?

When I was in Kabul in March 1979 the common figure for prisoners
in Puli Charki, cited by expatriate Westerners, was 12,000. I was unable
to find any documentation for this figure and efforts to discover its
source led me repeatedly to the American Embassy. I therefore dis-
counted it as a further sample of the 'black propaganda' being spread
about the Afghan government. Then, in a report published by Amnesty
International in September 1979,[4] the figure of 12,000 appeared publicly for the first time. It was thereafter sanctified by this prestigious
international organisation. Amnesty International was particularly
critical of what it regarded as lack of co-operation from the Afghan
government, and of its alleged record of human rights violations. They
did acknowledge that the record of previous Afghan governments in
this respect also left something to be desired, but it is significant that
they never bothered to send a delegation to Afghanistan *before* the
April 1978 Revolution.

Press reports subsequently referred to a list published in Kabul of
12,000 'missing' persons, although the list has never materialised. Hafizullah Amin denied any knowledge of such a list, and also denied that
there were anything like 12,000 political prisoners in Puli Charki. He
did however acknowledge the existence of some political prisoners in
Afghanistan, estimating the number at 'about 1000' a rather unusual
candour, for government leaders seldom admit to holding political
prisoners at all.[5]

After the Soviet invasion, when the doors of Puli Charki were 'flung open' by the Karmal regime, 2000 political prisoners emerged. What happened, then, to the other 10,000? There was never any suggestion in the Western media that Amin's estimate of 1000 was a more nearly correct figure and that Amnesty International and the Western press had been wrong. No: the 'missing' 10,000 must have been executed by Amin, along with another 7,000 thrown in for good measure, a figure no one has ever attempted to explain!

The present Afghan government and the Soviet Union have also played a not inconsiderable part in perpetuating the image of Amin as a mass murderer, although Babrak Karmal has so far been completely unsuccessful in discovering even a single mass grave, despite his early exhortations to the Afghan people to search for the many he claimed existed. And yet the myth of Amin as a mass murderer persists, perpetuated by refugees who fled an Afghanistan no longer being run in their class interest; by Babrak Karmal's regime, which depends heavily on it in order to legitimise its own seizure of power; by the US which uses Amin's 'appalling human rights record' to excuse its failure to heed his appeals; and by a group of leftist intellectuals outside Afghanistan for whom the alternative is too embarrassing to contemplate.

The portrayal of Amin as a butcher, while the most vicious of them, is not the only persistent myth concerning him. Scarcely less dangerous, since it provides much of the basis for the other, is the myth that he was a ruthless megalomaniac unable to rest until he had destroyed all his rivals, and which identifies him as the real power in Afghanistan from the time of the April revolution or soon after. Amin was certainly a powerful figure, both in the party before the revolution and in the government afterwards, though his power has usually been exaggerated, was always under challenge, and was nowhere near decisive until he became President in September 1979.

His appointment as Prime Minister at the end of March 1979, whereby he is commonly assumed to have pushed Taraki sideways into the Presidency and grabbed supreme power for himself was in fact a neat manoeuvre on Taraki's part to isolate Amin, leaving him with the prestigious sounding title of Prime Minister, but retaining real power in the office of the President. Amin was in the unenviable position of being held responsible for the chaos which developed in Afghanistan during the summer of 1979, without being able to do anything to prevent it. Once he regained control of the Defence Ministry, and especially after he became President, far from losing his grip in the face of either a religious-inspired rebellion, or mounting internal chaos, he began to implement policies which showed every sign of stopping the rot and consolidating the revolution. But his efforts were cut short after only three months by the Soviet military intervention.

Another persistent belief among some Westerners, especially Americans, is that Amin was fanatically pro-Soviet. As a socialist, Amin could be expected to adopt a similar position on many international issues to that of the Soviet Union. Nor is it surprising that the PDPA government, of which he was an influential member, sought Soviet advice and assistance in economic planning and development. As a realist, Amin recognised that Afghanistan was, and had been, locked into a position of military and economic dependence on the Soviet Union long before the April 1978 revolution. His aim was to minimise this dependence, to keep other options open, and, at least from the end of 1978, to prevent further Soviet encroachment into Afghanistan. Most important he sought to keep control of the levers of power in Afghan hands.

Although the image of Amin as a Soviet stooge took a battering when the news leaked out of Soviet involvement in the attempt to kill him in September 1979, and was further shaken by the Soviet invasion in December in which he was overthrown, it is still propagated by Americans who use it to help explain their government's failure to hear and to heed the signals Amin was sending out long before September 1979.

It has been challenged from the left by the equally damaging allegation that Amin was a CIA agent. This has been taken up with enthusiasm only by Babrak Karmal who uses it as a device to legitimise his own regime. Despite his claim to have known that Amin worked for the CIA from the 1950s, and his assertion that he has documentary evidence to prove it, Karmal has so far failed to produce anything convincing to this effect. Some foreign socialists explain it away, privately, by claiming that the new regime wanted to discredit Amin, and the easiest way to do this among simple Afghan peasants was to say that he was working for the Americans. A more sophisticated explanation, from a source sympathetic to Karmal is that 'people in Afghanistan were so horrified by Amin's policies, which they thought were damaging the revolution, that the only explanation they could find was that he must be a CIA agent'.[6] Although the USSR was prepared to run this line to a domestic audience in a film on Afghanistan made early in 1980, it has been more circumspect in communications with foreign audiences. In an article on CIA interference in the third world, published in the monthly journal *International Affairs*, references to Afghanistan make no mention of Amin.[7]

The uncomfortable fact, for both Russians and Americans, is that Amin would not allow himself to be manipulated by either of them. If the conventional view of Amin is not supported by the evidence – and clearly it is not – what is the truth? If he was not a genocidal megalomaniac, a Soviet stooge or a CIA agent, what was he? What was his role in the Afghan revolution? And why was it so important for the Soviet Union to destroy him?

Notes

1. Those retained were Saleh Mohammad Zeary, Dastagir Panjsheri, Mohammad Ismael Danesh, and Mohammad Hassan Bareq Shafie, though only Danesh was given ministerial responsibility by Karmal. Zeary and Panjsheri remained members of the Politburo. Those executed were Mohammad Zarif, Mohammad Siddiq Alemyar and Sahib Jan Sahrayi.
2. Conversation with the author, December 1980.
3. 13 November 1978, pp. 1, 45.
4. Amnesty International, *Violations of Human Rights and Fundamental Freedoms in the Democratic Republic of Afghanistan: An Amnesty International Report* (London, September 1979), p. 8.
5. Interview, *Corriere Della Serra* (Milan) 3 July 1979, text *Kabul Times* (hereafter *KT*), 7 July 1979.
6. Conversation with the author, New Delhi, December 1980.
7. V. Petrusenko, 'The CIA and Imperialist Propaganda', *International Affairs* (Moscow), no. 4, 1980.

2 THREE REVOLUTIONARIES

In 1929, the year Hafizullah Amin was born, Afghanistan was convulsed by a tribal uprising. King Amanullah's ambitious plans for modernising his country were in shreds and every significant political force was arrayed against him. In January, with the charismatic Tajik bandit leader Bacha-i-Saqao ('Son of a Water-carrier') threatening Kabul, Amanullah abdicated and left for Kandahar, deep in Ghilzai Pashtun country, where he made a last-ditch attempt to rally support. Within days of Amanullah's departure from Kabul the city fell to the Bacha who proclaimed himself King. However much they disliked Amanullah, the Pashtun tribes, accustomed to ruling Afghanistan themselves, found the prospect of a Tajik on the throne utterly unacceptable. Seeing his opportunity Nadir Khan, the most prominent member of another branch of the Durrani Pashtun royal family, returned with his brothers from exile in France in March 1929 and began to rally the tribes in the eastern provinces bordering the British Indian North-West Frontier. By May it was clear to Amanullah that his situation was hopeless, his life threatened both by the Ghilzais and the Bacha's troops. He fled to the Indian border and later sailed with his family for exile in Europe.[1]

It was not until October, just before the coming of winter threatened to delay his campaign that Nadir Khan was able to gather enough support to mount a final, successful offensive against the Bacha. He received decisive assistance from two sources. Sher Agha, a prominent Ghilzai tribal leader and brother of Afghanistan's most powerful religious figure, the Hazrat of Shor Bazaar, decided that his political ambition would best be served by supporting Nadir Khan. He was able to bring with him the backing of the Ghilzai tribes, traditional rivals of the Durrani Pashtuns, as well as the religious establishment. Nadir Khan also received tacit assistance from the British, who turned a blind eye to his recruitment of the border tribes to his cause. With this powerful backing he entered Kabul in mid-October and was proclaimed king. The Bacha was captured and hanged. Nadir Khan, now Nadir Shah, proceeded to dismantle Amanullah's reforms.

Fifty years later Hafizullah Amin attempted to carry on where Amanullah had been forced to leave off. Like Amanullah, Amin was a romantic. Where Amanullah, having toured Europe, dreamed of giving Afghanistan the benefits of modern industrial civilisation, Amin's vision was a society 'void of exploitation of man by man'. Like Amanullah, he was also a nationalist – the dream was not to be achieved at the cost of subjugation to a foreign power. There, however, the resemblance ends, for Amin, although of a relatively privileged background did not have the access to power afforded Amanullah as a member of the royal family.

Amin's official biography describes his family as 'intellectual, and from the economic view-point . . . lower middle income group . . .'[2] They lived in a village in the district of Paghman, some 25 kilometres west of Kabul, and although Hafizullah spent much of his later life in the city, his roots were in the Afghan countryside. As a young boy he walked a distance of twelve kilometres to the government-run primary school at Paghman, where he received his elementary education.

His father, Habibullah, was a low-ranking civil servant, which suggests that he was well enough educated by the standards of his day (when only about two per cent of the population was literate) and had good enough contacts to get a civil service job, but that he lacked the influence necessary to rise high enough in the hierarchy to acquire wealth or power. The upper ranks of the civil service were the preserve of the Durrani Pashtun aristocracy, and Habibullah Amin, though a Pashtun, was a Ghilzai.

Although a powerful tribe, the Ghilzais had never succeeded in breaking the Durrani grip on power in Afghanistan.[3] A Ghilzai rebellion had been savagely suppressed by the Amir Abdur Rahman in the 1890s, after which many members of the tribe were bought off with grants of land. Amin's family was probably one of these, which might explain how they came to be living in Paghman, far from traditional Ghilzai territory in the south-east. Although 'pacified', the Ghilzais were never trusted, and were confined to the lower ranks of the civil service and the officer corps, where they remained a constant, potential source of opposition to Durrani dominance. It is not surprising, therefore, that Habibullah Amin failed to gain promotion, or that Hafizullah grew up in a radical household.

Little more is known of Habibullah, who died when Hafizullah, his younger son, was still a child. His elder son, Abdullah, now took responsibility for the family. A school teacher himself, Abdullah probably persuaded his younger brother to follow suit. Hafizullah gained entry as a boarder to the Dar-ul-Mualimeen Teacher Training High School in Kabul, one means by which intelligent children of less well-off or influential families could gain access to higher education. The oldest and most prestigious of Afghanistan's teacher training institutions, entry to Dar-ul-Mualimeen was by competitive examination; and only those who had completed at least nine years schooling were accepted. Teaching qualifications guaranteed employment in Afghanistan where there was a serious shortage of teachers at all levels. They had civil service status and, although salary levels were low, certain fringe benefits such as subsidised food and fuel were important. An added incentive was that six years' service as a teacher carried exemption from military service.

Amin's official biographers are reticent on the subject of his family, but there is evidence that he relied heavily on them, especially in his later political career. In 1954 he married a Pashtun girl. They had seven children, the eldest of whom, a daughter, was married to Abdullah's son, Assadullah. Though radical in most other respects, in this at least the Amin family adhered to tribal custom, for, according to Pashtun tradition, a first cousin is the preferred marriage partner.

After the April 1978 Revolution, Abdullah Amin was made head of the Spinzar Company, the big government-owned textile enterprise and the largest manufacturing concern in Afghanistan. In the difficult days of August 1979 Hafizullah appointed his brother Chief of Security for the four northern provinces of Samangan, Kunduz, Takhar and Baghlan, which straddled the highway south from the Soviet border to the strategic Salang tunnel on the road to Kabul. His nephew and son-in-law Assadullah, a doctor of medicine by profession, was first appointed Deputy Minister for Public Health, and later Deputy Minister for Political Affairs in the Foreign Ministry. After Hafizullah became President in September 1979 he put Assadullah in charge of the Security Police. His eldest son, Abdur Rahman, scarcely out of his teens, acted frequently though informally as his father's representative; officially he was a member of the Central Board of the Khalqi Organisation of Afghan Youth (KOAY) and later its Deputy President. In his tendency to place his greatest trust in members of his immediate family, Hafizullah Amin remained true to one of the oldest Afghan traditions, but it was a practice that would eventually, in the hands of his enemies, serve as a weapon against him.

By coincidence the man who was to become Hafizullah Amin's greatest rival, and who would ultimately defeat him, was also born in 1929, a few miles away in Kabul city.[4] But Babrak Karmal's background was entirely different. His family were members of the Durrani Pashtun aristocracy, highly urbanised and alienated from their tribal roots. They spoke Dari, a variant of Farsi and the language of the Persianised Durrani court, rather than Pashtu, the tribal language. While Hafizullah Amin could appeal to the tribes in their own language, Babrak Karmal was never accepted by them. 'He is not a Pashtun, he speaks only Dari', was a frequent comment.

In contrast to Amin, Babrak Karmal enjoyed all the privileges that flowed from membership of a prominent aristocratic family associated with the royal house. His father, Mohammad Hussain Khan, was a senior army officer who subsequently became a general, Commander of the Armed Forces in southern Afghanistan and Governor of Paktya.

Karmal was educated at one of Afghanistan's oldest secondary schools, the Amani High School, founded in 1923 as part of King Amanullah's campaign to westernise education, at least of the Kabul elite. Three such schools were established by him: Amaniyeh in 1922, modelled on the French system and later re-named Lycee Istiqlal; Amani in 1924, on the German pattern and staffed by German as well as a few Afghan teachers; and Ghazi in 1927, using English as the medium of instruction.

After Amanullah's overthrow, the Amani High School, many of whose students remained loyal to Amanullah and his aims, became a centre of opposition. Amani students had a history of violent political activity directed both against the new royal family and the British. In 1933 former Amani students were responsible for the assassination of the Afghan Ambassador to Germany, Mohammad Aziz, a brother of Nadir Shah and father of Daoud. Later that year an Amani student assassinated Nadir Shah himself, and another made an attempt on the life of the British envoy in Kabul.[5] Mohammad Hussain Khan's decision to send his son to the Amani High School suggests that he had some sympathy with Amanullah's attempt at modernisation, and that there was also a degree of radicalism in the family atmosphere in which Babrak grew up, although of a different kind from that surrounding Amin. Babrak's later political activity caused his father considerable embarrassment, and resulted eventually in estrangement between them, ending only after Babrak became President.

Meanwhile, in the small village of Sur Kalai (Red Town) in Ghazni province, the twelve year old boy who would one day found the People's Democratic Party of Afghanistan, was attending one of the very few primary schools then in existence in rural Afghanistan. Nur Mohammad Taraki came from a far less privileged family than either Amin or Karmal. Ghilzais, the family was described by Taraki's official biographer as 'semi-peasant, semi-shepherds'.[6] The biography emphasises the family's poverty — for example it claims that Taraki, at the age of five 'was hired as a hand by a widow, running her errands and looking after her house', and that his father Nazir Mohammad Taraki, an illiterate semi-nomad, 'was always bothered by problems arising in connection with his precarious mode of living.' Despite these problems the young Taraki managed to secure a primary education which he completed in 1932, and this at a time when primary education was barely established in the cities, let alone the villages of Afghanistan. Furthermore, his father had also managed by this stage to become literate, a remarkable achievement for one in his position.

It is likely that Taraki's biographers, in the interests of revolutionary mythology, exaggerated his family's poor economic circumstances and emphasised his peasant-nomad connections, also for political reasons. But it is clear that, if he was not poor in Afghan terms, neither was he among the privileged of his society. After leaving school in 1932 Taraki took a job as an office boy with the Pashtun Company in Kandahar. He was later sent as a clerk to the Bombay Branch of the company, where he learned English and completed his matriculation at night school. It was in Bombay that he first became acquainted with the principles of Marxism. In 1939 he moved to Kabul where he joined the civil service. He did not fit easily into the system and was soon transferred to Badakhshan, surely the Siberia of Afghanistan and a penance, as was any provincial appointment, to a Kabul bureaucrat. The publication of a number of socially critical articles and novels did not endear him to the authorities, but despite this he managed to return to the capital where he was involved in the political ferment that developed in the late 1940s.

Not until Habibullah became king in 1901 was a conscious effort made to open Afghanistan to European ideas and influences. The first newspaper was not established until 1911.[7] The first modern secondary school (for boys only) was established in 1904, and the foreign teachers brought in were mostly Indian Muslims. Habibullah did plan to send some students to Europe but World War I and internal opposition prevented him. In 1921 and 1922 Amanullah sent some members of the royal family and other aristocratic families to France and Germany for study. With the establishment of the first faculty of Kabul University in 1932 – the School of Medicine – European teachers began to be employed, a trend that gathered momentum as the education system expanded and insufficient Afghan teachers were available to fill the posts.[8]

One result of this slow development was that an urban intelligentsia receptive to ideas of European radicalism did not develop until the 1940s. The appointment as Prime Minister in 1945, of Shah Mahmud, the youngest of the King's uncles, initiated a period of political ferment. Under the influence of the new Western-educated elite, Shah Mahmud

made an attempt to hold elections less rigidly controlled than previously, leading, in 1949, to the so-called 'liberal parliament'. He also
relaxed press censorship, and immediately a number of opposition
papers appeared, with political groups forming around them. The revo-
utionary movement in Afghanistan had its roots in what became known
as the Wish-i-Zalmaiyan period. Wish-i-Zalmaiyan, or 'Awakened Youth'
was the most important of the organisations that sprang up during Shah
Mahmud's brief flirtation with liberalism. Established in 1947,[9] it had
roots in Kandahar but attracted a broad cross-section of Kabul's newly
emerged intelligentsia who supported radical political and social reform.
The Soviet historian Akhramovich described it in the following terms:

> Not possessing a distinct organizational structure and noted for its
> mixed membership, the movement at first was more like a trend
> made up of the most diverse social views and sentiments, and often
> the only thing that was common to all of them was the desire to
> find a way to get rid of the confusion obtaining in the country. This
> movement became a centre of social ideas around which began the
> consolidation or polarisation of forces on a class basis.[10]

Several newspapers appeared, providing a platform for Wish-i-Zalmaiyan adherents. The best known were *Watan* (Homeland), *Nida'-yi-
Khalq* (Voice of the People) and *Angar* (Burning Embers).

Associated with *Watan* was a group many of whom rose to prominence during Zahir Shah's 'constitutional period' in the 1960s. The
assistant editors were Abdul Hai Aziz who became Minister of Planning
in the 1960s and Mir Mohammad Siddiq Farhang, a Deputy Minister of
Planning, and parliamentary leader in the Wolesi Jirga (lower house)
from 1965-9,[11] and who can be regarded as forming the right-wing of
Wish-i-Zalmaiyan. *Watan* emphasised legal reform and

> wrote that it would endeavour to defend the common interests of
> civil servants and peasants, workers and pensioners, to work for 'the
> passing of democratic legislation to cover all civil matters,' equal
> rights for all, freedom of choosing an occupation, freedom of move-
> ment, the inviolability of the person and property and observance
> of the law by the courts.[12]

Nida'-yi-Khalq, a Persian language bi-weekly also took a conservative
approach, accepting the necessity of the monarchy at least for the time
being and supporting the government's foreign policy (which claimed to

be non-aligned but tended then to be pro-American) though it argued for real non-alignment. It did however emphasise its demand for freedom of the press, legal reform and universal suffrage. In July 1951 the publishers of *Nida'-yi-Khalq* established a political party called Hizb-i-Khalq (People's Party), with the aim of achieving a 'secure social life', political rights, free speech and press, impartial courts, 'fair conditions for the employed' and universal education.[13] In consequence the government closed the newspaper and banned the party.[14]

Not surprisingly, Kabul University provided a focus for much of this political activity. The Students' Union in particular took a central role debating a wide range of topics in a thoroughly uninhibited fashion Students were also involved in the writing and production of plays attacking the royal family and Islam, activity which the government found intolerable, and which led in 1951 to the dissolution of the Students' Union.

The upsurge of political activity alarmed the ruling group and before the next elections in 1952 Shah Mahmud took steps to crush this liberal movement.[15] When Daoud became Prime Minister in 1953, although he pursued radical policies in other respects, he suppressed political activity altogether.

The revolutionary movement in Afghanistan had its roots in the Wish-i-Zalmaiyan period. The disillusionment which accompanied the abrupt termination of the experiment in liberalism was an important factor in the radicalisation of the men who later established the PDPA

Hafizullah Amin's student career gives an early indication of his preference for low-key, long-term organisational work at which he excelled, and which was to become characteristic of his political style in contrast to the high profile, high visibility approach adopted by Babrak Karmal.

After graduating from Dar-ul-Mualimeen, Amin went on to study mathematics and physics in the Science Faculty of Kabul University completing his degree, without interruption, in 1951. There is perhaps some exaggeration, designed to improve his revolutionary image, in his later claim to have taken an 'important' (though not a leading) role in the student movement.

> During the years of his education in Kabul University, he served as a teacher in Kabul Darul Muallimin, Kushal Khan and Rahman Baba high schools, [the] boarding high school and the financial course where he was held in deep affection in the hearts of all the students enlightening their socio-political understanding and making the

democratic movement among the students and teachers highly power-ful.[16]

It would have been unusual for a young man of Amin's intelligence and background not to have been influenced by and involved in the activity around him, particularly in the light of his later commitment to revolutionary politics. The fact remains that he did not attract the adverse attention of the authorities as did his more flamboyant con-temporary and later political rival, Babrak Karmal.

In 1952 Amin returned to Dar-ul-Mualimeen as a teacher, and in 1955 became teaching vice-principal. Soon after, he was appointed principal of Ibn Sina High School, another big teacher training establish-ment in Kabul. He was then in his mid-twenties.

These were the heady days of Sardar Mohammad Daoud's early premiership. In 1953 Daoud, in alliance with his cousin the King, staged a palace coup which removed their uncle, Shah Mahmud from the Prime Ministership and transferred power to the younger generation of the royal family. Daoud's appointment as Prime Minister signalled many changes. One of the most important was the abandonment of the old 'pay as you go' method of financing economic development. Given Afghanistan's limited revenue and the government's timid approach to direct taxation, 'pay as you go' and dependence on private investment condemned Afghanistan to slow and capricious economic progress. It was Daoud's intention to speed up this process under government direc-tion, and to finance the development by borrowing from whoever was prepared to lend the required sums. He proposed to modernise and expand the armed forces, since King Amanullah's experience had shown that a central government bent on modernisation was lost without a strong reliable military machine with which to enforce its will on the tribes. Such financial assistance might have been available from the United States, but the price was signature of a Mutual Security Agree-ment and membership in the anti-Soviet Middle East defence pact that the USA was trying to construct at the time. Daoud was also a national-ist, and well aware of Afghanistan's precarious position on the USSR's southern frontier. Membership of a US-backed anti-Soviet pact seemed to him a high price to pay for the assistance he sought. Furthermore Afghanistan had a long-standing territorial dispute with Pakistan regard-ing the border – the Durand line – which arbitrarily divided the Pashtun tribes in the frontier area and which Afghanistan refused to recognise.[17] Kabul argued that, just as Indian Muslims had been given the option, in a plebiscite, of staying with India or joining Pakistan, the Pashtun population should have been given a similar choice, i.e. of opting to become part of Afghanistan, where the Pashtuns are the dominant ethnic group. Afghanistan continued to call for 'self-determination' for Pakistan's Pashtun population. To enter a US-sponsored pact specifically directed against Afghanistan's most powerful neighbour, and of which Pakistan was also a member, did not appear to Daoud a useful way to advance Afghanistan's interests.

The Soviet Union, alarmed at the success of US pact-building with Turkey, Iran and Pakistan was anxious to encourage Afghanistan's independent approach. In December 1955 Bulganin and Khruschchev visited Kabul and endorsed Afghanistan's Pashtunistan policy and the following year concluded an aid agreement for $100 million — the largest amount of aid committed by the USSR outside the Soviet bloc. Soon after, agreements were reached regarding the provision of Soviet military training and equipment. This was the beginning of the Soviet Union's large-scale involvement in Afghanistan.

As a Pashtun, Hafizullah Amin apparently approved of the Prime Minister's foreign policy. One former student testified to Amin's political persuasiveness among those in the schools where he taught, recalling that he was in this period an advocate of Pashtun dominance and of Daoud's aggressive policy on Pashtunistan.[18]

Amin remained a nationalist, but later exposure to formal training in political science and economics, and to socialist thought and literature broadened his awareness and changed the direction of his political commitment and activity. Ironically, this development took place, not in the USSR where many young Afghans went for further education, but in the United States.

Despite the ambitious plans of successive Afghan governments to make education universal, free and compulsory, the country continued to suffer a chronic shortage of teachers, particularly in the villages. In 1954 the government, in co-operation with UNESCO and Columbia University Teachers' College, embarked on a plan for reorganising teacher training. The exercise was only partially effective, but the links with Columbia University continued. In 1957, Amin, now more involved in the administrative side of education than actual teaching, was sent to Columbia as a post-graduate student.

During the summer of 1958, while still working for his Master's degree, he took courses in political science and economics at the University of Wisconsin. He also joined the Socialist Progressive Club. This seems to have been a turning point. He later told an interviewer that he came to understand 'the situation in my country in which there was prevailing a feudal socio-economic system', adding 'I closely watched capitalist conditions too.'[19]

Back in Afghanistan he lectured for a time at the Education and Training Faculty of Kabul University, and in 1959 took over once more as principal of Ibn Sina High School. The following year he was appointed principal of Dar-ul-Mualimeen and then, six months later, transferred to the newly established Teacher Training Institute in the Ministry of Education. During this period all of Amin's appointments were in some way related not simply to teaching, but to teacher training, which placed him in an excellent position to communicate his political philosophy as widely as possible among one of the most important groups of people in Afghanistan: those responsible for the education of the youth of the country. It was through these people that the ground would gradually be prepared for the revolution Amin was convinced must take place. His was a long-term strategy, aimed first at the radicalisation of Afghan teachers, and through them the radicalisation of the Afghan population, especially the rural population.[20]

There could, of course, be no formal organisation. Daoud was still Prime Minister, and while in many ways he had an enlightened approach to economic and social development, politically his regime was extremely repressive. Amin had to move with caution. One means he used to raise the political consciousness of the student teachers was the production of dramas and sketches with a political theme, many of which he wrote himself and later published under a pseudonym.[21] Another method was to hold conferences, in the course of which he was able to communicate directly with the participants. His activities were not confined to Kabul. In 1961, for example, he was involved in a science teachers' workshop in Kandahar, which brought him into contact with teachers, men and women, already working in the province. By the early 1960s Amin had laid the foundations of an important power base in the rural areas as well as in Kabul where his influence was already considerable, not only among teachers, many of whom were his former students, but through them, among the new generation of students at the major schools in the capital.

The revolution must have seemed a long way off, as indeed it was, when in 1962 he won a scholarship for further post-graduate study at Columbia University, this time for a doctoral degree. Amin's decision to go a second time to the United States had incalculable consequences for his later political career, but at the time he could not have known that within a year Daoud would be removed from office and the political climate would change sufficiently to permit the formation, for the first time in Afghanistan, of a party committed to socialist ideals.

Hafizullah Amin's early career gives scarcely a hint of the formidable figure who would later emerge to assume the leadership of the PDPA. His political activity was directed towards the radicalisation of a generation of Afghan teachers and, through them, of the rural population. His success depended on his ability to maintain a low profile, to avoid attracting the attention of the authorities. In the process he was building for himself, almost incidentally, an important power base which would make his bid for the leadership possible. But at the same time, he was unable to acquire the revolutionary credentials that more overt political activity would have provided, and which would have made his claims to the leadership credible in the eyes of his contemporaries.

In contrast Babrak Karmal had every opportunity to obtain the appropriate credentials for revolutionary leadership. The Amani High School, from which he graduated in 1948, provided a springboard for his entry into radical student politics. His active role in the Kabul Students' Union, then the centre of student activity, is said to have resulted in his failure to gain admission to the Faculty of Law and Political Science in 1950. He was, however, admitted the following year.

His choice of the Law and Politics Faculty placed him in the mainstream of Kabul radical chic: it was the principal training ground for that westernised intellectual elite who provided the core of the country's politicians and diplomats. His political activity, at the time judged more dangerous than that of Amin, led to his arrest and imprisonment in 1953, before he completed his degree.

While in prison, Babrak Karmal met Mir Akbar Khyber, a recent graduate of the Military Academy a few years his senior who had also been imprisoned for his political activities. Khyber was one of the few Afghans already committed to Marxism, and under his influence Karmal's youthful rebelliousness against a repressive government acquired ideological direction. A close friendship developed between the two men who later formed the nucleus of what would become the *Parcham* faction of the PDPA.[22]

On his release from prison in 1956 Karmal worked briefly as a contract translator of English and German before being sent to the military reserve school in 1957 to undergo his two years' compulsory military service.

After this somewhat chequered career he returned to the Faculty of Law and Politics at Kabul University, finally taking his degree in 1960. Babrak Karmal, considerably older than his student contemporaries and with the glamour which attached to involvement in the earlier student movement followed by a spell in prison, must have been an attractive figure. It was during this time that he built up his following among Kabul's university students.

In 1961 he joined the Compilation and Translation Department of the Ministry of Education. Later that year he was transferred to the Ministry of Planning, whére he remained until his election to the Wolesi Jirga (People's House) in September 1965. He was therefore in Kabul during the vital eighteen months when the PDPA was taking shape and, despite later differences, had sufficient sympathy with Taraki's objectives to participate in the founding congress of the party.

Nur Mohammad Taraki, the man chosen as the first Secretary-General of the PDPA, had also been involved in the political activity of the earlier period, although he was never prominent among the activists seeking political change in Afghanistan.

Taraki's claims to the key role in both the Wish-i-Zalmaiyan and the newspaper *Angar* − his official biography states that he was responsible for the establishment of both − were no doubt made in order to build his image as 'Great Leader of the Revolution' and are not supported by the available evidence.

Neither Dupree nor Akhramovich mentions him. Both describe Wish-i-Zalmaiyan as a loose group of like-minded individuals, rather than the more highly organised party Taraki's biographers suggest. *Angar*, according to Dupree was 'a Persian and Pashto biweekly . . . published by Faiz Mohammad Angar, a noted Qandahari "Pashtunistan" advocate'.[23] There is disagreement over the date of *Angar*'s establishment: while Taraki claims he gained permission to publish it in 1949, the first issue did not appear until 1951. His biographers reveal no details of the Wish-i-Zalmaiyan 'programme' *What We Want?* published in the first issue, but Akhramovich records that

> Angar stated in its very first issues that to improve the condition of the people it was essential that the government should be a representative one, and that required the opportunity of establishing political parties and their free functioning and their right to take part in the elections to the National Assembly, which should be conducted without interference.[24]

A radical enough programme in Afghan terms, but there is no hint of the 'maturity as far as class consciousness was concerned' which Taraki is said to have attained and which presumably was reflected in *Angar*.[25]

To deny Taraki's extravagant claims to leadership, however, is not to deny his involvement, and it is not remarkable that neither Dupree nor Akhramovich appear to have failed to notice his existence, for no one, then or much later, took the Afghan left seriously. Dupree was concentrating his attention on the more moderate critics of the system, while Akhramovich studiously avoided dealing in personalities. Further evidence of Taraki's minor role at this time is the fact that he was not, like the editor of *Watan*, Mir Ghulam Mohammad Ghubar, among those imprisoned as a consequence of his political activities.

Instead, he was sent, in 1953 as Press Attaché to the Afghan Embassy in Washington: 'exile', according to his biographers, because of 'his great fame and popularity'. It is more likely that it was an attempt by the government to buy him off. If so the ploy was only temporarily successful. When Daoud assumed the Prime Ministership six months later Taraki called a press conference at which he attacked the monarchy, the government and the social system.[26] Not surprisingly he was recalled to Afghanistan. If Taraki obeyed seeking martyrdom – which seems to have been the case in the light of his reported telephone call to Daoud on his return: 'Shall I go home or to prison?' – he was disappointed. Taraki claimed that since his case attracted international attention, Daoud was afraid to undertake any reprisals, and there may be some truth in this. But it is also fairly certain that Daoud did not perceive Taraki as a major threat to the system. When he did, twenty-five years later, Daoud showed no such hesitation in imprisoning Taraki and his associates.

The subsequent ten years were frustrating ones for Taraki, ignored as he was by the authorities, who while keeping him under surveillance and (presumably) refusing to employ him, took no further action.

> From 1953 to 1963, Comrade Taraki primarily did odd jobs to eke out a living. However, as soon as he would land a good job, he was suspended through the intelligence service then called 'Zabt-i-Ahwalat'. So he was forced to run a translation bureau under his own name, 'The Noor Translation Bureau' doing translation work for some people and organizations or writing for the press.[27]

Although his official biographers do not mention it, one of his 'odd jobs', between 1955 and 1958, was as translator for the United States Overseas Mission, a forerunner of the US Agency for International Development (US AID), and another, between May 1962 and September 1963 was as translator for the American Embassy in Kabul.[28]

During these years Taraki wrote many novels and short stories usually dealing with the hardships suffered by the Afghan peasantry, a subject with which he was familiar and could write with feeling. The arguments were presented in the simple homely terms he used in his speeches after the April revolution. Here was no great intellect at work, but a man of warmth and humanity whose aim was to improve the condition of the peasant masses by raising the political consciousness of his readers. It is not clear how wide his audience really was: many of his works could not be published inside Afghanistan; others were published in Kandahar, where he seems to have had a considerable following; most probably circulated clandestinely among the small but growing circle of young intellectuals attracted by radical socialism.

Although not especially distinguished, Taraki seems to have been a well-liked, non-controversial figure and it was probably this together with the fact that at 47 he was among the oldest of the group of Marxists who formed the PDPA, which led to his election as the party's first leader. Despite his apparent simplicity, Taraki showed himself to be a shrewd and capable politician, well able to exploit the growing rivalry between Hafizullah Amin and Babrak Karmal.

Notes

1. For a splendid account of Amanullah's ill-fated attempt at modernisation, see Leon B. Poullada, *Reform and Rebellion in Afghanistan, 1919-1929* (Cornell University Press, Ithaca, 1973).

2. Democratic Republic of Afghanistan, Ministry of Information and Culture, *Comrade Hafizullah Amin's Short Biography* (Publications Department, Afghanistan Publicity Bureau, Government Publishing House, Kabul, 16 September 1979), p. 6.

3. For a useful history of Afghanistan see Vartan Gregorian, *The Emergence of Modern Afghanistan: Politics of Reform and Modernisation, 1880-1946* (Stanford University Press, Stanford, California, 1969) pp. 163, 187-8, 309-10.

4. Babrak Karmal, Official biography, *Kabul Times* (hereafter *KT*), 5 July 1978.

5. Vartan Gregorian, *Modern Afghanistan*, pp. 239-40, 338-9.

6. Nur Mohammad Taraki, official biography, *KT*, 30 Oct. 1978; see also Ludwig W. Adamec, *First Supplement to the Who's Who of Afghanistan: Democratic Republic of Afghanistan* (Akademische Druck-u. Verlagsanstalt Graz, Austria, 1979), pp. 15-16.

7. *Siraj al-Akhbar Afghaniyah* (The Lamp of the News of Afghanistan).

8. Gregorian, *Modern Afghanistan*, pp. 163, 187-8, 309-10.

9. Louis Dupree, *Afghanistan* (Princeton University Press, Princeton, 1980), p. 496; R.T. Akhramovich, *Outline History of Afghanistan After the Second World War* ('Nauka' Publishing House, Moscow, 1966), p. 46; *Taraki: Official Biography*.

10. R.T. Akhramovich, *Outline History of Afghanistan*, p. 46.

11. Dupree, *Afghanistan*, p. 495.

12. *Watan*, 23 March 1951, cited in Akhramovich, *Outline History of Afghanistan*, p. 55.

13. *Nida'-yi-Khalq*, 9 July 1951, cited ibid, pp. 59-60.

14. The editor and founder of the party, Dr Abdur Rahman Mahmudi, was imprisoned. He died of a kidney complaint three months after his release. Dupree was right (*Afghanistan* p. 497): one day Mahmudi would be resurrected as a martyr. *The Kabul Times* on 13 and 14 June 1978 published a two part biographical profile doing just that.

15. Dupree, *Afghanistan*, pp. 494-7.

16. DRA, *Comrade Hafizullah Amin*, pp. 8-9.

17. For an account of the 1893 agreement between the Amir Abdur Rahman and Sir Mortimer Durand, and the controversy surrounding it see Gregorian, *Modern Afghanistan*, pp. 158-9. The United States now appears anxious to deny that there was ever any question of signing a Mutual Security Agreement with Daoud. A senior American diplomat told the author that although Daoud himself had been anxious to sign such an agreement, the United States just was not interested. 'Afghanistan was too far away. Iran had a border with the Soviet Union; Pakistan we saw as relevant; but Afghanistan was too remote, a bottomless pit. We didn't want to get into supplying arms to Afghanistan. We knew that Daoud would turn to the Soviets and we accepted that.' If true, this statement has interesting implications for US perceptions of Afghanistan's non-aligned status, especially in the light of President Carter's hysterical reaction to the Soviet action of December 1979.

18. Cited in R.S. Newell, 'Revolution and Revolt in Afghanistan', *The World Today*, vol. 35, no. 11, November 1979, p. 435.

19. Interview with *New York Times* (*NYT*), broadcast by Kabul Radio in English, 9 September 1979, BBC *Summary of World Broadcasts*, (*SWB*), part 3, The Far East, FE/6219/C1/1, 14 September 1979.

20. The significance of this activity was later alluded to by Louis Dupree, though he was not writing directly of Amin, but of student disturbances in general:

> . . . the involvement of Afghan students and teachers . . . becomes a logical development if one remembers that the impassioned student demonstrations of *sehum-i-aqrab* in 1965 have now mostly become teachers and officials in the provinces. Naturally they maintain contacts with old friends and get together as often as possible. Thus cells are born, ideas proliferate, and action begins. Disgruntled at being away from the intellectual centre, Kabul, and nursing a grudge against the 'Establishment' which first brought them to the capital and then sent them back to rural areas, these teachers pass on their attitudes, together with their special knowledge, to their students – and sometimes, indeed, to their students parents. Dupree, *Afghanistan*, p. 621.

21. DRA, *Comrade Hafizullah Amin*, p. 11.

22. After the newspaper *Parcham* (Banner), established in 1968, edited by Suleiman Laeq and Mir Akbar Khyber.

23. Dupree, *Afghanistan*, p. 495.

24. Akhramovich, *Outline History of Afghanistan*, p. 54.

25. *Taraki: Official Biography*.

26. *New York Times*, 12 Nov. 1953, p. 6.

27. *Taraki: Official Biography*.

28. His connection with the US was cause for some friction in intra-party

disputes in the early 1970s, but it is to be noted that Babrak Karmal, since his installation as President in December 1979, while using Hafizullah Amin's American associations in an attempt to discredit him, chose to suppress those of Taraki.

3 A HOUSE DIVIDED: THE PDPA, 1965-1973

On 1 January 1965 a small group of Marxists met at Taraki's house i
Kabul and formed the People's Democratic Party of Afghanistan. Th
immediate impetus for the foundation of the PDPA was King Zah
Shah's proposal, on the basis of the new 1964 constitution, to broade
the scope of political activity permitted the Wolesi Jirga. It was widel
believed that legislation permitting the establishment of political partie
would be approved, and in anticipation groups spanning the politica
spectrum came into being. The PDPA was one — and, as it turned ou
the single most important — of them, although it received little atter
tion at the time.

The late development of a Marxist-oriented party in Afghanista
may be attributed to that country's isolation from Europe and th
mainstream of European radical thought. It was not until the late 194C
that a Westernised intelligentsia made its presence felt, finding expre
sion in the political activity of the Wish-i-Zalmaiyan period, whicl
brief as it was, provided an important experience for many of the part
cipants in the founding congress of the PDPA. The frustrations of th
succeeding years had hardened their radicalism, and the Congress agree
that the goal of the party should be the construction of a socialis
society in Afghanistan on Marxist-Leninist principles.

Although the USSR does not appear to have been directly involve
in the establishment of the PDPA, Taraki's analysis of Afghanistan'
historical development and of the international situation revealed hi
intellectual debt to Soviet theorists:

> In the last two years we have fully understood the ideology of eac
> other and our path is explicitly clear. We know that we are strugglin
> for some classes against some classes and that we are going to buil
> such a society on the basis of social principles in the interest of th
> toilers and void of individual exploitation.[1]

He made it clear that 'Our party will be among the world proletaria
parties and we will firmly maintain our fraternal ties with them.' H
argued that, while over the previous fifteen years productive forces i
Afghanistan had grown, the bourgeoisie had not developed to the exten
where it could become 'the vanguard class of our country'. Certainl

under Daoud most industrial development had been the result of government investment, with the result that instead of the development of a
classical bourgeoisie, there had emerged a bureaucracy in whose hands
economic power lay. Taraki might have added that, while an industrial
proletariat had developed, it was only a tiny minority of the population (estimated at 20,000 in 1962)[2] and that, as in other third world
countries, the party's problem would be to win the allegiance of the
peasantry. He did however implicitly acknowledge the problem:

> The foundation stone of our party rests on those classes which pro-
> duce material and moral wealth. But all the wealth is used up by the
> parasites and exploiting classes. If our party could get the toilers
> and their intellectuals together, and teach them the ideology of the
> workers and get them united on the basis of this ideology it would
> then be certain that our dear Afghanistan will be revived from all
> hardship and suffering.[3]

According to Taraki, only through a strong and disciplined party
could such deliverance be brought about. It was his intention to make
the PDPA such a party. Here he was to encounter serious problems. The
unity of purpose exhibited at the founding Congress did not extend
beyond the very general goal of the establishment of a socialist Afghanistan. The factionalism which eventually led to the fragmentation of the
party developed as a result of ethnic and policy differences shot through
with personal rivalry. One group, fearing Pashtun dominance, broke
away altogether and formed a separate party, Settem-i-Melli (National
Oppression) under the leadership of Tahir Badakhshi. The differences
over the proper strategy to be adopted vis-à-vis the regime of Zahir
Shah soon involved the PDPA in a bitter internal conflict which it was
never able to resolve. Much of the bitterness flowed from the intense
personal rivalry which developed between Hafizullah Amin and Babrak
Karmal, the most talented and ambitious of the younger members of
the party, who found themselves on opposing sides on all of the issues
that arose.

The identity of those attending the first Congress of the PDPA is not
known, nor is there any certainty about how many were present,[4] but
Hafizullah Amin was not among them. He was in the United States,
completing his doctoral dissertation, the final requirement for his degree.
During this second period in the United States he became deeply involved in Afghan student politics, and in 1963 was elected president
of the Union of Afghan Students. The same year he formed a leftist

political organisation in New York from among the most radical of his contemporaries, but this could not compensate for his absence from Afghanistan at the time of the formation of the PDPA, as a result of which he missed any opportunity of gaining early influence in the party hierarchy. The Congress elected a Central Committee of eleven, seven full members and four alternate members, with Taraki as Secretary General.[5] It was more than a year before Amin became an alternate member of the Central Committee and 1968 before he was promoted to full membership.

The fact that he was not a foundation member of the PDPA enabled his opponents to question his revolutionary credentials. He sought to defend himself by claiming that, even though he was in America, he considered himself to belong to the party:

> In 1342 (1963) Hafizullah Amin got the news that the revolutionary friends in Afghanistan were preparing for the establishment of a progressive workers' party. He informed [them] through correspondence that in New York too, with full adherence and loyalty to the workers movement and the leadership of the working class, he was carrying out activities and considered this organisation as part of a party which was later established as the People's Democratic Party of Afghanistan . . .[6]

In any case his political activity in New York led to his expulsion from the US in 1965 before he completed his degree. The circumstances of his expulsion were something of a mystery, even apparently to Amin himself:

> I did not know whether I was ousted or summoned. The American authorities said that I had been summoned by the Government of Afghanistan, and in Kabul they told me that the American authorities had ousted me. I demanded to continue my study at my own expense but my demand was turned down.[7]

His assertion that he sought to return to Columbia to complete his degree should perhaps be treated with caution. For a man whose political activity had become so important to him, who had (if the claims of his official biography are correct) gone to considerable lengths to establish his bona fides as a member of the newly formed PDPA, and whose political ambition was soon to become apparent, to wish to turn his back on the scene of the action in order to complete a doctoral thesis on secondary education in Afghanistan would be uncharacteristic to say the least. His expulsion from the United States, wherever the initiative came from, was for Hafizullah Amin a blessing in disguise.

While Taraki had been elected Secretary-General of the PDPA, Babrak Karmal secured the Secretaryship of the Central Committee, an influential post in terms of party administration which he no doubt hoped to use as a base from which to dislodge Taraki from the leadership. His other power base was clearly intended to be the Wolesi Jirga (where he could display his prowess as a demagogue) and, through it, Kabul's student population. In so moving, Karmal placed himself in opposition, not only to Taraki, but also to Hafizullah Amin, who himself had a considerable power base among Kabul's students and teachers.

Although he was absent for the founding Congress of PDPA, Amin returned to Afghanistan in time to contest, unsuccessfully, the seat of Paghman (his home district) for the party in the first elections held under the new constitution in August-September 1965.

After that he returned to teaching, but no longer in the prestigious and influential posts he had occupied before his departure for America in 1962. The political climate had changed under Zahir Shah, and Amin's political activities were by this time known and distrusted. The government would never again permit his involvement in teacher training.

He was appointed instead to a teaching post at Rabia Balkhi Girls' High School. It was clearly a demotion, and given the low priority which the government accorded women's education, seems to have been regarded as a position from which he could do little harm. In this the authorities made a serious error. Amin turned his attention to the recruitment of the girl students to the revolutionary cause. Afghan women were among the most oppressed members of their society, and it is not surprising that Amin received an enthusiastic response from his students at Rabia Balkhi. Nor was it any accident that educated Kabuli women were later to be among the PDPA's most enthusiastic supporters. It was during his term at Rabia Balkhi that the periodical *Khalq* (People) with which he was associated, made its brief appearance before being banned. According to his biography, *Khalq* and the ideas expressed in it circulated widely among the students at Rabia Balkhi High School and, through them, to other girls' schools in Kabul.

Realising that they had made another blunder, the authorities attempted to transfer Amin out of the education system to some other, less sensitive branch of the civil service. He successfully resisted this effort to curtail his activities, but had to be content with an appointment in the Elementary Education Department of the Ministry of

Education. No longer able to work among students and teachers, Amin concentrated on politicising the lower ranking civil servants among whom he worked. Here too there was considerable frustration, especially among the lower paid contract employees, but also among those on the bottom rungs of the bureaucratic rank structure for whom promotion, if it came at all, would be long delayed. Lower and middle ranking government employees were another group from which the PDPA drew support following the April Revolution.

Meanwhile, Babrak Karmal who, along with Dr Anahita Ratebzada, had secured election to the Wolesi Jirga in the 1965 elections, joined with her to form the nucleus of a left-wing group. The first two weeks of the Wolesi Jirga session in October 1965 were given over to unbridled attacks by the newly elected members on previous ministers for their alleged corrupt activities. An outpouring of legitimate resentment that had built up over the years, the attacks created an atmosphere of tension in which the new government was unable to operate, and which led to the student riots of 25 October (Sehum-i-Aqrab in the Afghan calendar) in which three people were killed by troops called in to quell the disturbances.

Much of the responsibility for this disaster must rest with Babrak Karmal,[8] a gifted orator, who encouraged radical students to appear in parliament on 24 October, the day the new Prime Minister was to present his cabinet for approval, and 'exercise their constitutional rights' by disrupting proceedings. The ploy succeeded and the Wolesi Jirga was forced to adjourn, having decided to hold a closed session the following day. Student demonstrations began early in the morning of 25 October and continued until the tragic intervention of the army. That many of the student leaders involved were Amin's followers is suggested by Louis Dupree's subsequent observations regarding *Khalq*, the newspaper with which Amin was identified: 'Each Monday during its short life, I visited the Khalq office to buy my copy of the paper and chat with the staff and its supporters, who included student leaders of the Sehum-i-Aqrab demonstrations.'[9]

Amin's reaction to Karmal's irresponsible manipulation of the party's young supporters, inciting them to actions which placed them, literally, in the firing line is not recorded. There are indications that he attempted to counter Karmal's growing influence among the students, as one of the latter's supporters, a major in the pro-Karmal remnant of the Afghan army testified in January 1980: 'The major had known Amin well. Amin had been a schoolteacher and had taught the major algebra in different days. But Amin was always a "troublemaker" who had "set people against each other, and thought only of himself" . . .'[10]

Babrak Karmal's flamboyant style of politics was again demonstrated after the brawl in the Wolesi Jirga in December 1966, as a result of which he was taken to hospital. When the students heard of this some of them rushed to the hospital where they held a demonstration in Karmal's support. The wounded hero allegedly seized additional bandages, wound them about his head, then limped bravely to the balcony to acknowledge the cheers of his fans.[11]

The student strikes and demonstrations of 1969, initiated by students of Ibn Sina and Dar-ul-Mualimeen, the institutions with which Amin had been most closely associated, were further evidence of his influence, although by this time the student radicals were divided, reflecting the split in the party itself.

Babrak Karmal's crude power play, which led to the Sehum-i-Aqrab tragedy in 1965, also helped forge the alliance between Taraki and Amin. Though a gifted orator, with a touch of charisma, Karmal was no match for Taraki and Amin in terms of organisational ability, or when it came to playing the numbers game. It was not until this alliance began to disintegrate that he was able to exercise more than a disruptive influence over the affairs of the PDPA.

The first major issue dividing the PDPA was the stand to be adopted towards the Zahir Shah regime. Two factions developed around rival newspapers *Khalq*, the official organ of the PDPA associated with the party's Secretary-General, Nur Mohammad Taraki, and *Parcham*,[12] associated with Babrak Karmal and Mir Akbar Khyber. The split came over the proper response to the government's action in banning *Khalq* in 1966, after only six issues had appeared. Subsequent disagreement related to the interpretation of the party programme as it applied to the formation of a 'national united front'.

Among the immediate tasks assigned the Central Committee (apart from contesting the 1965 elections in which it had little hope of success) were the preparation of a party programme and constitution and the establishment of an official party newspaper.

As Secretary-General of the party and chairman of the editorial board of the weekly *Khalq*, Taraki took the drafting of the PDPA Manifesto into his own hands.[13] The draft was first adopted by a committee set up by the Central Committee, and subsequently at a party conference (of which Taraki's biographers offer no details) and then published in the first two issues of *Khalq* in April 1966.

The manifesto identified the 'economic and political hegemony of the feudal class' as the source of Afghanistan's misery and backwardness,

and saw the immediate solution as the establishment of a 'national
democratic government', the political foundations of which would 'be
based on a national united front of patriotic, democratic progressive
forces, viz. workers, peasants, progressive elite, artisans, small bourgeois
(small and average class landlords) and national bourgeois (national
capitalists) who are struggling for national independence, popularisation
of democracy in social life and making the anti-imperialist and feudalist
democratic movement successful.'[14]

While at that particular stage of history the PDPA declared itself to
be struggling for the establishment of national democracy, it pledged
itself not to ignore 'our primary objective of creating a socialist society
which is imperative for our social accomplishment'. The PDPA manifesto thereby demonstrated the party leaders' intellectual debt to Marx
and Lenin, as well as to later Soviet authors of the theory of national
democracy. It also distinguished it from other political groups which
saw a solution to Afghanistan's problems in free elections, or a free
press, or legal reform, or reform of the bureaucracy. The PDPA acknowledged the need for such measures, but saw them, on their own, as
merely tinkering with the system when it was the system itself which
needed to be changed. It proposed not merely to limit the power of
the ruling class (in itself an unacceptable proposition) but to destroy it
altogether.

The government's response was predictable: since the party was
already clandestine it could not be banned. Its members – and the
government boasted that it was fully aware of the activities of most
prominent leftists[15] – were not considered sufficiently influential and
therefore dangerous to warrant arrest. But publication of *Khalq* could
not be allowed to continue. After the appearance of only six issues the
paper was closed, on 16 May 1966.

It was at this point that the dispute within the party flared into open
conflict. Despite his record as a student militant and his presence at the
founding congress of the PDPA Babrak Karmal had something less than
impeccable socialist credentials. His family background, together with
that of his close associates, and his equivocal attitude to the royalist
regime made him suspect in the eyes of the other party leaders. Karmal
himself was the son of one of Zahir Shah's generals. Dr Anahita Ratebzada, his long-time companion, was the wife of Dr Qamruddin, a former
President of Kabul University and surgeon in the Royal Household. His
closest associate, Mir Akbar Khyber had spent the ten years since his
release from prison in the Ministry of the Interior in the para-military
police force.

Karmal's proposed solution was a compromise: *Khalq* should darken the red colour on the masthead and 'assure the king we'are not communists'. It is unlikely that such a simple device would have altered the government's attitude, as a letter to Taraki from the Ministry of Information and Culture suggests: 'As your magazine entitled *Khalq* has already been banned and since you want to issue a magazine having the same aims and object, you cannot be given permission to re-issue the same or a new paper.'[16]

There had been no indication up to this point of any coyness on Karmal's part about identifying himself as a communist or in endorsing the Manifesto, drafted in unmistakable Marxist-Leninist terms. Was he, then, advocating a change in policy; for to reassure the king would have required more than a darker red masthead? Or was he making a suggestion he knew would be unacceptable, in order to provide an excuse to pursue an independent line designed to advance his own political career? The fact that he immediately began clandestine publication of *Parcham* (a carefully non-controversial title) and later gained permission for it to appear openly, while the Khalq group was never again permitted a legal mouthpiece, suggests that there was more than an element of opportunism in Karmal's stand. He was clearly prepared to split the party if he could not dominate it.

Babrak Karmal's willingness to co-operate and compromise suggested a degree of political opportunism which alarmed Taraki and his party colleagues, as did the possibility that Karmal might have a majority on the Central Committee, elected eighteen months earlier.

Taraki could only rely on Saleh Mohammad Zeary, while Sultan Ali Kishtmand was regarded as Karmal's supporter. Dastagir Panjsheri and Shahrullah Shahpur could not be counted upon by either (both changed sides several times before Panjsheri threw in his lot with Taraki and Shahrullah Shahpur left the PDPA). Tahir Badakhshi was also an unknown quantity who first sided with Taraki, before quitting the PDPA to form the Settem-i-Melli Party, directed specifically against Pashtun dominance of other Afghan nationalities, and against the concept of Greater Pashtunistan.

Taraki was in a stronger position among the alternate members, where Shah Wali, Karim Misaq and Dr Mohammad Zahir could be relied upon, and only Abdul Wahab Safi was a supporter of Babrak Karmal.

Taraki therefore moved to enlarge the Central Committee, bringing in eight new alternate members, 'in order to check unprincipled activities and rifts in the party'.[17] The device was only partially successful for a number of the new members turned out to be pro-Karmal — a fact acknowledged in the comment that, even after this 'Babrak Karmal did not give up his divisive policies'. Of the eight new alternate members only four could be relied on to support Taraki against Karmal. They were Hafizullah Amin, Ismael Danesh, Abdul Mohammad and Mohammad Zahir Ofaq. Karmal could count on Mohammad Hassan, Bareq Shafi, Nur Ahmad Panjwai and Suleiman Laeq. Hakim Sharai Jauzjani wavered, but ultimately sided with Taraki.

The Central Committee had now expanded to nineteen: the original seven permanent members, and a tail of twelve alternates. While only the votes of the full members counted, both sides had brought up their reserves.

Then Babrak Karmal made three tactical blunders. In order to allay the suspicions of the King, he made a speech in the Wolesi Jirga in which he declared Zahir Shah to be 'the most progressive King of Asia', affirmed his 'sincere and abiding faith in the King', and praised the budget presented by the Ministry on the grounds that Zahir Shah had himself devoted time to its preparation. The effect of this speech on the King is not known, but it apparently disturbed the PDPA leaders.[18]

Second, Karmal tried to have two of his supporters, Mir Akbar Khyber and Dr Anahita Ratebzada, neither of whom were at that stage PDPA members, elected to the Central Committee. To this end he actively lobbied other Central Committee members.

Finally, in order to force the issue, he made the cardinal error of submitting his resignation to Central Committee.[19] The six remaining full members divided evenly, three in favour of accepting Karmal's resignation, (Taraki, Zeary and Panjsheri) and three opposed (Kishtmand, Shahrullah Shahpur and Badakhshi). However, Karmal, having tendered his resignation, was counted as voting in favour. He thus found himself not merely out of the Central Committee but effectively out of the party.

This was apparently not the result he anticipated or intended, and there commenced a desperate power struggle which eventually split the PDPA. Karmal refused to accept what amounted to his expulsion from the Central Committee which resulted from Taraki's deft procedural footwork. He was apparently able to convince Dastagir Panjsheri of the justice of his position – an important coup, because Panjsheri was the only permanent member of the Central Committee who changed sides to support Babrak Karmal on this specific issue. Even he eventually lost patience with Karmal and rejoined the party. However, the numerical advantage was cancelled out by Tahir Badakhshi's move in the opposite direction.

In his efforts to rally support, Karmal looked once more to the student constituency, turning to advantage his hospitalisation after the brawl in the Wolesi Jirga. According to official party sources, 'the associates of Babrak without caring for the decision of the Central Committee invited University students to hold demonstrations in favour of Babrak Karmal'.[20] It is not clear if any of the student leaders were aware of the internal power struggle going on within the PDPA, or if it would have made any difference had they known. The object of the exercise was to enhance Karmal's public image and in this it succeeded.

Meanwhile the alternate members of the Central Committee were as deeply divided as the permanent members. When it came to the crunch three permanent members left the party in support of Karmal: Kishtmand, Shahrullah Shahpur and Panjsheri. They were followed by five of the twelve alternate members: Abdul Wahab Safi, Bareq Shafie, Hakim Sharai Jauzjani, Nur Ahmed Panjwai and Suleiman Laeq.

Some members of each group, anxious to heal the rift, opened negotiations in the following months. The participants were Panjsheri and Jauzjani on behalf of Karmal and Shah Wali and Karim Misaq for the Khalq group. They apparently met at Taraki's house, which could hardly be regarded as neutral territory. According to Khalq sources an agreement was reached 'to secure unity of action at the first stage and later to strengthen this unity. Since this argument ran counter to Babrak's designs he turned down the agreement.'[21] What was meant by 'unity of action at the first stage'? A common policy with regard to opposition to the Zahir regime? Or did it refer to the competing publications? In either case the split had proceeded too far for either side to compromise. After the suppression of *Khalq*, the party began publishing clandestinely two journals, *Jumbish* and *Rahnuma*. Karmal and his supporters while ostensibly supporting efforts to secure permission either for *Khalq* to re-open, or for another paper to be established by the PDPA, began clandestine publication of *Parcham* in which Karmal expressed his own viewpoint. By the time the 'agreement' was worked out, Karmal's policy of reconciliation with Zahir Shah's Court had paid off and *Parcham* was allowed to appear openly, with Suleiman Laeq and Mir Akbar Khyber as joint editors (14 March 1968). Now Babrak Karmal had not only a platform in the Wolesi Jirga, but his own mouthpiece in *Parcham*. Already a well known public figure among Kabul's university students Karmal at this stage saw greater possibilities of gaining political power by remaining at the head of his own faction, than in sinking his differences with Taraki and the Khalq. Compared with his apparent advantages they seemed to have little to offer. A further disincentive to reunification, from Karmal's point of view, was the Khalq's adamant refusal to accept Mir Akbar Khyber and Anahita Ratebzada, along with Karmal, as members of the Central Committee.

Although most of those who had followed Karmal out of the PDPA remained with him, he lost the support of two important figures, Panjsheri and Jauzjani, both of whom, it appears, had left the party in protest at the way in which he had been forced out of the Central Committee but who were ideologically in sympathy with the Khalq and who had genuinely sought a reconciliation. When they realised that this was not possible they rejoined the PDPA.

With the split now apparently permanent, the PDPA in the summer of 1968 re-organised and streamlined its Central Committee. Taraki of course remained Secretary-General, with Zeary still a permanent member and Panjsheri back in the fold. Shah Wali had already been promoted from alternate to permanent status following the exodus of Parchamites the previous summer. Four other alternate members now became full members: Hafizullah Amin, Abdul Karim Misaq, Ismael Danish and Hakim Sharai Jauzjani. Seven new temporary members were appointed: Mansour Hashemi, Abdul Ahad Wolesi, Rashid Aryan, Mohammad Soma, Hassan Paiman, Mohammad Yaseen Bumjadi and Abdul Karim Zaghoorn (later expelled).[22]

After the split of 1967 the Khalq virtually disappeared from public view, quietly 'performing its political, ideological and organisational duties among peasants, workers and intellectuals of the country'.[23] Party activities were based on the Leninist principle of democratic centralism which meant that the PDPA was highly centralised and tightly disciplined, as befitted a party forced by a hostile political environment to operate in a clandestine fashion.

So low was its profile in contrast to that of Babrak Karmal and the Parchamites, that Louis Dupree, a seasoned observer of Afghan politics, seemed unaware that Taraki's group existed and regarded *Parcham* as *Khalq*'s successor: surely the effect Karmal had hoped to achieve. Dupree did, however, note a significant change in Karmal's political position as revealed in the pages of *Parcham*.

The writers of *Parcham* include such well-known socialists as Babrak Karmal and Dr Anahita . . . both of whom seem to have calmed down appreciably since the December 1966 Wolesi Jirga fight . . . Currently . . . Babrak and *Parcham* appear to be agreed that a milder evolutionary approach to socialism is to be preferred to violent overthrow. *Parcham* believes that all sectors of the Afghan population

can contribute to the defeat of 'feudalism and imperialism' and pro-
motes the creation of a 'United Democratic Front', to work for a
change *within* the constitutional system . . .[24]

As the newspaper campaign continued through 1968 and 1969 (until
the government clamped down on political activity before the 1969
elections) an interesting newcomer appeared on the scene: *Shola-i-Javid*
(Eternal Flame), edited by Dr Rahim Mahmoudi and Dr Hadi Mahmoudi, began publication on 4 April 1968, a few weeks after *Parcham*.
Like the Settem-i-Melli, its politics were radical left but anti-Pashtun.
The logic of international politics was such that both tended to be pro-
Chinese — China supported Pakistan which opposed 'Pashtunistan',
while the USSR supported Afghanistan which was 'pro-Pashtunistan'.
The intrusion of the Sino-Soviet dispute into the politics of the Afghan
left further complicated an already complex situation. *Shola-i-Javid*'s
relations with Khalq seem ambivalent. On one hand an anti-Parcham
alliance appeared to have developed during the student unrest of 1969,
as observed by Dupree who described in detail one of the major demonstrations:

> Shu'la-yi-Jawed forces raised a large banner with the red-lettered
> word *Khalq* ('The Masses', the name of the leftist paper banned in
> May 1966). This new gambit plus the shouting of another slogan
> (Long Live the democratic movement of the Khalq and Shu'la-yi-
> Jawed!) precipitated a fight between the two factions.[25]

Later, Khalq sources blamed the *Shola-i-Javid* 'Maoists' for the death
of one of their members during the Sehem-i-Aqrab demonstrations in
Herat in 1971. Hostility towards 'leftist opportunists', as the Khalq
called *Shola-i-Javid*'s supporters, continued, but essentially the only
issue dividing the two groups was their difference regarding the Soviet
Union. Khalq was much less committed to the idea of Pashtunistan
than Karmal's Parchamites which represented a common enemy for
both. It only required Khalq disillusionment with the USSR for its
leaders to turn to *Shola-i-Javid* as a natural ally and a channel of communication with China and Pakistan. It appears that such a development occurred in 1979 and was a significant factor in persuading the
USSR to intervene in Afghanistan.

The 1969 election campaign, officially announced by the King on
21 April signalled a marked shift even further to the right in Afghan
politics. Zahir Shah was determined not to permit the wave of criticism

of the government and in particular of the monarchy to continue. Babrak Karmal's conciliatory tactics were not enough to save *Parcham*, which was banned on 15 July, a few days after the government closed *Shola-i-Javid*. He did manage to secure re-election, perhaps because of his modified position. Dupree described him as a 'putative leftist', adding that despite the *Shola-i-Javid* campaign accusing him of being a government stooge, 'those who know him believe that, if he is not really a leftist, he is independent'.[26]

Karmal remained suspect, particularly in the light of the arrest of three members of the new Khalq-controlled PDPA Central Committee: Zeary, Misaq and Panjsheri.[27] Dupree records that Misaq and Panjsheri were sentenced to two and ten years jail respectively, but that Misaq suffered a nervous breakdown and was released.[28] He makes no reference to Zeary or to their identity as Khalq supporters. Zeary and Panjsheri remained in prison until the coup which overthrew the monarchy in 1973.

Although Babrak Karmal was the only one of the old Parcham group in the Wolesi Jirga to secure re-election, Hafizullah Amin successfully resisted the conservative tide, winning the seat of Paghman which he had contested in 1965, giving the Khalq its first and only representative in Parliament. His biographers record that Amin took an active part in the proceedings of the Wolesi Jirga.

> During his four years as a deputy he continued his sound struggle as a representative of the PDPA against imperialism, feudalism and reaction and exposed the corruption and treason of the Zahirshahi court and the tyranny of the rotten regime. As a deputy he made maximum use (of his position) in the interest of the people, movement and his party . . .[29]

Despite these activities on behalf of the PDPA Amin and the party were looking beyond the Wolesi Jirga in their opposition to the monarchist system. Amin later recalled that all their efforts were directed to 'the acceleration of their struggle to bring the class war to a head.'[30]

Emphasis continued to be placed on agitation. The Khalq claimed to have 'led about two thousand meetings and demonstrations throughout the country from the year 1965 to 1973 in defending the democratic rights and liberties of workers, peasants, students, teachers and women and thus played a vital role in the political re-awakening of the masses'.[31] Certainly there was an upsurge of worker and student unrest during 1968, documented by Dupree, in which the PDPA, if not solely responsible, at least took a leading part.[32]

A major concern of the PDPA after the 1969 election was to forge a united front against the Zahir Shah regime.

> The People's Democratic Party of Afghanistan decided that all progressive, democratic and national forces be united under a single banner of a united front composed of patriotic elements to protest against the Zahir Shahi regime in nation-wide meetings and demonstrations.[33]

If the PDPA hoped that Karmal, his newspaper driven underground, himself isolated in the Wolesi Jirga, would be sufficiently disillusioned with the King to join forces with his old rivals, they were sadly mistaken. He was indeed disillusioned with the King, but he had other irons in the fire, and the formation of a united front with the Khalqis formed no part of his plan. Years later Amin made an angry reference to Karmal's refusal to co-operate:

> ... Babrak Karmal who then led a faction composed of (false) patriots, feudal court lackeys and dependents of the oppressors in order to continue his historical role made the formation of this front impossible by creating a rift among the patriots and thus nipped in the bud this collective effort.[34]

Relations were certainly as bad as they had ever been. Both the Parcham and Khalq factions were claiming to be the real PDPA. The Khalq complained that when Jai Prakash Narayan invited Karmal to visit India, Karmal did so claiming to represent the Khalq party, the PDPA.[35] The Khalq responded categorically to Karmal's claims. The Central Committee declared that 'there was only one party, named Democratic Khalq Party in Afghanistan and that Babrak was not the leader of the Party'.[36] Since Taraki, the first Secretary-General of the PDPA still held that office there was considerable justice in the Khalq group's claims to constitute the legitimate PDPA, but given their unconciliatory attitude it is not surprising that Babrak Karmal and the Parchamites looked for allies elsewhere. Karmal had not abandoned the idea of forming a united front, but it was to be formed with Sardar Mohammad Daoud and a group of disaffected army officers, not with the PDPA.

Notes

1. Address to the First Congress of the People's Democratic Party of Afghanistan, January 1965, *Kabul Times (KT)*, 1 Jan. 1979.

2. Leon B. Poullada, *Reform and Rebellion in Afghanistan, 1919-1929* (Cornell University Press, Ithaca, 1973), Table 1, Social Stratification of tribal and religious groups in Afghanistan, pp. 17-18.

3. Address to the First Congress.

4. The official account (*KT*, 30 Oct. 1978) claims that there were 'about 30 young men' but informal estimates suggest there were fewer. An earlier account, attributed to Khalqi sources makes no mention of the number attending the founding congress, merely noting that it elected a Central Committee. 'Democratic Khalq Party of Afghanistan: Pioneer of the Working Class', *Tariq-ul-Shaab* (Baghdad), July 1976.

5. The permanent members were Taraki, Dastagir Panjsheri, Saleh Mohammad Zeary, Shahrullah Shahpur, Babrak Karmal, Sultan Ali Kishtmand and Tahir Badakhshi. The temporary members were Shah Wali, Karim Misaq, Mohammad Zahir and Abdul Wahad Safi, ibid.

Fred Halliday ('Revolution in Afghanistan', *New Left Review*, no. 112, November-December, 1978, p. 23) produces a different, longer list of names. In addition to those included above he names Nur Ahmed Nur and Shah Wali among the permanent members and Bareq Shafie, Suleiman Laeq, Hafizullah Amin, Ismail Danish, Hakim Sharai Jauzjani, Abdul Mohammad and Zahir Ofaq among the temporary members. Unfortunately Halliday gives no indication of the source of his information. The list seems to correspond more nearly to the later (1968) enlarged Central Committee. Louis Dupree, ('Afghanistan Under the Khalq', *Problems of Communism*, July-August 1979, p. 40) produces yet another set of names, also without reference to any source.

6. Democratic Republic of Afghanistan, Ministry of Information and Culture, *Comrade Hafizullah Amin's Short Biography* (Publications Department, Afghanistan Publicity Bureau, Government Publishing House, Kabul, 16 September 1979), pp. 13-14.

7. Press conference, broadcast by Kabul radio in English, 9 September 1979, BBC, *Summary of World Broadcasts (SWB)* Part 3, The Far East, FE/6219/C1/3. Official American sources claim that Amin 'returned home because he did not qualify', see Louis Dupree, *Red Flag Over the Hindu Kush Part II: The Accidental Coup, or Taraki in Blunderland*, American Universities Field Staff Reports, Asia, 1979, no. 45, p. 5.

8. Not all however. Mir Akbar Khyber was also apparently involved. The *Kabul New Times* (17 April 1980) states that he was banished to Paktya for his part in the disturbances.

9. Louis Dupree, *Afghanistan 1966*, American Universities Field Staff Reports, South Asia Series, vol. X, no. 4, (Afghanistan), July 1966, p. 13.

10. David Selbourne, 'Conversation in Kabul', *New Society*, 31 Jan. 1980, pp. 225-6.

11. Louis Dupree, *Afghanistan* (Princeton University Press, Princeton, 1980), p. 615.

12. *Khalq* (People) and *Parcham* (Banner).

13. Taraki, official biography, *KT*, 30 Oct. 1978.

14. *The Aims and Objects of the Democratic Khalq Party*, (unofficial English translation, Kabul, March 1979).

15. Louis Dupree, *Afghanistan 1966*, p. 13.

16. 'Democratic Khalq Party of Afghanistan'.

17. Ibid.

18. Ibid.
19. Ibid.
20. Ibid.
21. Ibid.
22. Ibid.
23. Ibid.
24. Louis Dupree, *Afghanistan: 1968, Part III: Problems of a Free Press*, American Universities Field Staff Reports, South Asia Series, vol. XII, no. 6 (Afghanistan), August 1968, p. 6.
25. Louis Dupree, *The 1969 Student Demonstrations in Kabul*, American Universities Field Staff Reports, South Asia Series, vol. XIV, no. 5 (Afghanistan), May 1970, p. 11.
26. Louis Dupree, *Afghanistan Continues Its Experiment in Democracy: The Thirteenth Parliament is Elected*, American Universities Field Staff Reports, South Asia Series, vol. XV, no. 3 (Afghanistan), July 1971, p. 7.
27. Democratic Khalq Party of Afghanistan.
28. Dupree, *Afghanistan Continues Its Experiment in Democracy*, p. 7.
29. DRA, *Comrade Hafizullah Amin*, p. 20.
30. Speech on the anniversary of the Sehum-i-Aqrab demonstrations, *KT*, 26 Oct. 1978.
31. 'Democratic Khalq Party of Afghanistan'.
32. Dupree, *Afghanistan*, p. 620.
33. Amin, speech, *KT*, 26 Oct. 1978.
34. Ibid.
35. 'Democratic Khalq Party of Afghanistan'. Room for confusion exists since the word 'Khalq' (People) appears in the title of the PDPA — Jamiyat-i-Demo-kratiqi-Khalqi-Afghanistan — as well as referring to the party's newspaper *Khalq*, and the name of the faction associated with it. The confusion is increased by the Khalq faction's tendency to refer to the PDPA as 'the Khalq Party'.
36. Ibid.

4 THE MAKING OF A REVOLUTION: THE PDPA, 1973-1978

Ousted from the Prime Ministership by his cousin the King in 1963, Daoud had remained uncharacteristically quiet through the remainder of the 1960s, watching the development of policies he had instituted gradually lose momentum as the Afghan political system seized up. The election of a much more conservative parliament in 1969 placed the provincial and tribal elite in an even stronger position. The effect was to paralyse the central government still further, probably their fundamental objective since the power struggle between Kabul and the provinces was an ongoing feature of Afghan politics. While the weakness of the king secured the ascendancy of the feudal-tribal ruling class, and ensured that no measure would be adopted likely to undermine their position, other groups were increasingly discontented.

Those who could remember the 'liberal parliament' of 1949-52, and whose hopes had been dashed in the repression that followed had had a similar experience in the 1960s, when Zahir Shah's Constitution of 1964 promised so much and gave so little. Instead of power being transferred to the hands of the impatient, educated elite, what little influence they had gained under Daoud's premiership from 1953 to 1963 was being whittled away in favour of the traditional conservative power centres.

Of the new educated urban elite dissatisfied with Zahir Shah, probably the most important section was the officer corps of the army and the air force. Under Daoud the armed forces had acquired special prestige. More than any other leader he had modernised and expanded the army and the air force, sent many young officers for training in the Soviet Union, equipped them with modern Soviet weapons. Many of the officers therefore shared Daoud's commitment to modernisation and development of a new Afghanistan, in which they saw themselves in a central role. Since most of the senior officers were members of the Pashtun aristocracy they also supported Daoud's aggressive policy on Pashtunistan.

The Parchamites, who also had links with the Pashtun ruling class, found the armed forces a fertile field in which to recruit support. In the period 1969 to 1973, while the Khalq was concentrating on raising the consciousness of the masses, Parchamite efforts, under the direction of Mir Akbar Khyber, sought to attract a following within the officer corps. As the Parchamite network spread, and as dissatisfaction with Zahir Shah grew, not only within the armed forces, but also within the royal family, excluded from political activity under the 1964 constitution, it was only a short step to an alliance between Daoud, Parcham and the military.

While Daoud's need of the armed forces is self-evident, the Parchamites also had a role to play in his scenario, for if he was to implement the reforms he planned Daoud needed a dedicated cadre to send into the provinces to replace the old, inefficient and corrupt bureaucracy. For Babrak Karmal and his supporters the alliance offered the possibility of speedy access to political power, denied under Zahir Shah's regime and, it seemed, likely to be indefinitely delayed if they followed the example of Khalq: 'The party has faith in the principles of Marxism-Leninism and proletarian internationalism against opportunism (of left and right) and always keeps our party purified of alien elements.'[1]

It is not clear how close the links between Karmal and Daoud actually were. Dupree claims that some Parchamites were central to the planning of the coup.[2] One source suggests that 'knowledgeable circles in Kabul regarded Parcham as Sardar Daoud's own "communist party"'.[3] Some Parchamites were appointed to the Revolutionary Council, and others became Ministers: Major Faiz Mohammad was Minister of the Interior; Pacha Gul Wafadar became Minister of Frontier Affairs; Major Abdul Qadir, believed by some to be 'close to Parcham' became Vice-Commander of the Air Force; while Major Zia Mohammadzai Zia, a Parcham sympathiser belonging to the royal family became Chief of the Republican Guard.[4] Some 160 leftists were appointed to bureaucratic posts in the provinces.[5]

If he had hoped that alliance with Daoud would provide a short-cut to personal power, Karmal was disappointed, for he was left outside the new Republican regime, as effectively as his Khalq rivals in the PDPA proper.

By the time of Daoud's coup in 1973 Hafizullah Amin had more than recovered from the set back he suffered as a result of his absence in the United States during the vital period of the formation of the PDPA. Promoted to full membership of the Central Committee in 1968, he became one of the mainstays of the party after the arrest of Zeary and Panjsheri in 1969. Along with Shah Wali, who alone enjoyed seniority to him on the Central Committee, he shouldered the major burden of the organisational work. His pre-eminence in the party hierarchy survived the release from prison of Panjsheri and Zeary in 1973 and their return to active politics. Both these men, by virtue of their standing as members of the original Central Committee, and of their experience in prison, had arguably better revolutionary credentials than Amin. Both could, with some justification, have felt aggrieved that he had taken advantage of their enforced absence to advance his own position in the party. But despite this potential for friction, it appears that from 1973 until the re-unification of the party in 1977 Amin's authority within the PDPA was accepted as second only to that of Taraki.

The relationship between Amin and Taraki is one of the most intriguing aspects of the history of the PDPA. The official, and widely accepted view is that Amin was Taraki's protégé, that Taraki's role was almost a paternal one, with Amin portrayed as the devoted disciple of the great leader, faithfully carrying out Taraki's instructions. A close reading of the relevant documents reveals Amin's more central, independent position, and suggests that the alliance between the two men was founded on something far less sentimental than the official histories would imply. Soon after the establishment of the party Taraki recognised and cultivated Amin's 'tactical and strategical talents'.[6] Taraki needed, and came to depend on, Amin's organisational ability, the more so after the latter developed his power base in the armed forces. It was a skill that Taraki, an old fox on committees and in intra-party skirmishing, lacked.

Amin's need of the alliance is more obscure, but there is a clear indication that Babrak Karmal, although the bitterest of them, was not Amin's only enemy. Taraki having discovered Amin's ability

> defended him against all sorts of intrigues and propaganda. He always shielded Comrade Amin against the treacherous or erroneous blows dealt him by some elements who meanwhile took pride in belonging to the party, safeguarding his loyal disciple against all intrigues resorted to by some colleagues consciously *or sub-consciously* which eventually proved to be in the interests of the enemy.[7]

Amin needed Taraki, the old fox, to protect his back. The other more senior Central Committee members might have accepted Amin, as Taraki's protégé, acquiring increased authority. They would have been much less likely to accept him in his own right. The only avenue through which Amin could hope to realise his ambition was to accept Taraki's protection and the role of 'loyal disciple', working through Taraki who then took most of the credit. It was a role that would, and obviously did, grate on a man of Amin's temperament, and one that he threw off, with apparent relief, several years later. But for the time being Amin and Taraki needed each other in the struggle against their common enemies: President Daoud and the Parchamites.

The PDPA welcomed the proclamation of the republic by Daoud in July 1973 and declared its readiness to 'defend democracy against reactionary forces and imperialist conspiracies'.[8] While approving the objectives outlined in Daoud's address to the nation, the PDPA argued that no progress could be made unless Daoud cleared the government of 'reactionaries and corrupt bureaucrats' and formed a united front, presumably including the PDPA.

Having been upstaged by the Parchamites, the Khalq group, now somewhat optimistically, sought a piece of the action:

> The Khalqis reject the system of one party government in Afghanistan under present conditions ... It is vital that all patriotic and democratic elements should get united for the construction of new Afghanistan, the future of which definitely lies with socialism.[9]

Not surprisingly, they were ignored. Daoud had entered a temporary alliance with the Parchamites solely for convenience. He had no long-term commitment to democracy or socialism, and proceeded to dump the left as soon as he could safely do so. He could not have been expected to give even passing consideration to the extension of this alliance to include a group as ideologically committed as the PDPA. Babrak Karmal also, as he had done on previous occasions, rejected the call for a united front. Believing his alliance with Daoud had brought political power within his grasp Karmal had no incentive to share it with his old rivals. Indeed, he endeavoured to use what influence he had to persuade the PDPA that, since the revolution had now taken place, there was no need for other parties and that the continuation of PDPA activity amounted to 'treachery to democracy'.[10] The clear implication was that the PDPA should dissolve itself and its organisation. Neither Taraki nor Amin had any intention of committing political suicide on Babrak Karmal's request and this further attempt by him to destroy the PDPA only intensified the hostility between the two groups.

The Khalqis later claimed that their correct application of Marxist-Leninist theory enabled them to analyse correctly the political situation following the Daoud coup, and that they were thereby saved from Daoud's deception, in contrast with the Parchamites, whose opportunism led them into the trap. This is, of course, self-flattery, for the Khalqis' exclusion from political power, while certainly related to their ideology, was not self-imposed, but entirely fortuitous. It was, never-theless a remarkable stroke of luck for it meant that Taraki, Amin and their colleagues, unlike Babrak Karmal and the Parchamites, were not discredited by association with the Daoud regime. They represented an alternative focus of loyalty and source of leadership for those radicals in the armed forces, formerly followers of Karmal, who quickly became disillusioned with both Daoud and the Parchamites. It was this shift in allegiance of a significant proportion of the Afghan left that enabled Taraki and Amin to seize power in 1978.

In the meantime, having been rejected as partners by the new regime, the PDPA set about strengthening its organisation, continuing its oppo-sition to the government. Three clandestine publications which were attributed to the Khalq group criticised the government for not 'living up to its announced ideals'. Publication ceased only when the govern-ment threatened to arrest the Khalqis.[11]

While maintaining its opposition to the regime, the party also under-took a far-reaching reappraisal of its strategy to date, from which emerged what was later presented as Taraki's special contribution to revolutionary socialist theory:

> Comrade Taraki had appraised Afghan society on a scientific basis and had intimated to the party since the 1973 coup that it was possible in Afghanistan for the people to wrest power through a short cut as the classical way in which the productive forces undergo different stages to build a society based on socialism would take a long time. This short cut would be utilised by working exclusively within the armed forces. Previously the army was considered as the tool of dictatorship and despotism of the ruling class and it was not imaginable to use it before toppling its employer.[12]

In effect, the PDPA finally acknowledged that the armed forces were the key to revolution, and that by rigid adherence to the Marxist-Leninist view of them as the helpless instrument of the ruling class the party had conceded victory to Babrak Karmal and the Parchamites with-out even a struggle.

Although Taraki claimed credit for the belated discovery of the revolutionary potential of the Afghan armed forces, the initiative for extension of party work in this direction was taken by Amin. From 1973 Amin conducted, within the armed forces, the same persuasive and effective campaign to recruit support for the party that he had formerly carried on among his colleagues and students in the schools in which he taught.

It was a remarkable achievement considering that with the exception of his brother-in-law Major Yaqub he had no obvious means of contact with the military as he had had with the teachers and students. The fact that Afghan officers, married or single, lived with their usually very large families instead of being isolated in quarters set aside for the military meant that they were integrated into the society around them. This made it possible for Amin to work among them without attracting undue attention to his activities. The official history of the revolution records that he 'met patriotic liaison officers day or night, in the desert or the mountain, in the fields or the forests, enlightening them on the basis of the principles of the working class ideology'.[13]

There were other factors besides Amin's skill and energy (and the vast amount of literature he apparently distributed) which contributed to the success of the PDPA campaign. The most important was President Daoud's swift and transparent double-cross of the left, and of the radical army officers who put him in power. At the time of the July 1973 coup, Dupree records the existence of two other plots, one centred on the Abdul Wali Shah, cousin and son-in-law of King Zahir, and the other on former Prime Minister Hashim Maiwandwal. The Daoud coup pre-empted the others. Abdul Wali Shah and Maiwandwal were both arrested, the latter dying in prison in October under mysterious circumstances.[14]

It was not until early 1974, with the other plotters tried and sentenced — five were executed — that Daoud felt sufficiently secure to dissociate himself from the left, gradually replacing radical ministers with relatives or former royalist ministers. Two important conservative appointments were the Minister of Commerce, Mohammad Khan Jalalar, a former Finance Minister, in January 1974 and Ali Ahmad Khoram as Minister of Planning in May 1974. In March and April the Frontier Affairs Minister Pacha Gul Wafadar and Communications Minister Abdul Hamid Mohtat were removed from office. By the end of 1975 the last Parchamite minister had gone: Faiz Mohammad was sacked and the important Interior Ministry, controlling security services and provincial administration went to Abdul Qadir Nuristani, the former Chief of Police noted for his brutality. Major Abdul Qadir, instrumental in bringing the air force in behind Daoud in 1973, was relieved of his post as Vice-Commander of the air force and sent to run a military abattoir. At the same time Abdul Wali Shah and the former Prime Minister Mohammad Musa Shafiq, both of whom had been condemned as traitors in December 1973 were released from prison.

These top level changes in personnel, combined with Daoud's obvious

disinclination to press the reform measures he had promised, had a
demoralising effect on the lower- and middle-ranking officers who,
hoping for genuine progress, had supported Daoud in 1973. Amin found
an eager audience and ready support among the angry young officers
seeking a coherent ideology and new political leadership.

Taraki and Amin also gained important support from young Parchamite civil servants whom Daoud had sent into the provinces to
explain and implement his policies, and then abandoned. They found
themselves confronted by what Dupree has aptly called 'the mud curtain', a wall of subtle (and sometimes not so subtle) non-co-operation
from hostile rural vested interests. They had neither the material nor
moral support of the central government in Kabul which had sent them
there. Dupree has suggested that it was rather clever of Daoud to have
used the young radicals in this way, for in dispersing them to the provinces in the first place, if 'the leftists wanted to plan a countercoup,
their most effective members were scattered outside Kabul', and later,
when they realised that their ideals had been betrayed, 'the disillusioned,
urban-oriented Parchamis straggling back to Kabul posed little immediate threat of an ultra-leftist coup'.[15] But they, along with the
middle-ranking army and air force officers, represented a time-bomb
beneath Daoud's regime: it was the left that he had betrayed which
eventually brought him down.

Despite the Parchamites' unfortunate experience with Daoud, their
second unsuccessful attempt to advance the cause of socialism through
co-operation with the royal family, relations between them and the
mainstream PDPA grew worse rather than better. There were reports of
a plan involving Major Zia Mohammadzai, the Parchamite head of the
Republican Guard, to arrest and kill the Khalq leadership which failed
when it was discovered by its intended victims.[16] There is no independent confirmation of the story, and the Parchamites understandably
deny it, although Babrak's subsequent activities lend credibility to
Khalqi accusations that Babrak was conspiring with Daoud to wipe
them out. The whole incident serves to illustrate – and if true, explain
– the enmity between the two factions and the deep distrust with
which Taraki and Amin regarded Babrak Karmal and his associates. It
also explains why Hafizullah Amin wanted to activate the plan to seize
power as early as 1976. Apart from regular weekly consultations with
Taraki, Amin had adopted the practice of preparing a progress report
twice each year, in January and May. In 1976, after Daoud had put the
axe through his radical ministers, and the Zia Mohammadzai plot had
been discovered, he wrote that the PDPA 'could with a certain amount

of casualties on the part of the armed forces, topple the Daoud government and wrest political power'.[17] Having worked closely with the military for three years, Amin believed that he had sufficient support within the armed forces to ensure a reasonable chance of success, and that the threats to their survival from Daoud and the Parchamites justified the risks involved. For once his powers of persuasion failed. 'Comrade Taraki, with his profound far-sightedness, asked Comrade Amin to wait till the objective and subjective conditions in the country were ripe enough and the party grew still stronger.'[18]

The timidity exhibited by Taraki and the rest of the Central Committee had unfortunate consequences for the PDPA. Two years later circumstances forced the party to seize power or face annihilation. But in the intervening period the Parchamites returned to the fold and, unreliable as they were known to be, they had to be accommodated in the revolutionary government.

There are various reports that the reunification of the PDPA, eventually achieved in 1977, was negotiated through the good offices of a third party. Some credit Ajmal Khattak (a leftist Pashtun leader of the National Awami Party who fled Pakistan in 1973) with bringing the two factions together. Others attribute the successful intervention to the Communist Party of India or to the Russians. The CPI and the NAP both had close links with the Parchamites while the Russians, wherever their preferences lay, maintained contact with both groups through Alexander Pusanov, the experienced and formidable Soviet ambassador in Kabul. It is possible that all three were involved, but it was only under the direst of threats from Daoud who, tempted by Iranian gold, moved even further right, that Babrak Karmal sought accommodation with his old enemies, and the Khalq, having rejected Amin's proposal to go it alone, saw no alternative but a deal with the Parchamites.

The details are not clear, but it seems that neither faction trusted the other and each kept its own separate organisation intact. According to Taraki's biography in July 1977, 'unity was achieved . . . without taking into consideration the number [of] each side, popularity among the masses, organisational experience . . . with equal rights in leadership'.

In the agreement that emerged Hafizullah Amin was the main loser. The old Central Committee was replaced by a Politburo of eleven, including Taraki who made sure he retained the position of Secretary-General. The other ten positions were divided equally between the two factions. One condition on which the Parchamites insisted, and to which Taraki agreed with great reluctance, was that Hafizullah Amin be excluded from this top policy making body. Such was their dislike of him that a later attempt by Taraki to bring Amin into the Politburo nearly split the party once more.[19]

These manoeuvres by Babrak Karmal and Mir Akbar Khyber could not disguise the fact that the organisational strength of the PDPA lay with the Khalq, especially in the armed forces. And control of the military organisation was in the hands of Hafizullah Amin. The civilian and military organisations were apparently dealt with separately. On the civilian side unity was to be achieved on a strictly equal, power-sharing basis although 'facts brought to light recently [September 1978] indicated that Babrak Karmal had secretly kept an organised group of Parchamis for himself'.[20]

Hafizullah Amin was equally determined to keep his laboriously con-structed military power base untainted and under his personal control. It is clear that on this issue Amin had Taraki's complete support. When the time came to seize power, it was to be done by the Khalqi organisa-tion alone:

> In the military field, since the number of Parchami officers was much smaller than that of their Khalqi colleagues, the latter were told that, after Daoud, political power should be wrested by the Khalqis and should Daoud be toppled by someone else, this power ought to be transferred to the Khalqis notwithstanding . . .[21]

Taraki's biography later revealed in no uncertain terms the degree of distrust existing between the two factions:

> Also in the military field, the methods used by Khalqis and Parchamis differed greatly, the former based on wresting power from Daoud and the latter on completely defending the Daoud regime. Therefore Comrade Taraki believed that unity in the military field between the Khalqis and the Parchamis should not be on an equal footing, but should be somewhat delayed.

Amin's successful attempt to keep the PDPA military network separ-ate and intact laid him open to the charge, apparently well founded, that he was attempting to delay or sabotage the reunification of the party. Considering that he had tried to persuade Taraki to run the coup the previous year, it was to be expected that he would have severe reser-vations regarding any unity deal with the Parchamites. But when his own demotion in the party hierarchy was part of that deal his opposition was inevitable and entirely comprehensible.

Such was the fragile, not to say artificial, unity forged between the Khalq and Parcham factions of the PDPA in July 1977. One result was that Amin was forced to revise his timetable for the seizure of power. He told a press conference in Belgrade in July 1978 that the uprising of April that year had been run about two years ahead of plan. But in the early months of 1978 President Daoud's actions imposed a timetable for revolution not of anyone's choosing.

Daoud's policies, and his willingness to bow to Iranian pressure had already alienated several important and powerful groups in Afghanistan, especially within the armed forces. Many believed that the Shah had a hand in mediating the agreement that Daoud now concluded with Pakistan. In return for the release from prison of several Pashtun and Baluch militants by Pakistan's President Zia ul-Haq, Daoud agreed to scale down Afghan support for these groups and to expel by 30 April those who had taken refuge in Afghanistan. Many of these, such as Ajmal Khattak, had close links with the Afghan left, especially the Parchamites, but any sign of a concession on the Pashtun national issue was bound to harden opposition to Daoud from all Pashtun nationalists, an especially important group in the armed forces. Daoud was inadvertently forging a powerful coalition against his regime.

Then, on 18 April Mir Akbar Khyber was murdered. His killer was never identified and it is not clear whether this was an isolated incident or, as was later widely believed, the beginning of an attempt by Daoud's secret police to eliminate all the PDPA leaders.[22] In any case, Khyber's assassination set in train a series of events which led to the seizure of power by the PDPA nine days later. He had been a well known and popular figure, and his funeral procession developed into a large and angry anti-government demonstration, an expression of the hostility to Daoud's regime and policies which had until then been boiling beneath the surface.

This evidence of popular support for left-wing opposition to his regime provoked Daoud into moving against the PDPA leadership, although the slowness of his reaction — it was a week before Taraki was arrested — suggests that he suspected nothing out of the ordinary. The fact that Amin, the key figure in the subsequent uprising, was one of the last Central Committee members to be picked up indicates that Daoud's security forces had no suspicion of the existence of either the plan to seize power or of Amin's organisational network. They were certainly unaware that Taraki's arrest was the pre-arranged signal for the uprising to commence.

Taraki was arrested soon after midnight on 26 April, a Wednesday. At the same time the police raided the homes of four other Central Committee members, including that of Amin. Amin was awakened by his son Abdur Rahman in time to salvage the list of officers involved in the planned uprising, giving it to his wife to hide in the children's bedroom. The police seized his books and papers, but somewhat surprisingly merely placed him under house arrest. His children, including his adult son Abdur Rahman who was also an active party member, were left to move freely.

Abdur Rahman, sent to find out what, if anything, had happened to Taraki, returned at six o'clock with the news of the leader's arrest. In the five hours that remained before he too was arrested, Amin set in motion the plan on which he had worked for so long, giving instructions that the uprising was to begin at 9 a.m. the following morning, 27 April.[23] The timing was determined by the officers' daily routine of travelling by bus to their various units, a routine that was used to communicate the orders to start the revolution. Communication was apparently further assisted by orders given by Daoud's Defence Minister, General Rasooli, on learning of Taraki's arrest that

> all the armed forces detachments be on a war footing and celebrate the occasion the next morning with folk dances and meetings. This treacherous order proved very useful to the process of revolution as the Khalqi elements participated in these meetings where they contacted their unit commanders for instruction without rousing suspicion.[24]

Command of the ground forces was entrusted to Aslam Watanjar, while Abdul Qadir, by now reinstated as Chief of Staff of the Air Force, was in charge of air operations. Watanjar, having announced the commencement of operations to the Armour Corps was then to leave with two tanks for the airport near Kabul, where an air force cadre, Sayed Mohammad Gulabzoi would be waiting with Abdul Qadir. Upon his arrival, the airport would be captured; Qadir would leave by helicopter for Bagram airport to pass on instructions to the Khalqi officer, Hashim, who was to take charge there. Qadir would then return to Kabul and assume overall command of air operations. Radio Afghanistan was to be the first objective, after which the Air Force was to attack Daoud's palace — the Arg.

Things went more or less according to plan, although it was 11.30 a.m. before Watanjar, at the head of 250 tanks and armoured cars, was

eady to leave the Armoured Corps headquarters at Puli Charki for
Kabul and noon before he fired the first shots at the Defence Ministry.
As expected the 7th and 8th Divisions put up the stiffest resistance in
defence of Daoud, the 8th under the direct command of Rasooli. When
Rasooli and other senior officers left the headquarters of the Central
Forces the 8th Division surrendered. The scene of the fiercest fighting
was the Arg itself, attacked by the Armoured Corps and at 4 p.m. by
aircraft, while Radio Afghanistan did not fall into revolutionary hands
until 5.30 p.m. At this stage the 7th Division, belatedly making its way
to Kabul to support Daoud, and the 88th Artillery Detachment, were
still resisting.

Meanwhile, other revolutionaries were looking for the imprisoned
leaders. It was 5.30 p.m. before they found the right jail, demolished
the wall with tanks and armoured cars, releasing the members of the
Central Committee. There was tension beneath the euphoria. While
Amin, handcuffs still locked around one wrist, was congratulating
Taraki, Babrak Karmal asked where they were going, and if victory was
certain. Amin told him that if he did not want to come with them he
could stay in jail.

At Radio Afghanistan, where the party arrived half an hour later,
Amin's account makes it clear that Watanjar and Qadir immediately
handed over command of the revolution to him, and that he made radio
contact with Khalqi commanders, informing them of the victory of the
revolutionary forces. While civilian command over the armed forces was
apparently reasserted without problems, relations among the civilian
leaders were far from harmonious. The tension already existing between
Amin and Karmal was probably exacerbated by reports Amin received
on arrival at Radio Afghanistan to the effect that some Parchamite
officers were supporting Daoud. There followed a disagreement over
who was to make the victory announcement over the radio. Amin
argued that it should be Taraki, on the grounds that his voice would be
recognised by party members in remote detachments who would then
seize power locally.[25] Karmal allegedly strongly opposed this suggestion
and an argument developed between the two men, only settled when
Taraki proposed a compromise: why not let the two military commanders make the announcement? So, at 7 p.m., introduced by Amin,
Watanjar read the Pashtu text and Qadir the Dari version, which is how
the rest of the world came to share the confusion as to who actually
was running Afghanistan.

Babrak Karmal, with some justification, remained unconvinced that
victory had been secured, and wanted the party leaders to retreat from

Radio Afghanistan until all fighting had ceased. This suggestion pro
voked another quarrel between Karmal and Amin. Karmal succeeded
in persuading Taraki and other members of the Central Committee to
withdraw to the comparative safety of the airport. He failed, however
to budge Amin, who was clearly determined that at this critical point
such a vital weapon as the national radio station should remain in his
hands. But dawn had broken on Friday 28 April before the last resist
ance ceased, and the victory claimed at 7 p.m. the previous evening wa
finally assured.

Another matter which seems to have occasioned some disagreement
among those Central Committee members who withdrew to the airport
was the fate of Daoud: 'Karmal insisted that Daoud should be kept
alive, which outraged the Khalqi officers.' The official account is care
fully neutral on this question, placing responsibility for Daoud's death
on the former president's own resistance.[26]

One of the remarkable aspects of the seizure of power by the PDPA
is that, in the official account, *On the Saur Revolution*, we have, as it
were, the inside story. No author is named, but since the pamphlet wa
published by the Political Department of the PDPA in the Armed Force
in Afghanistan, the official title given Amin's organisation after the
revolution, it can be assumed that he at least approved the document
if he did not actually write it. As Amin's personal account (howeve
disguised) of the events surrounding the April revolution it must be sus
pect in certain respects. But despite the bravado, it provides importan
insights into the conduct of the coup and, perhaps more significantly
into Amin's own style of operation.

It reveals that Amin was rather careless about putting things in writ
ing: had his son been a little less alert, the whole plan of action, and the
identity of the Khalqi officers would have fallen into government hands
And yet, twice again that morning, Amin wrote out detailed instruction
for party cadres to pass on. The first of them was Faqir Mohammad
Faqir, who, overwhelmed by events, felt he could not trust his memory
The question of how Faqir Mohammad Faqir was allowed to visit and
leave Amin's house (with the vital list in his possession) while the latter
was under house arrest must remain a mystery. It was only after the
second Central Committee member arrived within half an hour of the
first, at 8 a.m. on Wednesday morning, that the police guard became
suspicious.

When Mohammad Zarif left the house to dismiss the taxi which had
brought him, the police refused to let him re-enter. He managed to con
vey a message to Amin, through the latter's younger son Khwazak, that

ie would await instructions in a nearby restaurant. The instructions, in writing, were duly delivered by Abdur Rahman, with additional copies or Saleh Mohammad and Kheyal Mohammad Katawazi, who was to ake charge of Radio Afghanistan. Apart from having a beautifully lisciplined and co-operative family, Amin was fortunate in having an obviously sympathetic police guard.

The account also suggests that in sensitive situations Amin tended o rely either on members of his immediate family or on close party associates. Widely regarded as an unusually suspicious man, he trusted few people, but those few he trusted absolutely. In making the initial contacts on the morning of 26 April he used his eldest son, Abdur Rahman; his brother, Abdullah; and a cousin, unnamed but quite possibly Yaqub, his brother-in-law, an army major later appointed Chief of the General Staff. Mohammad Zarif and Faqir Mohammad Faqir, the other two men who visited his house that morning and were trusted to carry the instructions to the military cadres, remained loyal supporters and were appointed respectively Minister of Interior and Minister of Communications when Amin eventually assumed the Presidency. The others included in the initial organisation were Saleh Mohammad, Katawazi and Gulabzoi. In Gulabzoi alone was Amin's trust eventually shown to have been misplaced.

On the Saur Revolution also makes abundantly clear the continuing distrust and hostility between the Khalq and Parcham factions. Although the Parchamite leaders took no part in the actual seizure of power — and with the organisation in his own hands Amin would have seen to that — because of the formal reunification which had taken place the previous summer it was necessary to accommodate them in the post-revolutionary power structure, but the old hostility was never far below the surface. The angry exchanges between Amin and Karmal, even before they left the prison, and again at Radio Afghanistan, revealed more than intense personal dislike. They were an indication of the fundamental differences which would soon, once again, shake the PDPA to its foundations.

Notes

1. 'Democratic Khalq Party of Afghanistan: Pioneer of the Working Class', *Tariq-ul-Shaab* (Baghdad), July 1976.
2. Louis Dupree, *A Note on Afghanistan: 1974*, American Universities Field Staff Reports, Asia, vol. XVIII, no. 8 (Afghanistan), September 1974, p. 7.
3. 'Babrak Karmal', *Impact International* (London), 11-24 Jan. 1980. Louis

Dupree refers to Parcham as the 'Royal Communist Party', in 'Afghanistan Unde the Khalq', *Problems of Communism*, July-August 1979, p. 38.

    4. Fred Halliday, 'Revolution in Afghanistan', *New Left Review*, no. 112, November-December, 1978, p. 29.

    5. Dupree, *A Note on Afghanistan: 1974*, p. 7.

    6. Taraki, official biography, *Kabul Times (KT)*, 30 Oct. 1978.

    7. Ibid., emphasis added.

    8. 'Democratic Khalq Party of Afghanistan'.

    9. Ibid.

    10. Ibid.

    11. Dupree, *A Note on Afghanistan: 1974*, p. 11.

    12. Taraki, biography.

    13. *On The Saur Revolution* (The Political Department of the People's Democratic Party of Afghanistan in the Armed Forces of Afghanistan, Government Printing Press, Kabul, 22 May 1978), p. 8.

    14. Dupree, *A Note on Afghanistan: 1974*, pp. 3-4.

    15. Ibid., pp. 7-8.

    16. Halliday, 'Revolution in Afghanistan', p. 30.

    17. Taraki, biography; *On the Saur Revolution*, p. 9.

    18. Taraki, biography.

    19. Information on the unity deal of 1977 was obtained in interviews conducted in Delhi in December 1980.

    20. Taraki, biography.

    21. Ibid.

    22. It is sometimes suggested that Amin was implicated. See, for example, Kuldip Nayar, *Report on Afghanistan* (Allied Publishers, New Delhi, 1980), p. 17 'The murder was pre-meditated and the assailant was reportedly Amin's man.' Most observers however, even those with Parchamite sympathies, dismiss this allegation, and it seems unlikely to be true in view of Amin's later reluctance to execute his most dangerous enemies.

    23. The official history, *On the Saur Revolution*, provides a detailed, blow by blow account of the uprising. Although no author is mentioned, it is likely that Amin wrote it himself, and it is very much his story. It apears to be an accurate account of what happened, although Dupree (*Red Flag Over the Hindu Kush, Part II: The Accidental Coup, or Taraki in Blunderland*, American Universities Field Staff Reports, Asia, 1979, no. 45) doubts the extent of the planning. Undoubtedly there was an element of luck involved, for instance in Rasooli's instruc tions to the armed forces to celebrate the arrest of the PDPA leaders, which disorganised and incapacitated the pro-Daoud officers. But such a complex operation could hardly have been executed so smoothly (and by and large it did go smoothly) without considerable planning and forethought. Another source, th Indian journalist P.B. Sinha claims that Amin had nothing to do with it, that the coup was organised by Gulabzoi, Watanjar and Qadir on the instigation of the Russians (*Afghanistan in Revolt*, Hescht Publications, Zurich, 1970, extracts published in *Der Spiegel*, 14 July 1980). However Sinha obtained his information in Kabul after the Soviet invasion, since which time Amin's achievements have been systematically discredited by the new regime. His account must therefore be suspect.

    24. *On The Saur Revolution*, p. 23.

    25. Taraki, biography.

    26. 'After the victorious revolution communique was broadcast the 88th Artillery Battalion fighting for Daoud under Khalil's command began to defend the revolution. However, firing continued from inside the Daoud's Arg on the Khalqis while the 7th Division in Rishkhor continued its resistance. At this time

when Kabul was getting dark, cloudy and rainy, the heroic Khalqi pilots began to fire on Daoud's Arg with their fighter planes, forcing its officers and soldiers to surrender themselves before dawn. However, Daoud, his relatives and servants were putting up a dogged resistance. Murmurs were heard inside the Arg that Daoud should not be killed. He should rather be caught alive. However, when the Commandos entered Daoud's Arg under the command of Khalqi officers and Daoud was told by Comrade Imamuddin that political power was wrested by the Democratic People's Party of Afghanistan and he ought to surrender himself, Daoud through sheer insanity wounded him with his pistol. Upon this incident, the Khalqi soldiers accompanying Comrade Imamuddin opened fire on Daoud and his associates as a result of which they were felled down and Daoud's Arg was thus captured . . .' *On The Saur Revolution*, pp. 32-3. According to one foreign diplomat, Assadullah Sarwari (nicknamed 'King Kong' in Kabul diplomatic circles) used to boast that it was he who had killed Daoud, though few believed Sarwari's claim.

5   THE INHERITANCE: AFGHANISTAN, 1978

The Afghanistan whose problems the PDPA now found itself con
fronting was one of the poorest countries in the world. Landlocked, it
trade access to the outside world corresponded to the traditional cara
van routes through the old trading cities of Herat, Kandahar an
Mazar-i-Sharif to Iran, Pakistan and Soviet Central Asia. As dispute
with Pakistan and Iran rendered these routes from time to time unreli
able, the transit route through the Soviet Union became increasingl
important.

Predominantly Muslim — 80 per cent Sunni, 20 per cent Shi'i — th
population was ethnically mixed. Dominated by the Pashtun tribes
themselves divided, other groups included Tajiks, Uzbeks, Turkomans
Baluchis, Hazaras and Nuristanis. Two major languages predominated
Dari, an Afghan variant of Farsi (the language of the Durrani court) an
Pashtu, the language of the dominant ethnic group. Although othe
languages were spoken by minority groups, only Dari and Pashtu ha
official status.

The PDPA government which took power in April 1978 was face
with a daunting task, not the least aspect of which was the near tota
absence of accurate or complete statistical information on which t
proceed. No national population census had ever been taken an
estimates varied wildly between that of 17.5 million by the *ancie*
regime[1] and that of a US assisted pilot survey of 12.5 million fo
1979.[2] The new government argued that, for a variety of reasons, th
figure shown by the Demographic Survey underestimated the tota
population. Official DRA estimates for 1978 were therefore place
at 15.1 million, of which the urban population accounted for 14.1
per cent (2.134 million). The rural population was estimated at 12.9
million, of whom some 1.449 million were classified as nomads.

On this basis, per capita income for 1356 (1977-8) was estimate
at 6563 afghanis[3] (approximately US $156) although such an estimat
is virtually meaningless, not only because it fails to take account o
unequal distribution of income, but because much of the rural labou
force received payment in kind. Since the rural sector was not full
integrated into the cash economy, and since there were wide region
variations in wealth, it was exceedingly difficult to make a realisti
estimate of average income.

The Rural Sector

Land Tenure

Any analysis of economic conditions in rural Afghanistan was further bedevilled by lack of accurate or comprehensive information on land ownership or land tenure systems. In 1978 no cadastral survey had even been taken. One Western observer commented somewhat naively: Land and animals are rarely taxed; hence there is no need for inventorying land at the national level.'[4] A more accurate explanation is that any attempt to undertake a cadastral survey was correctly interpreted as a preparation for the introduction of land tax or reform and resisted or sabotaged accordingly. Similarly collection of data on land tenure and related matters was resisted by the rural power centres suspicious of the use to which such information might be put. Successive Kabul governments, in any case short of resources, did not encourage such studies either by Afghan or foreign scholars. Consequently, such information as was available was far from complete. It did suggest, however, a land tenure system of considerable complexity, with important regional variations.

Of a total area of approximately 160 million acres, only about 12 per cent was arable. However, only slightly more than half of the arable land was actually under cultivation and it was estimated that 60 per cent of this was left uncultivated each year partly through lack of water, partly because of the feudal system which dominated the countryside.[5] Land tenure fell into two basic categories: privately owned (*melk*) land and land jointly owned by a tribe or village (*khalisah*). Private ownership was most common in the long cultivated river areas, in Nuristan, and among Tajiks. One estimate placed about half the cultivated land under private ownership, in lots of between 5 and 50 acres (10 to 100 jeribs) with the largest holdings being found in the Helmand and Arghandab valleys, in the three southern provinces of Kandahar, Helmand and Nimroz.[6] One of the reasons for the predominance of small landholdings was the Islamic requirement of equal inheritance among sons which leads to the fragmentation of land into increasingly small plots. According to 1968 estimates, only about 30 individuals owned more than 1000 jeribs (500 acres)[7] but this is not to suggest that very large private landholdings were not a major problem in Afghanistan. In 1978 the new government estimated that 45 per cent of arable land was in the hands of 5 per cent of the landowners.[8]

Collective ownership of land was most common among Turkomans and Uzbeks in the north (in Kunduz, Balkh, Jauzjan and Fariab

provinces), the Chahar Aimaks[9] of Ghor and Herat provinces in the
west, and the Pashtuns of the Safed Koh mountains in Nangahar
province south of Jalalabad.[10] It sometimes applied to agricultural or
pastoral areas acquired through customary use, or through conquest or
treaty. Theoretically land was owned collectively by the tribe or clan
with individual families having the right to a share in the use of the land
according to the number of shares owned by each family head. The
allocation of land was made by the tribal *jirga* (council). In practice the
situation was often very different:

> In certain regions tribal lands and flocks have become the property
> of the tribal chief, and members of the tribe have become tenant
> farmers on his lands and shepherds of his flocks. Their relationship
> with their tribal chief has been changed from one of kinship to one
> of occupation . . .[11]

In other words, a tribal relationship had developed into a feudal one.
   One of the important features of land tenure in Afghanistan was the
expansion of the Pashtun tribes at the expense of others, especially
the Hazaras. The dispossession of the Hazara tribes of the central uplands (the Hazarajat) dated from the relatively recent imposition of
Durrani Pashtun authority over modern Afghanistan by Amir Abdur
Rahman in the 1880s and 1890s. As a reward for their assistance in
suppressing the Hazara revolt of the 1890s, and in order to ensure the
continued subjugation of this group, Abdur Rahman encouraged the
Durrani and Ghilzai Pashtuns to settle in the adjacent Uruzgan region
of the Hazarajat. In addition, Hazara pastures, their main source of
livelihood, were seized by the state and sold to Pashtun nomads, who
gradually expanded into the Hazarajat. This, together with the destruction and dislocation of the war led to the dispersal and dispossession of
the Hazaras, many of whom fled Afghanistan altogether for Central
Asia, Khorasan (Iran) or Baluchistan and Sind. Still others sought an
alternative livelihood in the capital where they continue to constitute
an important minority. The impoverishment of the Hazaras at the
hands of the Pashtuns was one of the underlying causes of tension in
Afghanistan.[12]
   Whether the land was individually or collectively owned, income
from it was traditionally divided according to five inputs: land, water,
seed, capital and labour. In a country as arid as Afghanistan control
over the water supply was an important source of power for those
tribes or families traditionally engaged in the building or maintenance

of irrigation channels, whether underground (*karez*) or surface ditches
(*juis*). But frequently control of the water was in the hands of the landowner. In addition,

> the landowner also supplies the seed. Animal or tractor power (capi-
> tal) for plowing or cultivation may be provided by the landlord, the
> cultivator, or a professional oxen or water buffalo owner. In many
> instances the individual who plows, plants, weeds, tends, reaps and
> winnows the crop receives only the one fifth due for labour. With
> this he supports his family and usually dreams unfulfilled dreams of
> buying his own property.[13]

The size of individual landholdings varied widely from region to region.
For example, a joint FAO-Ministry of Agriculture and Irrigation study
carried out in Baghlan Province in northern Afghanistan in the late
1960s and published in 1972 revealed a pattern of relatively large landholdings.[14] Many of the landholders had migrated from Soviet
Uzbekistan in the previous fifty years, and had been encouraged by the
government's cheap land policy to settle in what was then malarial
marshland. Some farmers owned 300 jeribs or more — one village malik
owned 600 jeribs. The area was subsequently drained, the malaria
controlled, and, from the 1950s when the Daoud regime began to
encourage the industry, became a major cotton as well as sugar growing
area. Although there were several large landowners in the survey area,
only 10 per cent owned holdings of more than 30 jeribs.

In contrast, a study made by Louis Dupree of the town of Aq Kupruk
in an ethnically mixed part of Balkh Province, a comparatively rich
area, revealed a quite different pattern: an average holding of 10
jeribs with 70 per cent of adult males owning land.[15] It was a mixed
farming region, with wheat and corn the main crops, but some cori-
ander and cuminseed, as well as cotton, fruit and vegetables.

Another joint FAO-Afghan government study of the grape growing
region of Koh-i-Daman, a predominantly Tajik area in the Panjsher
valley north of Kabul showed 72 per cent of holdings were less than
8 jeribs (50 per cent less than 4 jeribs) with 28 per cent over eleven
jeribs — including one of 19 jeribs — and an average holding of about
8 jeribs.[16]

A fourth study relates to a survey sponsored by the Faculty of
Agriculture of Kabul University, published in June 1970, of 225
wheat farms, both irrigated and dryland, which revealed an average
holding of 45.7 jeribs — although this gives a slightly distorted picture

since holdings of irrigated land tended to be smaller than farms in dry
areas.[17] Figures for average area per farm given over to wheat are per
haps more useful: 19 jeribs of irrigated land and 49.6 jeribs to dryland
wheat. On these 225 holdings, only 27 per cent were being farmed by
owner cultivators. Another 17 per cent were part owner-operated; 56
per cent were farmed by tenants or sharecroppers.

The Rural Class Structure

Although four isolated studies are no substitute for a national agricul
tural survey, they do point to some of the problems that appear to have
been common to much of rural Afghanistan, in particular the precarious
nature of the livelihood eked out by many, and, related to this the high
level of indebtedness.

Only the report on Aq Kupruk, written in 1966, before the crippling
drought of the late 1960s and early 1970s suggested a prosperous
community apparently spared the hardship of other areas. There was
little indebtedness, and although the shopkeepers 'have thousands of
Afghanis . . . tucked away in their shops and often function as money
lenders . . . few require these services'.[18] Interest rates were usually
under 50 per cent, 'mild' when compared to those imposed elsewhere
by nomad money-lenders.

> In the past people had used their surplus cash to purchase more
> land. Now because most *capable* farmers (one tends to forget that
> many, although not all, of course, landless peasants are lousy farm
> ers, who couldn't hold land if it was given to them) own land, sur
> plus cash is used to purchase additional commodity and luxury
> items (radios, watches, clothing, furniture, glassware, gas lanterns
> flashlights, etc). Liberals may point out that the system bleeds the
> poor farmer, but I find this difficult to believe in *all* cases, for many
> sharecroppers I have known over the past sixteen years in Afghanistan
> now own land – that is, if they have proved to be good farmers.[19]

Even Dupree, however, was reluctant to assert that *all* landless peasant
and unsuccessful sharecroppers were 'lousy farmers' (whatever that
means) who presumably deserved all they got. A clue to the problem
lay in the wealth of the shopkeepers, prepared as they were to lend a
such generous rates of interest; who, Dupree informs us, had in most
cases become landowners as well, and who presumably employed some
of the 30 per cent of the adult male community not 'capable' enough
(or lucky enough) to have acquired their own land.

In discussing tenancy arrangements in Aq Kupruk, Dupree implies the existence of a three-tiered class structure. The crop was shared according to the common system of one fifth for every one of the five elements — land, water, seed, animals, labour — supplied. However, if a landlord supplied more than land, he usually supplied water, seed and animals as well. If the tenant supplied more than labour, he usually supplied animals, seed and water. In effect there were landlords, rich peasants (who owned their own work-animals) and poor peasants who presumably owned nothing. However, Aq Kupruk being a relatively rich district, the landless peasant received half the crop for his labour and Dupree notes that most of the tenants got one half or four fifths of the crop.

The Government/FAO survey of the area around Baghlan also reveals a picture of relative wealth, although rather greater inequality than further west in Aq Kupruk: 73 per cent of farmers surveyed owned 12 jeribs or less, 10 per cent owned more than 30 jeribs; 78 per cent had an income of less than 40,000 afghanis ($533), with 46 per cent earning less than 20,000 afghanis ($267). Only 19 per cent had an annual income of more than 40,000 afghanis. Thirty per cent of the farmers surveyed said their incomes were insufficient for their needs and 25 per cent were in debt. 'The major source of credit was the village itself or the shopkeepers in Baghlan,'[20] at interest rates of between 21 per cent and 50 per cent. Since the survey was specifically concerned with landowners it says little about landless peasants or tenancy arrangements, however only 20 per cent of the farmers surveyed did not hire any labour at all, while most hired labour on a daily basis during sowing and harvesting seasons.

The situation among the grapegrowers of Koh-i-Daman was much more grim. Although 75 per cent had an annual income of less than 40,000 afghanis and 47 per cent earned less than 20,000 afghanis (roughly comparable with the Baghlan sample) 88 per cent were in debt. Many had sought credit to meet their day-to-day expenses, such as food, clothing, furniture, marriage, sickness and water supply. Since there were no formal credit facilities 'all of them had borrowed from richer people in the area'.[21] Interest was sometimes paid in kind, and varied between 10 per cent and 30 per cent. Seventy-eight per cent of farmers in this sample had income insufficient to meet their needs while 68 per cent, when asked their major problem in increasing the yield of grapes, said they did not have money to invest. While only a small proportion (10 per cent) did not hire any labour at all, most (70 per cent) had one or two family members working full time, and from time to time hired labour on a daily basis.

The Kabul University survey on wheat farming revealed a similarly depressed situation, particularly when it is recalled that Afghanistan's main crop was wheat, that consumed as *nan* it comprised about half the Afghan diet, and, despite good seasons in 1967 and 1968 Afghanistan had been a net wheat importer since 1957.[22]

Most of the area planted under wheat was irrigated. Dry-farming was precarious in the extreme. Even though few expenses were involved — the wheat was simply sown and left, sometimes under guard — these might not be recouped because of low yields in years of unfavourable weather. In good seasons, of course, dry farming produced a bonanza, but the risk for the individual farmer was enormous, particularly since he was producing for his and his family's own consumption. The survey estimated that half the wheat produced on farms investigated was used for home consumption, and suggested that since many were above average in size, the proportion consumed at home throughout Afghanistan was much higher.[23]

The introduction of an 'improved' variety on a limited basis in 1968 proved successful in so far as increased yields were concerned, but for the small farmer involved other problems. Although the government sold 'improved' seed to some farmers at 40 afghanis per seer* 'other farmers paid a premium, of money or through barter, in order to obtain improved seeds from other farmers'.[24] The actual cost was usually 50 afghanis per seer in 1968 and, in 1969, 'some farmers in the eastern provinces bartered 2½ seers of local wheat for one seer of improved Mexipak'.[25] In addition 'out of pocket' expenses — cost of seed and fertilizer in particular — were higher by one third for the improved variety. 'Many small farmers have difficulty meeting these expenses, especially if they have no ready source of reasonable credit.'[26] Such credit, of course was not available.

The wheat survey revealed a somewhat different pattern from the regional surveys discussed above: in contrast with those, most of the farms included were worked by tenant farmers.[27] Hired labour, though used for harvesting and threshing was relatively less important, and was usually paid in kind, but family labour accounted for more than half the total. The introduction of tractors would have cut labour costs, but in 1968 there were only 400 privately owned tractors in the whole of Afghanistan. In any case, as a later study showed, the introduction of tractors brought other fundamental changes.[28] In 1966 the government

---

*One seer is approximately equal to seven kilograms.

began selling tractors to provincial farmers. The intention was that they would be bought by village co-operatives. Carrying the normal 100 per cent plus import duty, they were sold for 700,000 afghanis (about US $10,000 at 1973 rates), repayable in seven annual instalments. In Ghazni province, with which the study is concerned, the tractors were bought, not by co-operatives but by wealthy individuals. Some used them to bring more land under dry-wheat cultivation, marginal land that would otherwise have been uneconomic to sow; by this process big landowners became even bigger.[29]

Other tractor owners, preferring a more secure remuneration than that involved in dry-farming, hired out their tractors to other farmers at an hourly rate some ten times the going rate for unskilled labour. The tractors were worked day and night, and following the seasons, went south to Kandahar in winter, returning to the Ghazni plain in spring. The tractor owner could calculate on earning his annual repayment instalment of 100,000 afghanis in two or three months, after which, operating costs aside, he was making clear profit.

The mechanisation of dry farming in Ghazni had other important economic and social consequences. Bringing marginal land under cultivation reduced pasture available to local and nomad flocks which had to go further afield and cooking and heating fuel, formerly gathered in these areas, was no longer available. Shepherding had to be contracted out, fuel had to be bought. 'Two essential resources that had always been "free for the taking" were becoming commodities to be paid for in cash, forcing more and more people into a cash economy for basic necessities.'[30]

It also changed the structure of demand for agricultural labour. Under traditional methods of cultivation some additional labour was required at frequent intervals, leading to the establishment of long-term economic relationships involved in sharecropping, and accompanied by a set of traditional feudal social relations between landlord and tenant. The new tractor cultivation in drylands required a lot of labour, but only for short periods. This was hired on a daily basis, for payment either in cash or in kind, offering increased opportunities for the Ghilzai nomads who summer in Ghazni and traditionally provided this labour. It also attracted other nomads, migratory agricultural labourers rather than pastoralists. There was a decline in the number of share-cropping contracts let. The profits to be made from dry farming led to some irrigated fields being ploughed under, and irrigation water was diverted to fruit crops which required less — but more highly skilled — labour.[31] All these developments, amounting to the introduction of

agribusiness into the countryside around Ghazni, had profound implications for the local rural labour force. Feudalism in this region was
already in an advanced stage of decay when the PDPA came to power
in 1978.

One of the reasons that mechanised dry farming expanded so rapidly
in 1973 was that Afghanistan was still recovering from the prolonged
and severe drought of 1969-72, and grain prices were still high. Hardly
had Dupree completed his optimistic assessment of the prospects of
'good farmers' and Kabul University Faculty of Agriculture completed
its much more cautious report on the problems of wheat farming when
disaster struck.

The first, and possibly the worst affected province appears to have
been Paktya, where the 1969 harvest failed. According to an FAO
report the average per capita income of Paktya was significantly lower
than elsewhere in Afghanistan. There was a high level of unemployment
– and underemployment – and, when FAO assistance was sought by
the government in February 1970, some 48,000 people were affected
by the drought.[32]

For two successive winters – 1969/70 and 1971/2 – precipitation
was only 63 per cent and 57 per cent respectively of that normally
received.[33] The major rivers, Helmand, Arghandab, Hari Rud and Farah
Rud, fell drastically and the US *Area Handbook* records that 'some
important reservoirs held as little as 1 per cent of capacity'.[34] The
worst affected provinces were in the south and the east: the major grain
producing areas. The initial impact was a decline in the quantity of
wheat finding its way onto the market as peasants were barely able to
sustain themselves. In 1971 the price of wheat rose to three times the
1968 level.[35] Livestock numbers declined as animals were slaughtered,
either for food, or because there was no fodder for them. With the
second bad season came famine, reaching its height in April 1972.

> Deaths from starvation between January and June 1972 probably
> numbered at least in the tens of thousands and have been estimated
> as high as 500,000. During the worst month of the famine, April
> 1972, at least 500,000 persons were suffering from severe hunger . . .
> The area affected by the famine contains an estimated 20 per cent
> of the population.[36]

By September 1971, after the failure of the second successive harvest
throughout Afghanistan, Zahir Shah's Prime Minister Mohammad
Musa Shafiq finally acknowledged the seriousness of the situation– a

predicted grain deficit of 500,000 tons – and appealed for international assistance.

The government had initially tried to cope with the situation by initiating 'food for work' programmes in conjunction with the FAO World Food Programme.[37] But what was in effect a strategy designed to alleviate rural unemployment by paying (literally) subsistence wages for minor public works was quite unable to cope effectively with a famine of the proportions of that afflicting Afghanistan in 1972. Many people did starve.

Government insensitivity was compounded by other problems. Of the 500,000 ton shortfall, 300,000 was delivered, two thirds coming from the USA, but bad roads, lack of vehicles and the mobility of some groups hindered food distribution. Further, 'corruption within the Afghan government diverted some supplies from needy groups and . . . inefficiency prevented their speedy delivery. Throughout this period food prices rose precipitously . . . observers have commented that profiteering in food was not unknown.'[38]

The long term effects of the drought, in particular the further impoverishment of the peasantry, were to have serious implications for the class structure of rural Afghanistan. Many peasants already in debt at the onset of the drought found it impossible to meet the high interest payments, let alone repay the original debt, and, losing everything to the money-lender, were reduced to the status of landless labourers.[39] Others, previously able to make ends meet, were forced into debt to buy seed and animals to replace those lost. A similar pattern emerged among the nomadic population. The poorest among them lost their herds and joined the ranks of itinerant agricultural labourers. Others found their herds – and hence their income and security – much reduced.

The only gains made during this period were made by money-lenders, in Afghanistan a disparate group. The disorganisation of rural credit in Afghanistan has already been noted. Bank credit was highly centralised, and all loans had to be approved in Kabul. While much cheaper than non-bank credit, it was not readily accessible to peasants and small landowners, often isolated even from the provincial capital, not to mention Kabul, and bewildered by the bureaucratic procedures involved. So the poorer and less influential members of the rural community were forced to seek credit nearer home. They turned, as we have seen, to wealthy landowners in the district, to merchants in the towns, and, in some cases, to wealthy nomads who provided credit, but usually at crippling rates of interest.[40]

The situation was further complicated for the peasant who mortgaged his land under the *gerow* system, where the landowner borrowed against his land while the lender maintained usufruct until the mortgage was paid off. Since the borrower thereby lost his main means of repayment, he usually also lost his land for good.

A study of business and credit conditions in Afghanistan noted at the end of 1972:

> One of the less favourable findings was that respondents frequently felt that income distribution was becoming less equal; standards of living at the bottom end of the scale had already declined; the rich had become richer, the poor poorer.[41]

Referring to economic conditions in general, this observation applied even more strongly to the rural sector.

The Nomads

An important element in any consideration of rural Afghanistan is the nomadic population who form a significant group, though there is no certainty about their numbers. Estimates in 1978 varied between less than one million to two and a half million. Because of their mobility, and because of their integration into the settled rural economy however, their impact was far greater than their numbers would suggest. Although there was a high degree of interdependence between the settled and nomadic populations, there was also considerable distrust of the nomads on the part of farmers and villagers.[42]

Successive Afghan governments regarded the nomads as 'a problem', and the romantic Western view of the nomads, exemplified by Michener's novel *Caravans*, ignores the fact that most of the present settled population of Afghanistan were once nomads, and not so long ago.[43] The economic rationale of nomadism lies in the necessity for climatic reasons to travel to other pastures, and in trade.

However the history of Afghanistan reveals that, under favourable circumstances, nomads will settle. Provided with land grants by Abdur Rahman, many Pashtuns settled in the southern Hazarajat in the 1890s. The process of settlement has been especially noteworthy among the Ghilzai Pashtun 'gradually settling on and expanding over their summer pastures and shifting to a primary dependence on small scale, often marginal, cereal cultivation which in turn became increasingly commercial'.[44]

Gradually as the network of roads developed by Amir Amanullah brought the markets of urban Afghanistan closer, a new opportunity opened up. Previously the market to which the Ghilzais were oriented was the Indus valley — a rich grain-producing area providing a market for animal products. But as the roads brought Kabul and Ghazni closer, opportunities appeared for the profitable marketing of a grain surplus. So the Ghilzai gradually turned to farming, recent developments including, as we have seen, the introduction of tractors and the extensive cultivation of previously uneconomic dryland areas.

Amongst the nomads there were three definable groups. 'True' nomads, semi-nomads and 'local' semi-nomads.[45] The 'true nomads', estimated at not more than 300,000, were those who lived permanently in tents, and were located mainly in the south. Normally they did not have herds. They included the poorest nomads who had lost their herds for one reason or another. Their numbers were swollen following the 1969-72 drought, when many became itinerant farm labourers. Others used to be camel traders, but, as the roads improved, exchanged their camels for trucks. They remained 'nomads' but, at the other end of the scale from the itinerant workers, they represented merchant capital, and were among the wealthiest groups in Afghanistan.

The second group, semi-nomads, comprised those moving between two regular grazing areas, usually a long way apart: from the north, opened up by Abdur Rahman, down to the Pakistan border area. This group was seriously affected by the closure of the border with Pakistan in 1962, and, more recently, by the drought. Some, unwilling to challenge the border closure, settled and became 'local' semi-nomads. Their number was estimated at about half a million. They were not a wealthy sector of the population, their first requirement being simply survival, followed by the acquisition of goods which made life more comfortable — carpets, for example. Few of them became really well-off, but should he do so (and, with karakul skins fetching about 1500 afghanis in 1979 it was most likely to be the karakul owner) the semi-nomad most often bought land, though he probably did not farm it himself, farming being considered a low status occupation, and, compared with karakul growing, nowhere near as financially rewarding!

The third group, 'local' semi-nomads, Euro-Mongolian in origin, were confined to the nothern areas, and numbered about 200,000. These moved from the village to a temporary camp, often not very far away, for lambing or pasture. They moved with the flocks by virtue of their occupation in the village — they were essentially shepherds — rather than their membership of a tribe. In other words a tribe, located in one or several villages might be part nomadic, part settled.

The Malik, the Mullah and the Landlord: an Interlocking Power Structure

The traditional rural power structure in Afghanistan was fragmented, in part because of the physical character of the country, in part because of the importance of kinship in social, political and economic organisation. Although there were regional variations, however, certain characteristics were common throughout the country.

The basic unit in the power structure was the village, which comprised between ten and five hundred families, but usually was made up of forty to eighty. In this respect a nomad camp was essentially a mobile village. Estimates put the number of villages in Afghanistan at about twenty thousand.

Authority in Afghanistan had its basis in the family, the head of which was the oldest male member. This pattern was reflected at village level where the head of the senior lineage was usually also the village chief (*malik* or *khan*). This position in many cases was hereditary. Whatever the variations in wealth — some maliks were much wealthier than others although wealth relative to the village was a basic requirement for a malik — he guarded his position and the power it conferred jealously. The fragmentation which resulted from the emphasis placed on lineage or tribal groupings was reinforced by the topography of much of Afghanistan — small valleys isolated from each other by great mountain ranges and roads frequently (at least in the past) closed by snow for much of the year. This enforced isolation contributed to the creation of a deep suspicion of the outside world and reinforced dependence on kinship ties.[46]

In Pashtun tribal areas the authority of the chief or khan was limited in some respects by the *jirga* (or assembly of elders), a relationship described by one writer as 'combining aspects of egalitarian tribalism with hillbilly versions of oriental despotism'.[47] Authority within the jirga depended not only on family status and wealth, although these were usually decisive, but on other qualities such as prowess in battle; reputation as a sage, an arbitrator or mediator; piety or religious status; allegiance of a significant group within the tribe or the support of other higher authorities. 'Within the jirga the man with the best combination of these qualities usually speaks with the most authoritative voice and is elected by general acclamation as the chief of that particular council.'[48] He could not afford to forget, however, that he owed his authority to the jirga and must take care not to abuse his power lest he risk challenge from others aspiring to the khanship. Important decisions were made collectively — and usually by acclamation — within the jirga, after which 'the chief has almost unlimited authority to see that it is carried out'.[49]

While there were egalitarian – or 'anti-authoritarian' – aspects of the jirga system, it should be noted that the qualities which permitted the individual to 'speak with the most authoritative voice' and thereby secure election as chief also gave him an advantage in imposing his will on jirga members. It should also be noted that the jirga itself was composed of men already in positions of authority – usually family heads – and in possession of some form of wealth.

Outside the Pashtun areas there were no such limits on the power of the malik: he was very much a law unto himself, effectively beyond the supervision of the central government apparatus, which rarely attempted to impose any control. The malik's functions were to settle disputes, to mediate between the village and the outside world, whether represented by the next valley or the central government in Kabul. Since traditionally most Afghan men bore arms he usually had armed force, sometimes considerable, at his disposal. Central government attempts to disarm the tribes had consistently failed. The malik also had the duty to collect such taxes as might be imposed, and administer recruitment of military conscripts on behalf of the central government. The extent to which he co-operated frequently depended on the size of the armed force at his disposal and the accessibility of the tribe or village to central government authority. As a reward for their support in placing him on the throne in 1931, the Shinwari were exempted from military service by Nadir Shah and successfully resisted attempts by Daoud to reverse this in 1974 and 1975. Attempts by Daoud to disarm tribes around Jalalabad and Torkham also failed, as had an attempt to collect land tax in Kandahar province.[50] The mediatory role of the malik was reinforced by the fact that, apart from the mullah, he was likely to be the only literate in the village.[51]

The central government, outside Kabul, was represented by the provincial governor, the *woleswal* (the official in charge of a sub-province or *woleswali*) and at the district or *alaqadari* level by the *alaqadar*. The alaqadar, based in the largest town in the district would often be physically remote from many villages, but the gap between him and the malik was not simply one of physical separation. Between the malik and the alaqadar existed a 'we-they' relationship. Usually, and deliberately so, a native of another area, the alaqadar was very much an outsider and regarded, with a suspicion bordering on hostility, as someone to be avoided. This was especially true of Nuristan, where the 'Afghan' invasion of the 1890s was still a comparatively fresh memory.[52] From the point of view of the central government, where the alaqadar was the end of the line of paid (and therefore, presumably reliable) officials this created important problems. It meant, in effect, that for some 86 per cent of the population, the administration of local government was in the hands of individuals with their own source of wealth and power, with whom Kabul might negotiate but whom it could not control. At this level there was no way that the central government could ensure the implementation of its policies.

The malik's power with respect to his people was largely economic, in that he was the possessor of considerable relative wealth, either in the form of land or animals, not only in the crude sense, but also because of the status and authority such wealth conferred. As a land-owner, usually the largest in the village, tenant farmers were dependent on him for renewal of their contracts. Each year he allocated plots for cultivation and peasants were frequently moved from one to another, so that they rarely had the opportunity to establish any sort of claim to a particular piece of land. Unsatisfactory tenants could be excluded from the village.

The landlord also, as we have seen, often performed the function of money-lender to his own tenants, and to less well-off landholders. In the poorer regions this sometimes led to a situation where peasants found themselves in perpetual bondage to a village chief, with no pros-pect of any alleviation of their poverty. Such a situation was graphically described by an American observer visiting a village in the Helmand valley in the late 1950s:

> By dint of much probing, I found out that this inheritance of the good earth was not the primary factor that bound these people to him [the village chief]. If that was all they would never have re-mained. They were debtors! Their common bond to him was that they all owed him money.

Further investigation revealed that it was an inherited debt, not one they had incurred themselves:

> They had never been able to reduce the principal, after the cost of survival was deducted from their earnings; indeed, it was more than it had been years ago. How this came about none of them could tell. They only knew that custom, which was how religion was interpre-ted for them, obliged them to keep on paying it.[53]

The malik's economic power was reinforced by the prevailing ideology

— the traditional tribal code onto which Islam had been grafted — producing thereby a blend of tribal and Islamic values unique to Afghanistan. This gave rise to some serious distortions of Islam, the most notable being the Pashtunwali demand for blood vengeance which has no place in the Shariat (Islamic law). Yet an educated Afghan (a Pashtun), explaining the basis of Islam to a non-Muslim audience, once began by describing the pay-back system and insisted that it was central to Muslim beliefs.[54] As a result of Pashtun cultural and political dominance the values of the Pashtunwali have to a large extent been internalised by other ethnic groups. The Islamic attitude to authority strengthened the malik's position and the Quranic injunction to obey God, the Prophet and the Caliph (or ruler) tended to discourage rebellion which is only permissible when the ruler ceases to rule according to Islam. Determination of what was or was not in accordance with the Shariat was, at the village level, the function of the local mullah. The mullah did not derive his authority solely from his function of interpreter and upholder of the Shariat, though this was of great importance. He was also respected for his learning: as noted above he might be one of the few — or even the only — literate in the village. In many villages the only school was the *maktab* or mosque school in which the boys of the village received the only education they were likely to get. As a teacher, the mullah's role was to reinforce the prevailing ideology. Efforts by the Ministry of Education to establish government-run schools in the villages therefore represented a threat to an important aspect of the mullah's power.

Because of the general lack of specialisation at village level the mullah was frequently also a landowner of some consequence, which gave him a further common interest with the malik in the preservation of the *status quo*. The practice whereby one lineage usually provided the mullahs for a tribe further served to incorporate Islam into the tribal system: the mullah's authority derived from his tribal status as head of a lineage as well as from his religious role.

For these reasons the malik and the mullah constituted a formidable coalition through which Afghanistan's rural power structure sought to maintain itself. The coalition — and the power structure — was strongest in the Pashtun tribal areas in the east, although it was influential in most areas, with the possible exception of Nuristan.

Nuristan

Nuristan is a special case in many respects. It was the last region of Afghanistan to be forcibly converted to Islam, in the 1890s, as part of

Abdur Rahman's nation-building drive. He himself was under no illusions about the campaign: 'I do not want to make these people Mohammedan by force. What I do want is for them to acknowledge my rule.'[55] However, in his efforts to win the hearts and minds of the Kafirs, he made it clear that he would brook no opposition. On discovering some Kafir idols in a detention camp he informed the elders that 'if they did not become sincere Mussalmans, they would be blown from guns'.[56]

On conversion to Islam the Kafirs (infidels) were renamed Nuristanis (People of the Land of Light). Numbering about 60,000,[57] they live in the north of the province of Kunar, in the Kunar valley bordering Pakistan. They speak a local dialect and, only since the Afghan conquest, have been motivated to learn Pashtu or Dari, the language of the new rulers. The Kafir economy was basically pastoral, with goat herding the major source of wealth. Some agriculture was practised, but it was a low status occupation, commonly the preserve of low-caste artisans prohibited from ownership of goats. Individual land-ownership was common, and power in the village lay in the hands of the elders of the land-owning, goat-owning families who gained merit by holding ritual feasts for the village and by killing Muslims. After the Afghan conquest, and the forced conversion, Islam was grafted on to pagan Kafir custom, in much the same way that it had earlier been grafted onto the Pashtunwali. Except that, having happened so recently, the new plaster was still visible, and Islam was scarcely more than a veneer over old Kafir practices. Feasts were still held where the old ruling class could afford it. The killing of Muslims was no longer regarded as meritorious, although the killing of 'Afghans' (as the Pashtun tribes are known) remained socially acceptable. Certainly the Afghan incursion was still keenly felt, and much effort on the part of village elders went towards keeping 'Afghan' influence out of the region.

An example of the way in which Islam had been grafted onto local power structures was the enthusiastic adoption of performance of the Haj (the pilgrimage to Mecca) as a form of conspicuous consumption which, like holding of ritual feasts, attracted merit.[58]

With the Afghan conquest came not only the alaqadar, the cash economy and the Afghan money-lender, but also the mullah — and each was regarded as part and parcel of an intruding and competing power structure, threatening the traditional power and authority of the old Nuristani elite. Although Dupree records: 'For the sake of continuity (and the perpetuation of their own power) most Kafir priests become Muslim mullahs, and many of their sons, grandsons, and great-grandsons function as religious leaders today,'[59] it appears that the mullah was not always so well integrated into the old structure. Jones states, for example:

> In no village on the Kalashum [collective name for the villages of the Waigal valley of Nuristan] is a mulla in a position of political influence. Most of them are Afghans and are often landless, and maintained by villagers since they do not usually participate in the economic life of the community ... The mullas discourage all practices which appear to them to be associated with Kafir times, whether they are linked with the pre-Muslim religion or not ... In Kalashum villages a mulla will have a group of devoted adherents, but in general these are not people who would have much influence in the village ...[60]

The Nuristanis use of Islam to resist the authority of Kabul is if anything more cynical than that of the Pashtun tribal leaders, though their defence of their traditional tribal power structure is no less committed.

Disintegration of the Feudal System

As elsewhere in Afghanistan, the traditional tribal-feudal power structure, with the dominance of the wealthy class (either landowners or owners of livestock) underpinned by a whole range of reciprocal social relationships, was gradually disintegrating. In each of the studies discussed above (Aq Kupruq, Baghlan, Koh-i-Daman and Ghazni) the appearance of agricultural wage labour was noted. With the spread of the cash economy and the growing power of usury capital this trend was accelerated, particularly in the wake of the drought of 1969-72. In Ghazni the disintegration of the old feudal structure with the introduction of tractors operated on contract by individuals for profit was particularly notable. In the words of a local tribesman: 'Sahib Khan? He is no Khan. He has a tractor but plows only for himself. It is that way now with tractors. There are no khans anymore.'[61]

In Nuristan too, the old power structure was breaking down. The Afghan conquest which freed the lower caste from slavery also made it possible for its members to seek advancement outside Nuristan, either in the Afghan civil service or the army.[62]

With the appearance of the cash economy came the money-lender, and the progressive impoverishment of the community:

> Debt is one factor that threatens to erode the influence of the elders. If a man needs money, grain or goods which he cannot obtain

from members of his lineage segment, he goes to the Afghan Safi
shopkeepers and moneylenders in Ningalam to borrow at usurious
rates. When he cannot pay, the case goes to the Afghan courts where
it is to some extent out of reach of the elders.[63]

The feudalism that the PDPA was committed to destroy was showing
significant signs of disintegration by the time of the April 1978 revolution. But the tribal-feudal power structure which depended on it,
already on the defensive, was to prove a formidable and dangerous
enemy. In addition it had a powerful ally in the form of Afghan
merchant capital.

Merchant Capital

Despite the predominance of the rural sector in the Afghan economy,
merchant capital had long existed in Afghanistan and was a well-
established and powerful force by the time of the April 1978 revolution.
The major cities of Kabul, Kandahar, Herat and Mazar-i-Sharif were
located on trade routes established for up to three thousand years, the
routes that linked Europe and Asia before the days of shipping. These
cities were long-established trading centres. Trade between Afghanistan
and Iran passes through Herat; that with Pakistan through Kabul and
Kandahar; while Mazar-i-Sharif was the transit depot for trade with the
Soviet Union. Much of this trade was carried by nomads, 'remnants of
the merchant clans whose caravans travelled as far east as China and as
far west as Baghdad',[64] with whom Marco Polo made his voyage to
China. As all-weather roads were constructed along the old caravan
routes, many of the wealthier traders exchanged their camels for trucks.
Some of them bought and sold goods on their own behalf. Others
merely carried goods on contract for merchants in the towns. They
carried Afghanistan's traditional exports, karakul skins, leather goods,
rugs, grain, dried fruit, spices from the producers to the markets,
returning with tea, sugar and imported luxury goods, including second-
hand western clothing, and more recently such things as pens, watches
and transistor radios.

Traditionally the traders provided a source of income for many
Pashtun tribes who either plundered the caravans passing through their
territory or extracted *badraga* (a kind of protection money) from them,
and customs duties were imposed by individual rulers along all the
caravan routes. With the establishment of the centralised Afghan state,

the government in Kabul claimed the sole right to collect customs duty. In order to encourage trade and thereby increase its revenue, the government sought to improve roads and suppress extraction of badraga. Since the improvement of the roads made the caravans less vulnerable to the tribes, this activity was fiercely resisted by them. It was an issue in the power struggle between Amanullah and the Mangal tribe in the Khost region of Paktya in the 1920s and in the late 1950s the government was forced to send in troops to protect a road-building gang under attack from the same tribe.[65]

The collection of customs was especially important to the government since this was its major source of taxation revenue. Direct taxation such as land tax or livestock tax was especially unpopular with the tribal-feudal power elite upon whose collective support the government depended. In return for placing him on the throne in 1931 this group extracted a commitment from Nadir Shah that he would not increase such taxes without their consent. In 1966 direct rural taxation accounted for only 3.5 per cent of government revenue, while customs duties (import and export) provided 27 per cent. Despite the much smaller urban workforce, income tax and company tax combined supplied 8.6 per cent of revenue.[66] As late as 1977/8, although there are no directly comparable figures, a similar profile is revealed. Indirect taxes provided 46 per cent of domestic revenue, while direct taxes provided only 15.2 per cent and the statistical handbook noted: 'Land taxes which were expected to go up substantially were still very low during 1356 (1977/8).'[67]

While the taxation system bore most heavily on them, the merchants of Afghanistan were no less skilled than landowners and pastoralists in tax evasion. Customs houses were situated in the four major trading cities, and collection of customs duty was the responsibility of the provincial governor, on behalf of the Ministry of Finance. The US Army *Area Handbook* notes: 'Although customs duty is the best revenue producer, it is estimated that 50 per cent of the goods entering or leaving Afghanistan are smuggled.'[68] Since traditionally Afghanistan imported much more than it consumed — one estimate placed this at four times as much[69] — the balance being smuggled into Pakistan, the government managed to collect revenue on a significant portion of the smuggling trade. There existed an uneasy live-and-let-live relationship between the government and the smugglers.

One consequence of the development of the entrepôt function of Afghanistan's major cities was the simultaneous development of an international money market to service this trade.[70] The tolerant

attitude of the Afghan government to both, as other countries in the
region (especially India and Pakistan after 1947) took steps to exert
control over their trade and foreign exchange, served to enhance the
regional importance, and the wealth, of the Afghan merchants. Successive attempts by Afghan governments to control these activities were
singularly unsuccessful.

Until 1930 the money bazaars of Kabul and Kandahar (and, to a
much lesser extent Herat) represented the only banking system in
existence in the country. Not only was Afghanistan's trade financed
through the money bazaars, but they were used to satisfy government
banking requirements as well. In that year there were some thirty to
forty private exchange dealers in Kabul and ten to fifteen in Kandahar.

As a consequence of the revolt against King Amanullah and the brief
rule of Bacha-i-Saqao trade had been severely disrupted. King Nadir
Shah called on a wealthy Afghan merchant, Abdul Majid Zabuli for
advice on the means of economic recovery. Zabuli, the founder of
Afghanistan's first joint stock company, recommended the establishment of a bank. Such a proposal, put forward earlier by Amanullah,
had already been rejected by the religious establishment, who objected
to the institutionalisation of usury. As an alternative Nadir Shah
authorised the establishment by Zabuli of a joint stock company to
regulate foreign trade, and with a monopoly over sugar, petroleum and
motor vehicle imports and cotton, karakul and wool exports. This
proved ineffective, and in 1933 the company was reorganised as the
Bank Milli and given a monopoly over all foreign exchange dealings.
Two years later free market dealings were prohibited, and Bank Milli
opened offices in Kabul and Kandahar to take over the functions of the
money bazaars. This was the first sign of a government challenge to the
private foreign exchange dealers. It resulted in a drop in their numbers,
but in 1938 Bank Milli acknowledged defeat and placed its own dealers
in the money bazaars.

In 1939, a central bank, Da Afghanistan Bank, was set up, and in
1943 took over from Bank Milli responsibility for foreign exchange.
Immediately after World War Two its ineffectiveness in this regard was
demonstrated when a depreciation in free market exchange rates
occurred 'caused apparently by "a sudden and substantial increase in
imports . . . to meet unsatisfied demand during the war".'[71]

A renewed attempt to bring foreign exchange under central government control by new rules introduced in 1947 and codified in 1951
effectively restored the system prevailing in 1938, and in any case was
scarcely effective. It established a differential rate for the surrender of

foreign exchange earnings from karakul, wool and cotton below free market rates in an attempt to cream off some of the profit from these sales, but in consequence offered little incentive to merchants to use the bank rather than the bazaar. The introduction of a 'free market rate' based on that in the bazaar in 1965 did not substantially alter the situation.

The money bazaars continued to operate in a legal half-world, left to themselves by the government, except for occasional harassment of individuals, including opening dealers' mail, which made them 'reluctant to deal on anything other than a cash basis'. Fry refers to a police raid in 1969:

After questioning each dealer was obliged to show his trade permit, identity card and military service certificates, and to produce three photographs and a guarantee. It is also reported that fines were imposed. For a while after this event, dealers discontinued their exchange operations and the Afghani depreciated substantially.[72]

The situation made it extremely difficult to collect information on the methods and scope of dealers' operations, and Maxwell Fry's account remains the most comprehensive available.

Part of the explanation for the ineffectiveness of government attempts to control foreign exchange dealings lies in the inadequacy of its resources, particularly in terms of trained personnel, making it simply out of the question for the government to attempt to replace the bazaar merchants.

A more serious inhibiting factor was the political implication inherent in any serious attempt to assert control over foreign exchange. The money bazaars provided facilities for the vast smuggling trade. Any serious attempt to eliminate the private dealers would have severely curtailed the activities of this significant proportion of Afghanistan's foreign trade, estimated by Fry to have been worth approximately $106 million in 1972, or 40 per cent of total recorded trade.

It would have had the effect of depressing normal trading activity, as periodic attempts to crack down on the bazaars indicated. As the government's main source of taxation revenue derived from customs duties this would have seriously depleted the treasury. Until the government was prepared to reverse its policy of dependence on indirect taxes, and impose effective revenue raising taxes on land, livestock and agricultural income (tax exempt), a policy which would have brought it into direct conflict with the tribal-feudal power structure, it could not

move to establish effective control over its foreign exchange reserves.
In this way there was a *de facto* alliance between the tribal-feudal
power structure and merchant capital, which permitted the expansion
of the latter, and in particular the Kabul and Kandahar money markets,
which developed into significant international financial centres. In 1973
there were some 35 principal dealers, with 50 or 60 partners or agents.
Dealers had contacts with foreign exchange markets in Beirut, Bombay,
Delhi, Karachi, London, New York, Peshawar, Tehran and Zurich.
Many dealers operated their own private accounts in foreign banks,
most commonly in London, Hamburg and New York.[73]

The existence of the Kabul and Kandahar money bazaars was also
a thorn in the side of the Indian and Pakistan governments, both of
which exert tight control over their own foreign exchange, banning the
export of their own currency. The foreign exchange dealers of
Afghanistan not only facilitated the smuggling of goods into, but also
the expatriation of capital from, these countries, with the greater effect
being felt, because of its proximity, in Pakistan. They also, of course,
made it impossible for the Afghan government to prevent the flight of
capital from Afghanistan itself.

The Industrial Sector

The industrial sector in Afghanistan has been characterised by slow
development and a high level of government participation, for Afghan
capital has in general found more lucrative avenues for investment than
industry. Apart from the relative profitability of usury and commerce,
a factor discouraging Afghan capital from investment in industry was
the government policy of using customs duty as a revenue raising device
rather than as a means of fostering economic development. Local industry, with the exception of match production, received no protection
from imports. Since Afghan merchants were able to make substantive
profits from trade, they had little incentive to alter their investment
strategy.

In consequence Afghanistan's early industrial development was
undertaken by the government, and was usually militarily oriented. The
first workshops, established in the 1860s, produced guns and artillery.
These were destroyed during the Second Anglo-Afghan war but later
rebuilt by Amir Abdur Rahman who expanded their activities to
include boot-making, leather-stitching, soap and candle production, all
non-military, but designed to serve the army.[74] Much later Amanullah

made some haphazard attempts at expansion which failed through lack of planning and technological knowledge — no one knew how to operate the machinery he imported. Nor did Amanullah ever consolidate his position sufficiently to bring about the stability required for industrial expansion. Gregorian records that 'no important industrial projects were completed in Afghanistan in the 1920s ...'[75]

The next phase of industrial development took place with the encouragement of the government under the auspices of the Bank Milli and under the direction of its founder Abdul Majid Zabuli, in the 1930s. The first industries were related to the processing of Afghanistan's traditional agricultural products — textile mills, cotton ginning, leather goods, fruit processing. Then came construction-related industries: ceramics, cement, wood products. The enterprises were established as joint stock companies, financed by Bank Milli, in which the government retained only a 5 per cent share.[76] The private capital invested was concentrated in very few hands, many closely associated with the ruling elite.[77]

Other state-owned enterprises were leased to private interests. Having provided the initial impetus by assisting the establishment of Bank Milli, the government adopted a low profile, leaving the expansion of the joint stock companies, with their privileged monopoly status, in the hands of a few individuals. While displaying enthusiasm for economic development, the government had 'no clear views on how this should be achieved,' consequently most government activity was of an *ad hoc* nature.[78] This was in part administrative weakness for the government lacked trained personnel to undertake comprehensive economic planning, but more particularly it resulted from political weakness. The government might have opted for a combination of laissez-faire and German state socialism' (it relied heavily on German advice during this period), intervening itself 'only when individual action and initiative was deficient or absent,'[79] but given its taxation policy it was chronically short of funds and locked into continued support of revenue-producing commercial enterprises. Private capital would only invest where the return was substantial, assured and virtually immediate: it was not interested in long-term investment in the industrial infrastructure. In any case, to have interfered with investment in commerce would have been to threaten the golden-egg-producing goose. The government itself lacked the financial resources to develop either communications or electric power and its insistence on a 'pay-as-you-go' philosophy regarding national development designed to keep the country free of a large foreign debt, meant continued neglect of the infrastructure.

During the period 1933-46 a motorable road was constructed linking Kabul with the northern provinces but most of Afghanistan's trade over an estimated 18,000 miles of dirt tracks, was still carried by camel caravan. By the mid-1940s Afghanistan produced only 22,000 kw of power, most of it serving the capital.[80] At this time the government made its first big break with traditional policy, and concluded an agreement with the American firm Morrison-Knudson for the construction of two dams and supporting canal systems in the Helmand Valley estimated to cost US $63.7 million. The scheme ran into enormous problems, many of them stemming from administrative weakness on the part of the government.[81]

The palace coup of 1953 which swept the older generation of royal uncles from power, replacing them with Sardar Mohammad Daoud, the King's cousin and contemporary, signalled a change in the government's approach to economic development. Daoud was committed to rapid, planned development. Recognising the inadequacy of private capital to the task, Daoud, in his five year plans, placed emphasis on public sector industrial development. This expansion was financed by foreign loans, mostly from the USSR and the USA, but also from other Western and Eastern bloc countries as well as the World Bank.[82] Some fifty new state-owned enterprises were established by Daoud. The results were not impressive. Most factories worked below — sometimes as much as 60 or 70 per cent below — full capacity. Fry, somewhat predictably (given that his study of the Afghan economy was undertaken as part of a US AID project) considered the cause to be inherent in the nature of government-owned enterprise.

There were other factors, which he mentioned as impeding economic development, though he failed to make the connection in this case. These included the government's inability to mobilise an agricultural surplus — the failure to attain self-sufficiency in grain production 'acts as a critical constraint to economic development'[83] — and inadequate statistical information which made co-ordinated development planning an impossibility. The first Five Year Plan was prepared in 1956 'after a series of studies and investigations which have taken into consideration the lack of statistical data and experience in planning. Without this data and experience but with the help of God Almighty this plan has been formulated.'[84]

Although later plans utilised foreign assistance, the quality of statistical data remained poor. The plans were little more than lists of projects for which foreign assistance was solicited. Fry reserves his trongest criticism for the Afghan government's failure in domestic esource mobilisation, which leads him to question its commitment to lanned economic development. But no government could hope to nobilise domestic resources effectively without successfully challenging Afghanistan's tribal-feudal authority structure.

Following another palace coup in 1963 in which King Zahir Shah acked Daoud and took control himself, the policy of public sector nvestment was reversed. However, private enterprise did not show tself eager to take up the role abandoned by the government.

Certainly some development of the economic infrastructure had een achieved. In 1967 the road network was estimated at about 8,500 niles (including the Salang tunnel) of which some 1,250 miles were aved, providing for the first time a year-round road link between Kabul and the north. There were 3,000 miles of secondary dirt roads nd 4,000 miles of tracks that were not always passable. 'Camels and ack ponies utilising thousands of miles of caravan routes provide the sual means of distributing goods throughout most of the country.'[85] Fen years later (1977/8) of the total of 11,500 miles of road, some 4,800 miles were paved, with 5,500 miles of secondary dirt roads and .,150 miles of tracks.[86]

Another indicator of the development of the economic infrastruc- ure, electric power supply, reveals a similar pattern. The 22,000 kw of he 1940s had expanded by 1966 to nearly 60,000, though most still erved Kabul. By 1356 (1977/8) this had risen to 764 million kwh of vhich some 53 per cent was produced in Kabul Province. At the time *one of Afghanistan's villages was electrified*.[87]

One legacy inherited by the new government in April 1978 was an mmense foreign debt. Debt servicing charges amounted to between 15 nd 20 per cent of current expenditure.[88]

Despite the expansion that had taken place during and after the 1950s, the industrial sector accounted for only a small proportion of Afghanistan's economic activity. The Soviet historian Akhramovich oted that, 'The few light industry plants, all the country had could neet but 10 to 15 per cent of the *home demand* for textiles, sugar, ootwear, and so on.'[89] This critical view of Afghan industrial develop- nent was later endorsed by the US Army *Area Handbook*: 'In terms of vailable resources, industrial potential considerably exceeds the :ountry's present ability to mobilize capital for development.'[90] In 977/8 industry accounted for only 17 per cent of gross national pro- luct and only employed an estimated work force of approximately orty thousand.[91]

As with other aspects of Afghan society or economy, detailed and up-to-date statistics are not available. However, an industrial census taken for the years 1345-48 (1966/7 to 1969/70) provides some useful information.[92] It emphasises the highly concentrated nature of Afghanistan's tiny industrial proletariat — geographically in the Kabul region, industrially in the cotton ginning and textile industries and physically in large, usually government-run factories. Of the six industrial regions (based on six major cities), Kabul accounted for approximately 70 per cent of the industrial labour force, followed by 22 per cent in the second industrial centre of Kunduz in the north. The other four, Kandahar, Mazar-i-Sharif, Herat and Jalalabad accounted for the remaining 8 per cent between them, with factories in Herat and Jalalabad together employing less than one per cent of the workforce. Some 39 per cent of workers were employed in textile or cotton ginning works, 11 per cent in mineral products (including cement works) with food processing, mining, construction and electricity accounting for between 7 and 9 per cent each. And 66 per cent of the workforce was employed in the 14 factories employing five hundred or more workers, (with 50 per cent in the 7 factories with over one thousand employees).

Although trades unions were illegal — labour relations were regulated by a Labour Code, administered by the Ministry of Mines and Industries — there is some evidence of politicisation of the work force. After the split in the PDPA in 1966/7, the Khalq strategy was to carry on party work among the masses. The wave of strikes in 1968 and 1969 in some of the largest factories in the major centres suggests they may have had some success. Strikes took place in Kabul at the National Printing House and the Jangalak Industrial Workshop, the latter erupting into violence; at Jabal-as-Saraj, involving workers at the cement plant and other industrial workers, as well as the nearby Afghan Textile Co. factory at Gulbahar; at Pul-i-Khumri in the Afghan Textile Co. factory and the cement works; at Kunduz, at the Spinzar Company. In Kunduz and Pul-i-Khumri the workers were supported by peasants and students, and students also demonstrated in support of striking workers at Jabal-as-Saraj.[93]

The Bureaucracy

The bureaucracy that the PDPA inherited was a medieval model, geared to tax collection and maintenance of law and order, quite unsuited to complex tasks imposed on it by governments striving, however hap hazardly, for socio-economic development. The need for administrative reform had long been recognised by successive Afghan governments, especially that of President Daoud, as well as various foreign advisers, but the Afghan bureaucracy had proved particularly resilient.

The civil service in 1978 numbered over 100,000 and included anyone — teachers, doctors, lawyers, diplomats — receiving a salary from the government's budget. Recruitment was the responsibility of individual ministries. In a token attempt to control nepotism, an employing officer was not permitted to employ any relative (including brothers, sisters, nephews, nieces and in-laws, but not aunts and uncles) under his direct control. In fact, family connections were of prime importance in securing a civil service position. There was no civil service list or public advertisement of vacancies. High school (twelfth grade) graduates entering the civil service at rank ten did so by what one source referred to as 'informal interpersonal communication'.[94] Dupree has referred to the way in which the rural power elite sent what he described as their 'second line of power' to Kabul 'as a first line of defense' . . .

> The second line of power, after setting up shop in Kabul, began to build its power base with horizontal links to the government, in addition to the regional vertical tribal kin links. The men of the second line were able to feed brothers, sons, cousins and other relatives into the government bureaucracy, thus strengthening their position in a single generation.[95]

In this way the tribal-feudal authority structure, at one remove, infiltrated the bureaucracy. While they may gradually have lost control of 'their men in Kabul', the bureaucracy had meanwhile been white-anted by people whose first allegiance lay in regional, tribal or kinship links. The question of loyalty aside, this method of recruitment meant that those who gained civil service positions were not always the most able representatives of their generation.

Apart from problems created by nepotism, the government had difficulty in recruiting the most gifted and best educated young men and women who were attracted by the higher salaries offered in Europe and America and, after 1973, in Iran and the Gulf countries. While some aspects of civil service employment were attractive — not least being the status it conferred — there were serious drawbacks. Salaries (at least in the upper ranks) while comparatively high in Afghan terms, had not kept pace with inflation and civil service salaries despite increases

in 1977, had in 1978 in fact declined in real terms by 50 per cent sinc
the late 1960s. Many senior officials came from wealthy enough familie
to be able to survive low salary levels, but for others, particularly thos
below rank 4, or the lower paid contract employees, real hardship wa
involved.[96]

Civil servants did receive certain fringe benefits. They were able t
buy, through co-operatives, essential goods such as flour, tea, sugar an
heating fuel at subsidised prices, although subsidies did not extend t
housing, one of the most expensive aspects of life in Kabul. Cars wer
provided for the higher levels, but free transport to and from work wa
provided for all employees of ministries in Kabul. These privileges how
ever scarcely made up for the decline in real income.

One of the inevitable consequences of low salary levels was a hig
incidence of corruption − baksheesh payments for a whole variety o
permits, licences and other documents. This in turn led to the develop
ment of a vested interest in and hence the institutionalisation of ur
necessarily complicated bureaucratic procedures; at one stage it wa
necessary to apply to seventeen or eighteen offices for a licence to trade
with 'efficiency charges' imposed by each. Apart from the administrativ
inefficiency involved, this practice resulted in a poor relationship be
tween civil servants and members of the public who had to deal witl
the bureaucracy.

There were other frustrations involved in a public service career be
sides low salaries. Promotion opportunities came slowly, every two t
four years. Procedures were cumbersome, and advancement, especiall
in upper levels, was often blocked by incumbents who gained and hel
their positions through personal contacts. This created a log-jam an
with it demoralisation and discontent in the middle ranks. Anothe
problem contributing to low civil service morale arose from poor per
sonnel management. Apart from the rank structure, there were no jol
classifications or descriptions for positions in the various ministries
Appointments were made by the Personnel Department of the ministry
often without reference to the person being appointed or his supervisor
there was no procedure for matching special skills or qualities to th
requirements of the job. It also meant that, since they could be trans
ferred at any time, employees had little incentive to commit themselve
to the completion of a particular project.

Efficient administration was further hampered by the reluctance o
officials to accept appointments outside Kabul. This was especially im
portant in relation to technical personnel required for development pro
jects. Field allowances were inadequate to compensate for the expense

ither of maintaining two households or moving the family to another
)cation, or to compensate for the hardship and isolation often involved
1 work in the provinces. Failure to persuade good people to work in
ural areas had serious implications for many social and economic de-
elopment policies, particularly in the fields of medicine and education,
lthough there was also a serious shortage of engineers and agricultural
xtension workers.

Other factors contributing to inefficiency, frustration and ultimately,
emoralisation included exceedingly narrow and rigid audit procedures,
he institution of direct, personal responsibility for equipment as well as
lecisions and cumbersome procedures regarding government stores.[97]

Government stores were kept in warehouses operated by a *tawildar*
•r keeper — not a civil servant himself but a man who had paid a con-
iderable sum of money for the right to act as caretaker for that parti-
ular store. If the tawildar happened to be away for any reason no item
lowever small could be removed from the store. One instance was re-
•orted where a tawildar was brought from jail, under guard, in order to
•pen a store and release much-needed equipment. The tawildar usually
equired several signatures authorising the release of equipment — often
ight up to Director-General level. The situation arose occasionally
vhere equipment had been procured, stored and, because of a lack of
ffective stocktaking procedures, forgotten. The tawildar's reluctance
o release goods within his care was a direct consequence of the fact
hat he personally was held responsible for every single item in 'his'
•ondstore.

In a more generalised fashion the emphasis on personal responsibility
ed to administrative paralysis at lower and middle levels: no one wanted
o take the decision. In consequence senior officials spent a dispropor-
ionate amount of time taking decisions on minor matters that should
lave been within the competence of their subordinates, while at the
niddle levels of the civil service initiative was stifled. On other occa-
ions, rather than take responsibility for a possibly unpopular decision,
)fficials resorted to committees in an effort to achieve consensus. More
)ften they simply failed to reach any decision at all.

Apart from sheer bureaucratic inefficiency the Afghan civil service
vas hampered in its task of promoting economic and social develop-
nent not only by members of the rural power elite who had infiltrated
it various levels, but by members of the religious establishment (the
ilema) who had been recruited to the civil service, in particular the
Vlinistries of Justice and Education, by earlier governments.[98] The first
noves in this direction had been made by Amir Abdur Rahman with

respect to the Islamic legal system. His objective, in which he was to degree successful, was to impose secular control over the Muslim jurist to bring Afghanistan's legal system within the scope of the governmer in Kabul. He might, in the short term have limited their power. But i bringing them into the civil service and putting them on the governmer payroll, he bureaucratised them and gave them a vested interest in th maintenance of the system. In effect he provided them with a powe base in the bureaucracy in addition to the formidable power base the already enjoyed within the tribal-feudal authority structure. By so doin he made the path of future legal reformist governments immeasurabl more difficult, as his grandson, King Amanullah, found to his cost whe he tried to introduce a legal code based on a European model. Islai makes no distinction between law and theology, and Afghanistan' lawyers were graduates of Muslim theological colleges. By proposin the introduction of a European-style legal code, King Amanullah nc only offended the ulema's religious beliefs, he threatened the livelihoo of many of them. Small wonder that he had a 'religious' revolt on hi hands!

Having settled accounts with Amanullah, the religious establishmen secured important concessions from Nadir Shah.[99] The brother of th Hazrat of Shor Bazaar was appointed Justice Minister. The Shariat gaine a special place in the new Constitution. And graduates of the newl established Faculty of Theology at Kabul University established stranglehold on the Ministry of Justice.

The judiciary was not the only area in which the ulema establishe a bureaucratic power base. They came to regard the field of educatio as their preserve. As Islam recognised no distinction between Law an Theology, it recognised no scholarship outside the narrow confines o its own *madrasas*. The religious establishment secured for the villag mullah in his maktab not only a large degree of autonomy but a plac on the government payroll. As Abdur Rahman had attempted to tam the jurists by employing them, so Nadir Shah recruited the teachers t 'modernisation'. As the jurists were given a veto over draft legislation so too were the ulema given a veto over the syllabus adopted in Afghai schools.[100]

Many of the ulema who later opposed the PDPA first went under ground after Daoud's coup of July 1973. All Nadir Shah and Zahir Sha had achieved was to further entrench the religious hierarchy whose authority had a much more powerful base than 'the personal behaviou of the village mullah'. When Daoud appeared to threaten this base – their domination of the judiciary and education, and the tribal-feuda authority structure of which they formed an integral part — they went into revolt. They were still in revolt when the PDPA seized power in April 1978.

The revolution was not only confronted with powerful enemies, it had in the civil service an entirely defective instrument with which to implement its reforms. For nearly fifty years, since the accession of Nadir Shah, the civil service had been treated as the preserve of powerful and ambitious families — usually Pashtun — who had used it as a means of protecting and extending their original power base in the rural areas. At the upper levels it not only was not geared to the implementation of economic and social reforms, it was positively antipathetic to such measures. In the middle and lower ranks, where members of the new generation of educated young Afghans were to be found, along with members of non-Pashtun ethnic groups (usually Tajiks) — allies or potential allies of the revolution — there was frustration and demoralisation.

The first task confronting the PDPA government was to turn the civil service from a bastion of the old ruling class into an effective weapon of the revolution.

Earlier Attempts at Reform

The task confronting the PDPA was indeed formidable: it amounted to the imposition of central government authority throughout Afghanistan as much as social and economic reform — in fact, as a prerequisite for such reform. It was a task which King Amanullah attempted, and for which he was hopelessly ill-equipped, financially and technically. He dared to challenge the tribal-feudal authority structure, and, failing, was destroyed by it. Subsequent Afghan governments were careful to leave it alone, to carry out reform and modernisation *around it* as it were. Such a policy led eventually to a dead end: economic and social reform could only progress so far while the vast majority of Afghanistan's population lay in the grip of a reactionary tribal-feudal ruling class, and while the 50 per cent of the gross national product generated by the rural sector remained untapped. The stranglehold exerted by this class over more than four-fifths of the population and half the national income had to be broken. Of this Daoud seems to have had some inkling: after 1973 he initiated reforms which pointed in this direction.

In 1976 he introduced two new laws — the graduated land tax law and the land reform law.[101] The Seven Year Plan period (1976-83) was to be occupied with a cadastral survey. Payment of land tax was to be regarded as evidence of ownership. Ceilings were set of 100 jeribs of prime irrigated land, 150 jeribs of secondary (single crop) land and 200 jeribs of non-irrigated (dry farming) land. Larger land holdings were to be dealt with first, with surplus land being taken by the government. However, generous provision was made for compensation for any land expropriated, and landlords were given ample time to sell off surplus land before the ceilings came into effect − at the end of the seven year period set aside for the cadastral survey. Landless peasants would receive the surplus, but they would have to pay for it, although no provision was made to meet small farmers' credit requirements. At the same time the law made no attempt to modify traditional terms of share-cropping or tenancy.

The main thrust of the Daoud government's policy was revenue collection, rather than social justice − to impose an effective system of land tax, rather than redistribute land or improve the lot of the peasants. The number of landlords owning more than 100 or 200 jeribs was certainly small and under the 1976 legislation they had between seven and eight years to sell off surplus land, and the period of the Seven Year Plan to haggle with officials conducting the cadastral survey. In fact the landowners involved had every opportunity to subvert the reform and when the revolution took place in April 1978 no real progress had been made on the cadastral survey.

An attempt at administrative reform met a similar fate.[102] Aware of the need for such reform Daoud, at the end of 1974 embarked on a project, with UN assistance, directed to this end. In December 1976 a Special Commission reported on the need for reform, listing its major criticisms of the existing machinery. Following the release of this report a decision was taken in May 1977 to set up a Central Office of Personnel and Administrative Reform (COPAR) within the office of the Presidency, under Daoud's personal supervision. However, further developments were defeated by the bureaucratic inadequacies and the vested interests that were the targets of the new reform organisation. The organisation and functions of COPAR were not worked out until December 1977 and, when the revolution took place the following April, no one had been appointed to head COPAR and the organisation was completely inoperative.

The success of other measures which Daoud had embarked upon such as planned integrated rural development and the conduct of the first ever national census were compromised by his failure to press on with administrative reform and land reform. The snail-like pace with which the government moved in both cases gave the tribal-feudal and bureaucratic elite time to mobilise its resistance, to ensure, as they had done in the past, that their power remained untrammeled. Daoud's caution betrayed his lack of resolution: when it came to the crunch he was not prepared to challenge the traditional Afghan power structure — logically enough, for he and his family were part of it.

For the PDPA the lessons were clear. Taraki and Amin did not make the mistake of underestimating the enemy: the tribal-feudal ruling class and the bureaucracy that served it had, for over fifty years, successfully resisted attempts by the central government to implement reforms that represented the slightest threat to its power. If the Revolution was to succeed, if the quality of life of the vast mass of the Afghan people was to be improved there could be no half measures. The power of the old ruling class and the tribal-feudal authority structure on which it rested had to be smashed once and for all. And its destruction had to be swift and thorough.

Notes

1. Population projection estimates, Government of the Republic of Afghanistan, *First Seven Year Economic and Social Development Plan, 1355, 1361 (March 76-March 83)*, vol. 1 (Ministry of Planning, Kabul, 1355 (1976)), p. 53.

2. Democratic Republic of Afghanistan, Ministry of Planning Affairs, Central Statistics Office, *Estimate of the Population of Afghanistan in 1357 and Projection of the Population for the Years 1358-1362* (CSO Printing Office, Kabul, Sonbullah 1357 (August-September 1978)).

3. Democratic Republic of Afghanistan, Ministry of Planning, Central Statistics Office, *Statistical Information of Afghanistan 1975-1978* (Afghan Education Press, Kabul, December 1978), pp. 3, 41. For further illustration of the problems confronting the PDPA see Table 1: Afghanistan 1977: Some Social Indicators.

4. Nigel Allen, 'The Modernisation of Rural Afghanistan: a Case Study', in Louis Dupree and Linette Albert (eds.), *Afghanistan in the 1970s* (Praeger, New York, 1974), p. 117.

5. Saleh Mohammad Zeary, 'Feudalistic Relations, Democratic Land Reforms', *Kabul Times*, 15 Sept. 1978.

6. Harvey H. Smith *et al.*, *Area Handbook for Afghanistan*, 4th edn, US Government Printing Office, Washington 1973, p. 272.

7. Louis Dupree, *Afghanistan* (Princeton University Press, Princeton, 1973), p. 153.

8. Saleh Mohammad Zeary, *KT*, 19 July 1978. See Table 2, Distribution of Land in Afghanistan, 1978.

9. Dupree, *Afghanistan*, Chart 6. Dupree disputes the use of 'Chahar' to describe these people.

10. *Area Handbook*, p. 272.

11. Ibid., p. 272.

12. See M. Hassan Kakar, *The Pacification of the Hazaras of Afghanistan* (Afghanistan Council, Asia Society, Occasional Paper no. 4, New York, 1973).

13. Dupree, *Afghanistan*, pp. 148, 151.

14. Government of Afghanistan Ministry of Agriculture and Irrigation Programme on Agricultural Credit and Co-operatives in Afghanistan (PACCA Project) Badam Bagh Training Institute, *Farmer Characteristics in the Baghlan Pilot Area* (Food and Agriculture Organization of the United Nations (FAO/TF), Technical Report no. 8, Kabul, 1972).

15. Louis Dupree, *Aq Kupruq: A Town in North Afghanistan, Part 1: The People and Their Cultural Patterns* (American Universities Field Staff Reports, South Asia Series, vol. X, no. 9 (Afghanistan), Nov. 1966), p. 10.

16. A.P. Barnabas, *Farmer Characteristics in the Koh-i-Daman Pilot Area* (PACCA, Kabul, Technical Report no. 4, April 1970).

17. Khairullah Dawlaty *et al.*, *Wheat Farming in Afghanistan: Cost of Production and Returns*, Technical Bulletin no. 17 (Faculty of Agriculture, University of Kabul, Afghanistan, June 1970).

18. Louis Dupree, *Aq Kupruq: A Town in North Afghanistan, Part II: The Political Structure and Commercial Patterns* (American Universities Field Staff Reports, South Asia Series, vol. X, no. 10 (Afghanistan), December 1966), p. 9.

19. Ibid., pp. 14-15.

20. PACCA Report, *Baghlan*, p. 12.

21. PACCA Report, *Koh-i-Daman*, p. 11.

22. *Area Handbook*, p. 263.

23. Dawlaty, *Wheat Farming*, p. 15.

24. Ibid., p. 8.

25. Loc. cit.

26. Ibid., p. 6.

27. Most of the information was however provided by the landlords, or as the survey report felicitously puts it 'owner-non-operators'.

28. Jon W. Anderson, 'There Are No *Khans* Anymore: Economic Development and Social Change in Tribal Afghanistan', *Middle East Journal*, vol. 23, no. 2, Spring 1978.

29. Unplotted, unirrigated land was considered by the government to be public domain, essentially open to all with the right of disposal retained by the government. In practice, local Ghilzai regard it as a species of commons to which those with adjoining irrigated fields had a pre-emptive right. Within that category, furthermore, specific persons or families secured, by repeated use, customarily recognized planting rights to specific portions in some cases. Such rights could be inherited but not otherwise disposed of by selling or letting on sharecropper contracts. These arrangements were not always spelled out, as there was usually more dry land than could be traditionally farmed, and the status of unimproved land thus varied from place to place from 'spoken for' to 'free for the taking'. Ibid., p. 174.

30. Ibid., p. 175.

31. Ibid., p. 176.

32. World Food Programme Inter-Governmental Committee, Twenty-Fifth Session, Rome, 22-26 April 1974, *Community Development in Paktia (quasi-emergency), Terminal Report* (WFP/IGC:25/11 Add. B.5, Feb. 1974), p. 153.

33. DRA, *Statistical Information of Afghanistan*, p. 153.

34. *Area Handbook*, p. xx.

35. World Food Programme Inter-Governmental Committee, Twenty-Fifth Session, Rome, 22-26 April 1974, *Community Development (quasi-emergency), Terminal Report* (WFP/IGC:25/11 Add. B.6, Feb. 1974), p. 1.

36. *Area Handbook*, p. xx.

37. Referring to the scheme undertaken in Paktya, the WFP report states:

> The issuance of WFP wheat to the beneficiaries during the drought emergency was made dependent upon the participation to the extent possible of the able-bodied men in community development public works. The response was very positive. During April/July, when WFP wheat was distributed an average of up to 3,500 labourers volunteered daily for riverbed protection, improvement of irrigation channels, construction of wells, road improvement and other development works. (WFP/IGC: Add. B.5, p. 2.)

imilar programmes were introduced in other provinces in the spring of 1972 and later WFP report notes:

> The experience gained from this project brought out an important feature of the situation in Afghanistan, namely that a large number of small works can be executed by local communities if they are provided with their staple food (wheat in this case), which can sustain them during the period of work. That such a large number of works could be executed in widely scattered localities shows the response of the people to the incentive of food. (WFP/IGC: s5/11, Add. B.6, p. 5.)

t is indeed amazing what people will do to avoid starvation!

38. *Area Handbook*, p. xx.
39. See Maxwell J. Fry, *The Afghan Economy: Money, Finance and the 'ritical Constraints to Economic Development* (E.B. Brill, Leiden, 1974), p. 151.
40. Saleh Mohammad Zeary, Minister for Agriculture, told a journalist in July 978 that interest rates varied from 25 per cent to 300 per cent, but that 'when I 'as in prison I heard that peasants had paid as much as four hundred per cent in nterest . . .' (*KT*, 19 July 1978).
41. Fry, *The Afghan Economy*, p. 5.
42. Dupree, *Aq Kupruq, Part I*, pp. 26-8.
43. Anderson, 'There Are No *Khans* Anymore', p. 178.
44. Ibid.
45. I am indebted for this explanation to an informant in Kabul engaged in a tudy of the nomads.
46. See Leon B. Poullada, *Reform and Rebellion in Afghanistan, 1919-1929* Cornell University Press, Ithaca, 1973), for an excellent description of Pashtun ribal custom. Another useful source is M. Ibrahim Atayee, *A Dictionary of the 'erminology of Pashtun's Tribal Customary Law and Usages* (International Centre or Pashto Studies, Academy of Sciences of Afghanistan, Kabul, 1979).
47. Anderson, 'There Are No *Khans* Anymore', p. 168.
48. *Area Handbook*, p. 189.
49. Ibid., p. 189.
50. Dupree, *Afghanistan*, p. 538.
51. This liaison role was referred to by the FAO survey teams in both Baghlan nd Koh-i-Daman. The Baghlan report simply noted: 'The village (Tulabai) is amed after the present malik who has been so for the last thirty years. He is a ort of liaison man between the settlers and the Government officials' (PACCA Report, *Baghlan*, p. 5). The Koh-i-Daman report was more explicit regarding the mplications for the survey of the malik's role in the village: 'It is not easy to meet eople individually. As the Malik calls the people, he too is present while the espondents are being interviewed . . . When the Malik himself is there, it is difficult to ask questions about leadership . . .' (PACCA Report, *Koh-i-Daman*,

p. 24). See also Anderson, 'There Are No *Khans* Anymore', p. 170.

52. See Schuyler Jones, *Men of Influence in Nuristan* (Seminar Press, London, 1974).

53. Edward Hunter, *The Past Present: A Year in Afghanistan* (Hodder and Stoughton, London, 1959), p. 267.

54. At a seminar at Sydney University, April 1980.

55. Schuyler Jones, *Men of Influence*, p. 231.

56. Ibid.

57. Louis Dupree, *Nuristan: 'The Land of Light' Seen Darkly* (American Universities Field Staff Reports, South Asia Series, vol. XV, no. 6 (Nuristan), Dec. 1971), p. 1.

58. Jones at first found emphasis on the Haj

> curious among a people whose eyes still light up when they relate the
> (probably exaggerated) number of Muslims their fathers and grandfather
> killed . . . Contrary to expectations it was found that the *hajji* himself
> tends to be traditionally oriented; he is a member of an important family
> in the traditional sense; he is a wealthy *atrozan* (land-owner) and an
> influential elder . . . The respect that villagers have for the *hajji* is much
> involved with family reputation and the resources required to make the
> journey. His father and grandfather used their wealth to give feasts to
> achieve rank, and he has used his wealth to make the pilgrimage to achiev
> prestige . . .' Jones, *Men of Influence*, p. 249.

59. Dupree, *Nuristan*, p. 12.

60. Jones, *Men of Influence*, p. 234.

61. Anderson, 'There Are No *Khans* Anymore', p. 171.

62. Schuyler Jones, *Men of Influence*, passim.

63. Ibid., p. 251.

64. *Area Handbook*, p. 237.

65. P.J. Reardon, 'Modernisation and Reform: The Contemporary Endeavour in G. Grassmuch and L.W. Adamec (eds.), *Afghanistan: Some New Approaches* (University of Michigan, Ann Arbor, 1969), cited in Fry, *The Afghan Economy*, p. 56.

66. *Area Handbook*, p. 359.

67. DRA, *Statistical Information of Afghanistan*, p. 8.

68. *Area Handbook*, pp. 344-6, 358.

69. Interview, Kabul, March 1979.

70. For a discussion of the role of the Kabul and Kandahar money bazaars, se Fry, *The Afghan Economy*, p. 234.

71. Ibid., p. 235.

72. Ibid., p. 238.

73. The following incident, reported by Maxwell Fry, testifies to the significance of Afghanistan's money bazaars:

> In 1351 (1972) a representative of one of the big American merchant
> banks visited Afghanistan to entertain traders from Kandahar who held
> large deposits with his institution and to solicit more accounts. Althougl
> a 'wholesale' bank, this bank was keen to keep such personal accounts
> because its Afghan clients appear to have been content to hold demand
> deposits in excess of $100,000 each, with few demands for services apar
> from easily undertaken credit standing inquiries. A charge of $3 per tran
> action is made to discourage small traders from opening accounts. It
> would seem therefore, that dealers in the Kandahar Bazaar also finance

a substantial volume of trade from convertable currency countries. Ibid.,
p. 240.

74. Vartan Gregorian, *The Emergence of Modern Afghanistan* (Stanford
University Press, Stanford, California, 1969), p. 143.
75. Ibid., p. 253.
76. Ibid., p. 362. This was increased in 1949 to 25 per cent.

77. Between 1933 and 1946 Bank-i-Milli managed to attract the greater part
of the private capital in the country, and to invest it in some 50 trading
and industrial holding companies. The same important merchants who
held shares in the bank were the majority stock holders of these companies. In addition to a virtual monopoly in the major commodities of
the Afghan export-import trade, the Bank-i-Milli and its president, Abdul
Majid Zabuli, gained control of most of the industry of the kingdom,
both the well-established, state-owned enterprises and the budding new
firms . . . Ibid., p. 363.

78. Fry, *The Afghan Economy*, p. 84.
79. Gregorian, *The Emergence of Modern Afghanistan*, p. 362.
80. Ibid., p. 367.
81. Dupree, *Afghanistan*, p. 482.
82. Ibid., p. 630.
83. Fry, *The Afghan Economy*, pp. 52-3.
84. Ministry of Planning, *First Five Year Plan, 1956/57-1961/62* (Kabul:
Ministry of Planning, mimeo, 1956), p. 2, cited ibid., p. 79; see also pp. 80-1.
85. *Area Handbook*, p. 336.
86. DRA, *Statistical Information of Afghanistan*, p. 109.
87. Interview, Kabul, March 1979.
88. The Economist Intelligence Unit, *Quarterly Economic Review of Pakistan,
Bangladesh, Afghanistan, Annual Supplement 1979*, p. 36.
89. R.T. Akhramovich, *Outline History of Afghanistan After the Second
World War* ('Nauka' Publishing House, Moscow, 1966), p. 11.
90. *Area Handbook*, p. 292.
91. DRA, *Statistical Information of Afghanistan*, pp. 3, 169-70.
92. Royal Government of Afghanistan, Ministry of Mines and Industry,
German Economic Advisory Group, *Industry Survey 1966/67-1969/70* (Kabul,
September 1971).
93. Dupree, *Afghanistan*, p. 620.
94. Information relating to the Afghan civil service is drawn from interviews
and documents obtained in Kabul, March 1979.
95. Louis Dupree, *Afghanistan Continues its Experiment in Democracy*
American Universities Field Staff Reports, South Asia Series, vol. XV, no. 3
Afghanistan), July 1971), p. 8.
96. Civil service salaries, 1977 (based on information obtained in Kabul, 1979).

Rank	Title	Annual Salary $US
1	Presidents Governors Deputy Ministers	$1600
2	Presidents Governors Chief Province Finance Officers	$1360

Rank	Title	Annual Salary $US
3	Director-General	$1333
4	Director	$ 813
5	Director	$ 733
6	Supervisor	$ 667
7	Supervisor	$ 587
8	Head Clerk	$ 507
9	Head Clerk (Entry for University graduates)	$ 467
10	Clerk (Entry for High School graduates)	$ 440

97. The following instances will illustrate the problem. An official, unable to hire labour at the stipulated rate, paid more. As a result he was able to complete the project ahead of schedule and well within the budget. But he was reprimanded by the Audit Department for paying more than the set wage. In another case an engineer, out in the field, returned to Kabul for a brief period in connection with the project on which he was working. When he left he took with him a machine, vital to the project, but which had been issued to him and for which he was personally responsible. Work on the project came to a standstill until he returned.

98. For discussion of the bureaucratisation of the ulema see Gregorian, *The Emergence of Modern Afghanistan*, passim, and Richard S. Newell, *The Politics of Afghanistan* (Cornell University Press, Ithaca, 1972).

99. Gregorian, *The Emergence of Modern Afghanistan*, pp. 294-5.

100. This strategy was applauded by a leading American scholar writing in 1972:

> The present dynasty has achieved a large share of its stability from having successfully incorporated religious specialists into government service and by emphasizing the religious components of its authority. The regime has set out to enlist the clergy's support in the process of state-building and, profiting from Amanullah's example it has succeeded to a large degree. Religious authority is still primarily based upon the personal behaviour of the village mullah, and his hostility towards the growing power and secularisation of the central government appears to have softened. To some extent this has been achieved by permitting religious leaders to influence the functions of the Ministry of Justice. A similar effect has resulted from incorporating a large proportion of the village mullahs into service of the Ministry of Education as public school teachers. (Newell, *The Politics of Afghanistan*, p. 75.)

Within twelve months the dynasty of which Newell wrote was overthrown and the ulema showed just how much their 'hostility toward the growing power and secularisation of the central government' had in fact softened by opposing President Daoud's administration from the beginning.

101. For a discussion of these proposed reforms see Christopher J. Brunner, 'New Afghan Laws Regarding Agriculture', in *An Analysis of Several Recent Afghan Laws* (Afghanistan Council, Asia Society, Occasional Paper no. 12, New York, October 1977).

102. Information obtained in Kabul, March 1979.

6 STRATEGY FOR REFORM

The People's Democratic Party took up the challenge of reforming Afghanistan's social and economic system well aware that earlier reformist governments had been defeated by the system they tried to change. The PDPA sought to avoid the pitfalls that had engulfed its predecessors by carefully analysing the situation and defining the problems, identifying its allies and its enemies and then, having united the former under its leadership, moving with care, precision and determination to demolish the latter. Apart from the sheer enormity of the task, and the inadequacy of the existing tools, which meant that the PDPA was virtually starting from scratch, there were many problems.

One difficulty, inherent in the attempt at a scientific approach, was that objective conditions were continually changing and consequently the analysis and the party's response were subject to constant revision. From this arose the disagreement within the party between the Khalq and Parcham factions over the appropriate strategy. The PDPA manifesto 'Aims and Objects of the Democratic Khalq Party' published in *Khalq* in 1966 was no longer applicable in certain important respects after the April 1978 revolution and Taraki gave this as the reason for not re-publishing it. This was only part of the explanation. It was clear that the manifesto had ceased to be applicable long before, but the fundamental differences between the two groups which persisted after the reunification of the party in 1977 prevented the drafting of a new manifesto which might have been presented to the Afghan people after the April Revolution. Once the party seized power events moved so fast that the breathing space necessary to produce a new manifesto never presented itself. Instead the party put forward a brief outline of its programme, entitled *Basic Lines of Revolutionary Duties of the Government of the Democratic Republic of Afghanistan*, clearly based on the earlier document, but with some important differences.[1]

According to the analysis contained in the manifesto, Afghanistan was considered to have a feudal socio-economic system, the basic contradictions being between the feudal class and the peasants on the one hand and the people of Afghanistan and imperialism on the other. The poverty and misery of the Afghan people were attributed to the economic and political hegemony of the feudal class, which had to be broken before any progress could be made. The feudal class consisted

107

of 'compradores, hoarders, big businessmen, corrupt bureaucrats, monopolists, and international imperialists whose class interests run counter
to the masses of Afghanistan'. The first step towards the destruction of
the hegemony of this class was the formation of a 'national united front
of patriotic democratic progressive forces, viz. workers, peasants, progressive elite, artisans, small bourgeoisie (small and average class landlords) and national bourgeoisie (national capitalists) . . .' under the
leadership of the PDPA. Its 'strategic objective' would be the foundation of a 'national government'.[2]

The PDPA considered that such a government had been established
as a result of the successful uprising of April 1978, which marked the
beginning of the national democratic revolution in Afghanistan. It was
the duty of the new government to consolidate and complete this revolution.

The reference in *Basic Lines* to the 'abolition of old feudal and pre-
feudal relations' indicates that the PDPA had refined its former analysis
to take into account the existence of the tribal system which complicated Afghan feudalism, but the absence of any direct reference to it
and the assurance that the new government would respect 'desirable
national traditions and customs' suggests a) that they did not want to
confront the tribal system head on and b) that they expected that the
problems it presented would be overcome by the agrarian reforms they
intended to implement.

In contrast to the 1966 version, the PDPA in *Basic Lines* refrained
from listing those considered its enemies, concentrating instead on
identifying its allies, presumably in the hope (now it was actually in
government) of attracting the broadest consensus possible. The people
of Afghanistan, in whose interests it was working, included 'workers,
peasants, officers and soldiers, craftsmen, intelligentsia, patriotic clergy,
toiling nomads, small and medium classes and strata, i.e. businessmen
and national entrepreneurs'. The inclusion of members of the armed
forces reflected an important change in objective conditions as they
related to the PDPA since 1966. It is also significant that, in its reference to 'patriotic clergy' and its assurance of 'respect to the principles
of the Holy Islamic religion', the PDPA had, in the intervening twelve
years, recognised the importance of and the need to come to terms with
the religious establishment.

The PDPA attempted to gather these groups into a national united
front, but not, as the Parchamites advocated, by permitting their direct
participation in government. The Khalq leadership rejected any suggestion of forming a front with other political groups[3] because it feared

that the momentum of the revolution would be lost, basic reforms undermined and its prime and essential commitment, the destruction of the old feudal ruling class, would never be achieved. They had the example of Daoud before them and realised that delay or compromise would be both inevitable and fatal. In any case, there were no political groups of any consequence with whom a united front would have been practicable, as Babrak Karmal subsequently discovered. Instead the Khalqi government encouraged its supporters to join those organisations which had been established under PDPA leadership, such as workers' unions, peasants' co-operatives, KOAY and KOAW[4] (the youth and women's organisations) and later the Committees for the Defence of the Revolution, which were formed on a village or neighbourhood basis.

The party identified its class enemies readily enough when the time came, but in *Basic Lines* it chose merely to issue a warning in the form of a list of policy objectives. These included 'weeding out from the state machinery anti-revolutionary, anti-democratic elements . . . and the creation of a sound and democratic state administration to serve the people'; protection of domestic industry against foreign competition; reduction of dependence on indirect taxation and an increase in direct, graduated taxes; price control; and adoption of 'effective measures' for the elimination of 'bribery and red tape, hoarding, usury and smuggling . .' Corrupt bureaucrats, monopolists, compradors, hoarders and big businessmen were put on notice to shape up or ship out. Many who had been closely associated with the old royal family fled, leaving their often considerable property behind. Others, Afghan and foreign businessmen, gradually wound up their affairs and left, taking their capital with them, a simple matter since the government could not and did not attempt to control the money bazaars of Kabul and Kandahar.

The PDPA decided to slay one dragon at a time. It set itself a precise and limited — but by no means small — target: the abolition of feudal and pre-feudal relations in Afghanistan. The key to this campaign was the combination of agrarian reforms prepared and implemented as soon as the millstone of Parchamite obstructionism had been removed and the government's limited resources could be mobilised.

The first of the agrarian reforms was presented in Decree No.6 designed to break the vicious circle of perpetual and ever increasing debt which led to the impoverishment of growing numbers of small and medium landholders, as well as landless peasants, and to provide the machinery for implementation of this reform, and others then in preparation.[5]

The decree distinguished between different types of debt, and the

status of the landowners. It was designed in the first place to reverse the
damage done when peasants mortgaged their land under the *gerow* system.[6] The government estimated the return on agricultural land to be
20 per cent per annum, which meant that someone who had collected
the harvest of mortgaged land for five years or more had effectively
been repaid. Land mortgaged in 1353 (1974) or before was therefore,
after collection of the standing harvest, to be returned to its owner. For
land mortgaged after that date, the mortgagee was permitted to collect
the standing harvest and then, after one year, which provided the debtor
with some income, the principal was to be repaid on a sliding scale and
over a period determined by the length of the loan.[7] This meant that
the person who extended the loan to the peasant got his money back,
but without interest, unless the loan was more than five years old, in
which case he was not to be permitted further exploitation. No attempt
was made to impose special hardship on the mortgagee who was to be
permitted to collect the harvest due to be reaped as the decree was promulgated.

For other forms of debt the status of the debtor was taken into
account. Landless peasants or labourers were exempted from payment
of debts due to landowners and usurers and from payment of interest.
So too were those owning ten jeribs (five acres) or less of first grade
land, who had incurred the debt before 1353 (1974). Debts incurred
in subsequent years by this category of landowner were to be repaid on
a sliding scale similar to that provided for mortgage repayments. Again,
the principal was to be repaid, but not the interest. Debts of landowners
with more than ten jeribs were considered outside the scope of the
decree on the grounds that 'larger landowners usually borrow for re-
investment in buildings, in farm improvement, for trading, and the like,
and when they borrow they are likely to get richer [rather] than poorer
...'.[8] The ceiling of ten jeribs was chosen because those owning this
amount of land or less, estimated at 71 per cent of all landowners,
usually found it necessary to lease land from the middle and large landowners and were therefore regarded as more vulnerable. After the loans
were considered to have been repaid within the provisions of the decree,
the mortgage and credit documents were annulled.

Given the extent of rural indebtedness throughout Afghanistan,
Decree No.6 had far-reaching effects.[9] Zeary estimated that it benefited 81 per cent of rural families, returning the land of those who had
lost it to money-lenders, and giving all peasants and small landowners
the chance of making a decent livelihood. It was not designed as a punitive measure against money-lenders, whether they were landowners

themselves, merchants in the towns, or nomad merchants. No attempt
was made to control interest rates for other types of loans, or for loans
to bigger landowners.

To administer the reform, the government made provision for the
establishment of Committees for the Solution of the Problems of the
Peasantry at province and woleswali level.[10] It was the Woleswali Committee that was responsible for the implementation of Decree No.6, and
also for the settlement of disputes between landlords and peasants arising as a result. Should the Woleswali Committee be unable to settle a
dispute, it was to be referred to the Provincial Committee, whose decision was binding and final. In addition the Woleswali Committee was
charged with the preparation of a cadastral survey, based on land tax
records and such other documents as existed, to enable the government
to proceed with its plans for land redistribution.

Provision was made in August for the establishment of Peasants'
Assisting Funds and Peasants' Co-operatives through which the government could channel financial and other assistance — such as seed, fertiliser, technical assistance — to the peasants.[11]

The next major step in the agrarian reform was the promulgation, on
17 October, of Decree No.7, relating to marriage laws.[12] It placed severe
restrictions on the payment of *maehr* (bride price) and other marriage
related expenses, set a minimum age for marriage of sixteen for girls
and eighteen for boys, and made the consent of both parties mandatory.
The provisions of Decree No.7, innocuous and unexceptionable as they
appeared on the surface, probably hit harder at the tribal-feudal structure of rural Afghan society than any of the other reforms. Under the
Pashtunwali (the Pashtun tribal code), whose values, as a result of Pashtun cultural dominance, had been internalised by minority nationalities
and spread throughout the country, women were regarded as property,
first of their fathers (or their oldest living male relative) and subsequently of their husbands. The Islamic provision for maehr, originally
a sum paid on marriage to the bride by her husband, and intended as a
kind of security should he die or divorce her, was distorted under the
Pashtunwali. In Afghanistan it was paid to the bride's family, which
meant in effect that women became commodities in rural property
transactions. Their consent was not required — nor for that matter, was
that of their prospective husbands. The whole deal was arranged by the
elders of the respective tribes.[13] Apart from the de-humanising aspect
of the process, the payment of maehr and related marriage expenses,
which could and often did run into tens of thousands of afghanis, was
a major cause of peasants' indebtedness. By placing an upper limit of

300 afghanis on maehr and forbidding the former practice of compulsory gift-giving to the bride's family on major religious holidays, the
government was aiming not only at social reform, but also at removing
an underlying cause of much rural economic hardship.

The third agrarian reform measure, Decree No.8, providing for land
redistribution, took longer to prepare and implement than the others.
The decree itself was approved only at the end of November, and its
implementation began in January 1979 in the warmer southern provinces and the following month in the colder areas.[14] In the meantime
the Committees on Peasants' Problems had completed the cadastral
survey which permitted the reform to proceed, a remarkable feat since
the cadastral survey initiated by Daoud in 1976 had made scarcely any
progress by the time of the April 1978 revolution, and existing records
were therefore scanty and confused.[15] The government announced the
successful completion of the redistribution — the first phase of the land
reform — on 2 July 1979, only six months after it had commenced.

The government set a ceiling of thirty jeribs (fifteen acres) of prime
irrigated land, or its equivalent which, while considerably lower than
the hundred jerib ceiling set by Daoud (but never implemented) still
adversely affected only a small number of landowners, certainly less
than 17 per cent and perhaps no more than 400.[16] However, it involved
the redistribution of approximately half the arable land to families
classified as 'deserving', i.e. those owning ten jeribs or less, who made
up 81 per cent of the rural population.

Apart from bringing about greater social and economic justice, the
government envisaged that the redistribution of land would improve
agricultural output by bringing more arable land under cultivation.
Under the old system, many big landowners had not bothered to cultivate all the arable land in their possession. It was estimated that only
40 per cent of the arable land had been cultivated annually.

Allocation of water was almost as important as distribution of land.
Under the old system, maintenance of irrigation ditches and canals was
traditionally the responsibility of one family, and allocation of water in
the village the prerogative of one man, the *mirab*. Under Decree No.8,
control of the flow of water and its allocation was taken over by the
Ministry of Water and Power and the Ministry of Agriculture and Land
Reforms. Maintenance and improvement to irrigation systems was to be
the subject of agreement between the local Institute for the Improvement of the Irrigation System and the peasants' co-operative, and financed by loans to the co-operative by the Agricultural Development
Bank.

Actual implementation of the land redistribution was carried out by Khalqi Specialised Committees at woleswali and province level in co-operation with the Committees for the Solution of Peasants' Problems.

The agrarian reforms represented the core of the government's strategy for the destruction of the old feudal system, but if they were to be effective they had to be backed up by reforms in education, the judiciary and the administration.

One of the highest priorities was the government's literacy campaign, since so many of its development schemes depended on raising the overall educational standard of the entire population.[17] Previously the extension of literacy had been in the hands of the Functional Literacy Directorate, established with UNICEF and UNESCO assistance in 1348 (1969). It suffered from the ills afflicting the whole of the Afghan bureaucracy, and from the lack of interest displayed in social reform by previous regimes. By the time of the April Revolution, it had produced only 5,265 literates. After the revolution, a new body was established, the National Agency for the Campaign Against Illiteracy (NACAI), under the chairmanship of Shah Mahmoud Haseen. The appointment of Dilhara Mahak, President of KOAW as Vice-Chairman of NACAI was an indication of the government's commitment to extend the literacy campaign to women. In the first weeks after the revolution the regime concentrated its efforts on the armed forces, claiming by July that 6,000 soldiers had been distributed among various units, and would be taught (on a voluntary basis) by officers.[18] In July NACAI held the first of a series of seminars to train teachers and supervisors. The literacy campaign was seen by the government as an opportunity to explain the party's objectives and the aims of the revolution and the seminar was at least in part designed to raise their political consciousness.[19] At the time NACAI had 510 teachers and 60 supervisors on its staff. Teaching was to be done in the participants' mother tongue, and a board of editors was appointed to prepare material in Nuristani and Baluchi as well as the major languages of Dari and Pashtu.

The original NACAI objective of total eradication of illiteracy in five years was later recognised as over-optimistic and in October 1979 Amin announced a revised target of ten years.[20] The main problem confronting the literacy campaign was the shortage of resources in terms of both trained personnel and teaching materials. Although the literacy campaign probably did encounter some resistance, especially in so far as it attempted to draw women into its courses, Hafizullah Amin denied that this had been important and in an interview with foreign journalists in August 1979 appealed for international financial assistance, saying that if it were forthcoming the campaign could be extended. There were simply not the means available to encourage all women to go to schools.[21]

The problems which afflicted the literacy campaign were common to the entire education system, especially the shortage of trained manpower. One means by which the government sought to overcome the immediate problem was to appoint as teachers the many unemployed high school graduates in the provincial centres. This had the two-fold advantage of providing a pool of schoolteachers for the rural areas and winning the support and co-operation of this important segment of the country's youth. An attempt was made to overcome their lack of training by instituting seminars or short courses although these were aimed more at raising political consciousness than inculcating teaching skills.

A high priority was the revision of the school syllabus and the preparation of new textbooks more relevant to the revolutionary objectives of the new government. Not only was there a shortage of textbooks, there was a shortage of printing facilities. An early and much publicised move was commencement of construction of a textbook printing press at the Ministry of Education,[22] and in September 1978 the government nationalised all eleven printing presses in Kabul.

Revision of the school curriculum was the first area where the government ran up against the vested interests of the religious establishment which had been given a veto over what was included by previous regimes. An assurance that Islamic Studies would continue to be taught failed to mollify many of the ulema who saw an important source of their power being taken from them.[23]

There was a similar, but if anything more acute, problem in the judiciary. In *Basic Lines*, the PDPA committed itself to 'Promulgation of democratic laws in all spheres and abrogation of all laws and regulations and disbanding of all institutions which contradict the aspirations and principles of the revolution . . .' This had clear implications for the Afghan judiciary which was manned for the most part by graduates of the Faculty of Theology of Kabul University, who represented a formidable obstacle to any attempt at secular reform of the legal system. The PDPA was fortunate to have in Hakim Sharai Jauzjani, the Minister of Justice and Attorney-General, a theology graduate able to deal with the ulema in their own terms. He instituted a series of seminars and training courses designed to explain the new government's policies and objectives, and to appeal for their support. Early in June 1978 he told an audience of students from Kabul's religious schools that the government deeply respects all Islamic principles and values but it shall not allow anybody to beguile the people in the guise of Islam [or] to serve their narrow-minded and anti-national vested interests by using Islam as a toy. Islam will be hereafter duly respected. We will prove this in practice and the people would judge that our objects and actions will conform with the essence of Islam.[24]

The government received a mixed reception from the ulema. One report claimed that five hundred of them had left Afghanistan in the four months following the April Revolution,[25] but much later an Afghan alim* asserted that one of the factors influencing his village to leave for Pakistan was the appearance of 'mullahs from Kabul preaching communism'.[26]

The first step in another important area of reform — that of the bureaucracy — happened almost automatically. Following the warning issued in *Basic Lines*, Taraki specified the criteria which would be used for dismissing civil servants: 'sabotage and practical anti-revolutionary actions, corruption, ill-repute, bribery, tyranny and despotism, and inefficiency'. At the same time he expressed his confidence that the majority of civil servants, even if they did not support the PDPA, were neutral. Programmes for 're-educating' them were in hand, and they would be employed in conducting the affairs of the new government.[27]

It is not clear how many were dismissed. The *New York Times* of 9 May reported the sacking of sixty officials of the Foreign Ministry while a month later the right-wing Pakistani daily *Nawa-i-Waqt* reported that not only had the civil administration been 'totally replaced' since the April revolution, but that others on the state payroll such as 'priests, trustees and teachers in mosques are also being replaced'.[28]

Many did not wait to be sacked or re-educated. They already identified with the old ruling class who had long dominated the upper ranks of the bureaucracy, and seeing no future for themselves under the new regime, left their jobs. The result was not the disaster for the government that is sometimes suggested. Certainly there was a shortage of trained manpower, but that was not new in Afghanistan. Traditionally many young Afghans privileged to receive a higher education had been lured by bigger salaries elsewhere and had either left the country, or not returned on completion of their studies abroad. The loss of a few more whose commitment to the objectives of the revolution was in doubt and who, had they remained may well have jeopardised its survival either

*alim (s.), ulema (pl.).

intentionally (as some attempted to do)[29] or through sheer incompetence, was a blessing in disguise.

Their going broke the log-jam, and made possible the promotion of others in the lower and middle ranks who could be relied upon to support the reform programme. What they lacked in experience, they made up for in enthusiasm. The government attempted to raise civil service morale, eroded by the fifty per cent drop in real income brought about by inflation, by announcing across-the-board promotions in most ministries. Another measure was the initiation of a low-cost housing project in Kabul, where high rent was one of the greatest problems for civil servants, especially those in the lower ranks. But the manpower shortage remained acute.

Another measure, in line with the commitment to a 'democratic solution of the national issue', was the publication of newspapers, periodicals and books in the minority languages which were given equal status with Pashtu and Dari. The abolition of compulsory Pashtu classes and of the monetary bonus paid Pashtu speakers in the civil service was announced early in October.

The same month, in a gesture designed to make clear to everyone that the April Revolution represented an absolute break with the past, the government introduced a new national flag, red with a gold emblem, symbolising its commitment to the slogan 'Food, Clothing and Shelter' under which the revolution had been carried out.

Measures such as those introduced by the PDPA, designed to change the economic power structure of the countryside and affecting 86 per cent of the population were bound to result in some dislocation and to generate serious opposition from the old ruling class who were thereby deprived of the means of maintaining their dominance. Critics of the PDPA have argued that its reforms were inappropriate and implemented with undue haste and brutality which led to widespread opposition, not only from the old ruling class, but from the peasants themselves.[30]

Relieving the peasants of a crushing and otherwise inescapable burden of debt is one of the most important aspects of any socialist land reform. But the money-lender, however rapacious, performs an important function in providing necessary rural credit and it is equally important that an alternative should be provided. The PDPA, in providing for the formation of Peasants' Assisting Funds and Peasants' Co-operatives showed itself aware of this need and in August 1979 Hafizullah Amin said that in the period up to June 1979, nine hundred such organisations had already been established and this number was steadily increasing. Fifteen hundred tractors had been distributed, along with fertiliser and improved seed.[31] That the establishment of these bodies was slow and their resources pitifully inadequate is a valid criticism, but the reason was the government's own lack of resources and not its failure to confront the problem. To have delayed the implementation of Decree No.6 until adequately financed funds and Co-operatives had been established throughout Afghanistan would have been to leave the peasantry to carry indefinitely an already unbearable burden. To the extent that other agrarian reforms depended on this first one, it would have invited further problems arising from the delay.

In any case the greatest need for credit was to meet payment of interest on debts already incurred. The reform removed this source of debt and with it the need for credit to meet it. The next most common reason for peasant indebtedness was marriage related expenses, and this was removed under Decree No.7. Relief from this combined debt burden together with the return of mortgaged land gave the peasant a means of earning a living and a chance of meeting other expenses, such as the need to buy seed or to cope with family illness, without having to borrow money. As a result of Decrees 6 and 7 the need for rural credit was much reduced, and the gap arising from the inadequacy of government sponsored credit facilities was not as great as has been suggested.

Reports of disruption as a result of the land redistribution were also exaggerated.[32] In most cases the peasants received the deeds of land they had formerly cultivated as tenants, the major difference being that they now owned it and were entitled to the entire income from it rather than the percentage, sometimes as low as 20 per cent, that they had received previously. Those peasants who were resettled were landless labourers who were given plots of previously uncultivated land. This experiment was unsuccessful because many peasants did not have adequate tools to build houses for themselves or bring the land under cultivation. But they were a minority, and their failure to cultivate their plots merely meant that the total area under cultivation was not increased as the government had hoped.

One gauge of disruption is a drop in the area under cultivation, which shows up as a substantial fall in the size of the harvest. In an average year, Afghanistan needed to import 200,000 tons of wheat.[33] In 1979, the first harvest after the introduction of the reforms, the government announced a shortfall of 300,000 tons.[34] But the winter of 1978-9 had been unusually dry and this would have had some effect on the wheat yield, especially dry wheat cultivation. Babrak Karmal's regime claimed in February 1980 that the previous year one third of the dry-farming land had been left uncultivated along with much of the irrigated land.[35]

However, before the April 1978 revolution, it was estimated that 60 per cent of the land brought under cultivation was left uncultivated annually, which suggests that at worst the Khalqi government had been unable to improve the situation. Some peasants did not cultivate their plots but an awful lot did. Those who did not were more likely to have been victims of intimidation by former landlords than of dislocation directly attributable to the land redistribution.

It is often suggested that the reforms were implemented too quickly, that the government should have proceeded more slowly and taken more care to explain its reforms to the peasants and to win their support.[36] There is also inherent in this suggestion the belief that a more gradual implementation of the reforms would somehow have lessened the opposition of the old ruling class, a most dubious assumption. It was important that the government demonstrate to the peasants the benefits of its policies, winning their support, as the PDPA leaders never tired of saying, with deeds and not words. The longer this was delayed, the longer the old ruling class, for whom it was equally important that the reforms be discredited, and who were still *in situ*, had to manipulate and intimidate the peasants into withholding their co-operation from the government. All the evidence points to the fact that the peasants initially welcomed the reforms, and it was not until the spring and summer of 1979 that the government began to encounter relatively wide and serious resistance. By this time they had lost the propaganda initiative and the counter-revolution had found powerful allies outside Afghanistan. Given the extent of counter-revolutionary propaganda and intimidation, the PDPA could fairly be criticised for not moving faster and using greater force, earlier, against those who opposed them.

This opposition came from a small but extremely powerful group. Some big landlords simply abandoned their land, like the former owner of 500 jeribs of prime irrigated land in the Kunar valley who saw no point in remaining to work the 30 jeribs he was permitted to retain, but others stayed and fought. They were usually tribal leaders, with all the authority that that implied and they had the support of many ulema, often themselves big landowners and heads of tribal sub-groups, who used their considerable authority as men of religion in defence of the privilege of the old ruling class of which they formed an important part.[37]

When the Khalqi Specialised Committees went into the villages they encountered the suspicion that traditionally greeted representatives of the central government. The gap between the alaqadar and the village remained. There were no well established channels of communication or administrative machinery that they could take over. They had to build it themselves, in the face of much more desperate opposition from the doomed authority structure now fighting for its very survival, than any previous Kabul regime had encountered.

Despite the extensive network of supporters and sympathisers built up by the Khalq faction in the rural areas[38] and who provided the backbone of the Khalqi Specialised Committees, the PDPA lacked the personnel to provide a presence in all villages, to police the implementation of the reforms and protect the peasants from the retaliation and intimidation of their former rulers. When the Committee left the village, the peasant was on his own. He was told that the new government was *kafir* (infidel) and that its policies were anti-Islamic, that co-operation with it was a sin and resistance an obligation for pious Muslims. The local mullah was the traditional arbiter of what was and was not in accordance with Islam, and in the absence of any alternative interpretation, the peasant tended to believe him.

He was told that to accept the cancellation of a debt, or any part of it was not only a dishonourable act in terms of the tribal code in so far as it broke an agreement, but that it amounted to theft, with all the implications of the severe Islamic penalties involved. Acceptance of the deeds of confiscated land was also represented as theft. The marriage reform, also cynically condemned as un-Islamic, was especially difficult to enforce. Payment of large amounts of maehr or the giving of expensive gifts were matters of status, regardless of the hardship involved. Ironically, many girls reportedly felt devalued by the imposition of the ceiling of 300 afghanis on maehr, and even if they did not, to whom could they appeal if they were forced into unwelcome marriages?

There were also cases where peasants continued to repay usurious loans and others, though less frequent, of peasants returning the plots they had been given. Where persuasion failed as it often did other methods were used. In some areas peasants who planted crops or otherwise co-operated with the government had their houses burned and their crops destroyed. Some who pruned their grapevines had their ears cut off as a warning to others.[39]

The government's attempts to explain its policies to the peasants also met with fierce resistance from the old ruling class who recognised that this as much as anything else would undermine its position. The literacy campaign and attempts to expand education at village level, limited as they were from lack of resources, were regarded as especially dangerous. Schools and schoolteachers were a special target. Schools were burned and young party members sent as schoolteachers were

intimidated. One particularly horrible incident involved a woman schoolteacher in Herat who was kidnapped, mutilated and then murdered, and
her clothes sent to her family with the advice that they should 'pray for
her dirty soul'.[40]

Intimidation was not confined to schoolteachers. Party members
engaged in a United Nations road-building project south-west of Kabul
were shot dead and others in the group told that they too would be
killed if they returned. The UN abandoned the project.[41]

In some respects the Khalqi committees created problems for themselves. The benefits of the reforms were self-evident to the party members who explained them in terms of freeing the peasants from oppression
and exploitation, incomprehensible concepts to many peasants. The
opportunity of presenting them as also upholding the true spirit of Islam
from which the old ruling class had deviated was completely missed in
the early months, and an important weapon thereby surrendered to the
enemy. This was an error of judgement, not just of individual cadres,
but of the PDPA leadership. They contented themselves with assurances
that they respected Islam, and that their policies were not anti-Islamic,
a negative approach arising from their secularism and contempt for
what they regarded as superstition. Hafizullah Amin was as guilty as
the other PDPA leaders in this respect, although he later realised his
mistake and took steps to rectify it.

Other problems did arise from the actions of individuals. Some of
the younger cadres, enthusiastic and totally committed to their cause
sometimes became impatient with the suspicion and caution they often
encountered from the peasants. Others, older men with experience of
the early Daoud regime when they had been defeated by the 'mud
curtain' were determined, now that they had the full support of the
government in Kabul, not to be humbugged again. They tried to bully
where coaxing might have served their purpose better. There were some
who clearly believed that the government was being too soft on the
former oppressors. In one incident in Ghor province at the ceremony
handing over the deeds of confiscated land to the peasants, a party
official attempted to humiliate one of the landlords. A peasant (who
had just received the deeds to his plot) became angry and shot the party
official. Soldiers with the Khalqi Committee then killed the peasant,
and a deadly free-for-all developed. The peasants from that village,
though in complete support of the land reform, joined the rebellion
against the government. One who was later taken prisoner still had the
deeds to his plot in his pocket and had steadfastly refused to return
them to the landlord.[42]

In such cases the government was caught in a dilemma. It was obviously essential to put a stop to such incidents which did so much damage to the party, but at the same time it was also important not to undermine the morale of the party workers and other officials doing a difficult and sometimes dangerous job. Taraki and Amin both demonstrated their sensitivity to the problem. Taraki told a group of KOAY workers: 'Peasants are a nice lot. They don't nourish ill-feelings in their hearts. The only drawback they have is that they are illiterate.' He warned them not to talk too much about theory, but to tell the peasants about 'the benefits they derive from the state and the party'.[43] Amin, addressing the directors of the Rural Development Department warned them that any mistakes they made in their contact with the people would damage the revolution but he also sought to encourage them:

> If the people of Afghanistan do not believe in promises you should
> not be depressed . . . work and discharge your duties in such a way
> that you win the confidence of the people. The confidence of the
> people cannot be won only through radio and newspapers.[44]

At the same time the government tried to give backing and protection to its workers and supporters. Unable to maintain a permanent presence in every village, it attempted to make up for its limited resources by taking punitive action against those who openly and persistently defied it. Ulema who preached that the reforms were un-Islamic and urged the peasants not to co-operate with the government were dismissed. Some of the most outspoken were arrested, although the government moved with considerable caution and only after extreme provocation. In September 1978 Taraki declared '*jihad*' (holy war) against 'the Ikhwan',[45] but it was not until the end of January 1979 that the most strenuous opponent of any kind of reform, and the most influential religious figure in Afghanistan, Mohammad Ibrahim Mujaddidi (the Hazrat of Shor Bazaar) was arrested along with several members of his family, despite the fact that his nephew, Sigbhatullah Mujaddidi had assumed leadership of a counter-revolutionary coalition based in Peshawar four months earlier. In February government forces eventually attacked the compound of another religious leader, Mian Gul Jan, who had been in open revolt in the Panjsher region since before the April 1978 revolution. Despite immediate reports that he and his followers had been massacred, he reached Peshawar a couple of weeks later along with hundreds of his disciples.[46]

Some ulema probably were executed, although the government never

made any public statement to this effect. Again it was faced with
dilemma. Not to take action against outright rebellion was to abdicat
its responsibility as a government, to undermine the morale of its sup
porters and to give the peasants little encouragement to trust it. But t
carry out reprisals, especially against religious figures was to provide th
counter-revolution with fuel for its propaganda that the governmen
was against Islam and was persecuting the faithful.

On one occasion the government does appear to have over-reactec
though again after much provocation. This incident involved the villag
of Kerala in Kunar province, near the provincial capital of Assadabac
Rebels from near the village had been harassing the provincial capital fo
several weeks, to the extent that a United Nations hydro-electric projec
in the vicinity had to be abandoned. In the wake of the Herat mutin
in March 1979 and the declaration of jihad by counter-revolutionar;
leaders based in Pakistan, government forces entered Kerala and execute
all the adult male inhabitants, said to number about 1,700. Whethe
this was a local initiative by government forces in Kunar is not known
though the fact that it was an isolated incident (even the most bitte
critics of the PDPA have been unable to produce evidence of simila
massacres) suggests that this was the case.

A careful evaluation of the reform strategy of the PDPA reveals tha
much of the criticism levelled at it has been unfounded or misguided
Reports of dislocation were exaggerated as were those of popular oppc
sition, which, to the extent that it occurred was attributable to th
government's loss of the propaganda initiative rather than to the allege
inappropriateness of the reforms, or the supposed haste and brutalit;
with which they were implemented. Indeed it could well be argued tha
the government moved too slowly and with too much restraint, thereb;
leaving the old ruling class free to mount a serious counter-attack. Prob
lems there most certainly were, and blunders too, which the governmen
for the most part acknowledged and attempted to rectify,[47] but th
reforms were not the unmitigated disaster that is frequently claimed

For the scale and intensity of the counter-revolution that develope
in the summer of 1979 it is necessary to look elsewhere. The loss of th
propaganda initiative in the first weeks after the April 1978 revolutio
was a disaster attributable as much to the power struggle between th
Khalq and Parcham factions that engaged the party's attention for tha
vital period as to later miscalculations on the part of the Khalqi leader
ship. Even so, had the counter-revolution not found allies outsid
Afghanistan, in the reactionary military dictatorship in Pakistan an
the aggressive Islamic oligarchy in Iran, the situation would not hav

eteriorated as it did through the summer of 1979.

Notes

1. Democratic Republic of Afghanistan, *Basic Lines of Revolutionary Duties f the Government of Democratic Republic of Afghanistan, May 9, 1978* (Government Printing Press, Kabul, 1978).
2. 'Aims and Objects of the Democratic Khalq Party' (unofficial English translation, Kabul, 1979).
3. Taraki interview with Iraq News Agency, 6 June 1978, *Kabul Times* henceforth *KT*), 10 June 1978.
4. Khalqi Organisation for Afghan Youth (KOAY) and Khalqi Organisation or Afghan Women (KOAW).
5. For text of Decree No.6 on relief of peasant debts, see *KT*, 17 July 1978.
6. See Ch. 5 p. 78 above.
7. Saleh Mohammad Zeary, Minister of Agriculture, interview with *Anis* Kabul), reprinted *KT* 19, 20, 22 July 1978. The following table illustrates the liding scale of repayment:

Year of mortgage	Proportion of mortgage money to be repaid	Period of repayment (after first year)
1356 (1977)	90%	5 years
1355 (1976)	60%	3 years
1354 (1975)	40%	2 years
1353 (1974)	20%	1 year
Before 1353 (1974)	None	

8. Zeary, *KT*, 20 July 1978.
9. Fred Halliday, 'War and Revolution in Afghanistan', *New Left Review*, 19, Jan-Feb 1980 is quite wrong in asserting (p. 24) that Decree No.6 merely cancelled the debts of peasants to other farmers and landlords . . . The debt cancellation decree did not touch, nor could it have, the main area of rural debt, riz. debts to bazaar merchants and moneylenders.'
10. Appendix No.1 of Decree No.6, Text *KT*, 17 July 1978. The Provincial Committee comprised the Governor, the provincial Auditor General, the Director General of Settlement and Properties, the Director General of Agriculture, the Director of Education and three peasant representatives. The Woleswali Committee comprised the woleswali, the official in charge of properties, representatives of the Attorney General's Office, the Education Department and the Agriculture Department, and two peasant representatives.
11. Charter of the Assisting Fund for Landless Peasants and Agricultural Laborers, text, *KT*, 15 Aug. 1978 and Charter of Cooperative for Provision of Agricultural Services, text, *KT*, 22, 23 Aug. 1978.
12. Text, *KT*, 18 Oct. 1978. In the text of the decree *maehr* is incorrectly referred to as 'dowry' instead of 'bride price'.
13. See Erika Knabe, 'Afghan Women: Does Their Role Change?' in Louis Dupree and Linette Albert, *Afghanistan in the 1970s* (Praeger, New York, 1974), pp. 146-9.
14. Text, *KT*, 2 Dec. 1978.
15. Fred Halliday is again mistaken in stating ('War and Revolution', p. 24): The land reform was not based on any cadastral survey of the Afghan countryside

or even on a minimal preliminary investigation of landownership.'

16. See Table 2: Distribution of Land in Afghanistan 1978, p. 222. The lower estimate of 400 was made by Hafizullah Amin in a conversation with a foreign ambassador in June 1979. In the light of Dupree's estimate (see p. 69 above) 400 is a plausible figure. A UN official in Kabul told the author, in March 1979, that 4 per cent of landowners were adversely affected by the land redistribution, and that they included most of the chiefs of Afghanistan's 20,000 villages.

17. See Table 3, Literacy in Afghanistan, p. 222.

18. Shah Mahmoud Haseen, interview, *KT*, 18 July 1978.

19. 'NACAI as an important literacy propagation organ can play an important role in enlightening the masses and it was on this basis that is was deemed necessary that teachers and supervisors of the literacy courses in Kabul province take the course.' Ibid.

20. *KT*, 27 Oct. 1979.

21. *KT*, 4 Aug. 1979.

22. To stress the government's commitment to the project and to underline the need for the participation of the entire population in the development of the country, Amin and the Education Minister Dastagir Panjsheri were photographed carrying (rather self-consciously) a tray of cement. *KT*, 22 June 1978.

23. Amin, interview, *KT*, 5 Oct. 1978.

24. *KT*, 8 June 1978.

25. *Jang*, 30 Aug. 1978, *Urdu Press Summary* (Australian Embassy, Islamabad)

26. Conversation with the author, Peshawar, January 1981.

27. Interview with the Indian weekly, *Current*, *KT*, 27 May 1978.

28. *Nawa-i-Waqt*, 15 June 1978, *Urdu Press Summary*.

29. For example:

> Djamal Sultani, haut fonctionnaire dans un ministère de la capitale afghane, dut se résoudre, lors du coup d'Etat d'avril 1978, à collaborer officiellement avec le nouveau régime. En fait, durant cette année de collaboration, il a centralisé toutes les informations de la résistance au pouvoir mis en place par Mohamad Nour Taraki . . . Francois Missen, *Le Syndrome de Kaboul* (Edisud, Aix-en-Provence, 1980), p. 6.

'Djamal Sultani' (his real identity was withheld allegedly to protect his family still in Afghanistan), gave Missen what appears to be a highly coloured account of his activities before he was discovered and fled to avoid arrest.

30. See for example, Fred Halliday, 'War and Revolution'; Richard S. Newell, 'Revolution and Revolt in Afghanistan', *The World Today*, vol. 35, no. 11, November 1979; and two interviews, 1. Feroz Ahmed, editor of *Pakistan Forum* and 2. an 'unidentified Afghan Marxist', *MERIP Reports*, July-August 1980, reprinted in *Intercontinental Press/Imprecor*, 15 Sept. 1980.

31. *KT*, 1 Sept. 1979.

32. The 'unidentified Afghan Marxist' (*Intercontinental Press*, 15 Sept. 1980) while critical of other aspects of the government policy acknowledged that the implementation of the land reform 'with some irregularities, here and there, was accomplished'.

33. Finance Minister Misaq, announcing that the 1978 harvest had been 'satisfactory' (*KT*, 25 May 1978).

34. Taraki announced that the government was importing 300,000 tons 'as a precautionary measure'. The Soviet Union had agreed to supply 100,000 tons as a grant-in-aid, India 50,000 and the USA 'a few thousand tons' (*KT*, 3 May 1979) In August Amin told a press conference that Afghanistan had not yet solved its wheat import problems, but that the harvest that year had raised hopes that

\fghanistan could become self-sufficient 'in the next few years' (*KT*, 1 Sept.
979). A few days later he said that Afghanistan would obtain 300,000 tons of
vheat from the Soviet Union for the year 1979-80 (*KT*, 12 Sept. 1979). This
mplies that the total shortfall for 1979 was 350,000 tons. Halliday's assertion
that Afghanistan was facing 'a grain shortfall of up to 1.4 million tons this year,
r nearly half its normal requirements', and that the country was facing a famine
uch as it had suffered in the early 1970s ('War and Revolution', p. 28), appears
o be without foundation. It implies a shortfall nearly three times as great as that
of 1971, the worst famine year. Had this been the case the stream of refugees
rom Afghanistan would have been much greater than the (probably exaggerated)
'akistan government estimate of 300,000 in November 1979. Furthermore, none
f the refugees entering Pakistan has shown signs of starvation, nor has shortage
f food been among the reasons given by them for leaving Afghanistan.

35. *Kabul New Times*, 12 Feb. 1980.
36. Feroz Ahmed (*Intercontinental Press*, 15 Sept. 1980) remarks somewhat
condescendingly:

> Unless you know your own country very well – know the geography, the
> political complexity, the social structure, the class structure, the political
> dynamics – things are going to be very difficult. This party (the PDPA)
> did not know that much about its own rural society. In fact, some
> peasant workers across the border in Pakistan looked at developments
> with great frustration because they had tremendous experience in work-
> ing with peasants. They used to say 'If only they would leave this area to
> us for three months, we'd show them how land reforms are carried out.'
> They had the experience of mobilizing people, of taking the people along.

\part from the quibble that conditions in Pakistan, even in the border areas, are
ery different from those in Afghanistan, its own track record scarcely qualifies
he Pakistani left to lecture the Khalqi leadership. A Pakistani who had been involved in the implementation of the much milder Bhutto land reforms told the
author that he completely endorsed Taraki's and Amin's approach: 'If you don't
move quickly the feudals evade the measures and you never achieve anything.'
37. Those like Richard Newell ('Revolution and Revolt', pp. 436-7) who argue
that the PDPA mistook 'what are frequently social relations for economic relations' themselves fail to recognise that these social relations have an economic
underpinning. To assert, as Newell does that 'Afghan khans and other local leaders
are expected to protect their clients from intrusions by the central government.
Hence institutions of land control, tenancy and labour service are often linked to
the performance of local leaders in maintaining local autonomy on the basis of
consensus within the community . . .' is to ignore the fact that 'the intrusions of
the central government' were usually (and in the case of the PDPA certainly)
designed to improve the conditions of the 'clients' at the expense of the 'khans
and other local leaders' and that the 'consensus' to which he refers is obtained by
the use of a combination of crude economic force and an ideology based on a
distorted version of Islam, in order to manipulate the ignorant and illiterate
clientele'.
38. A common view, even among leftist critics of the PDPA, was that it was
an urban-based party with no support outside the main cities, yet both Feroz
Ahmed and the 'unidentified Afghan Marxist' (*Intercontinental Press*, 15 Sept.
1980) acknowledge that initially the revolutionary government had the support
of between 80 and 90 per cent of the population. While it may be true that support for the Parchamite wing of the party was confined to the urban population,
this was not the case with the Khalq. It is interesting that in conversations with

the author in December 1980 several pro-Parcham leftists in Delhi tried to explain the continuing failure of the Karmal regime to consolidate its position in terms of the strength of the Khalq in the provinces! Furthermore, an Afghan exile previously associated with the royalist regime told the author that, in 1973, before the Daoud coup, the then Prime Minister Mohammad Musa Shafiq wanted to postpone the elections due later that year in order to give the regime time to build up a mass base in the countryside which could 'compete with the communists'.

39. This last example of the methods used by the old ruling class to intimidate the peasants was cited by *Time Magazine*, 28 April 1980, p. 11. Milder forms of persuasion apparently met with little response from the peasants. A Pakistani official told the author that an Afghan mullah had described the Soviet invasion of December 1979 as 'a blessing in disguise', because 'before that we had trouble persuading the people that they should oppose Taraki and Amin'.

40. From an Afghan rebel source in Delhi, 1980.

41. Information obtained from UN sources, 1980.

42. From a source sympathetic to the PDPA, Delhi 1980.

43. *KT*, 13 March 1979.

44. *KT*, 11 Jan. 1979.

45. *KT*, 23 Sept. 1978. Ikhwan ul-Muslimin, or Muslim Brotherhood, an illegal Egyptian party with strong fascist characteristics, wide international connections in the Muslim world, and known for its use of terrorism and assassination as weapons against its political opponents. Taraki was referring in particular to two of the Peshawar based Afghan parties, the Jamaat-i-Islami and the Hizb-i-Islami (to which he gave the name 'Ikhwanul-Shayateen' or 'Brotherhood of the Devil') both of which are closer to the Egyptian party than they care to admit. See Beverley M. Male, 'Afghanistan: Rebels Without Policies', *The Bulletin* (Sydney), 17 Feb. 1981.

46. *Nawa-i-Waqt*, 5 March 1979, in *Urdu Press Summary*.

47. See for example Amin's speech to members of the Administrative Education Co-ordinating Commission, *KT*, 20 March 1979:

> I draw the attention of the scholars to this reality that some of our khalqi colleagues are not much experienced in the affairs of state. They may have taken decisions on the spur of the moment, in certain cases, carried away by the sentiments emanating from their struggles dating back to the past few years. They might not have treated some of our compatriots in consonance with their social standing or failed in behaving in a specific manner as the stand of these men . . . called for. But I can assure you that our khalqi government and colleagues have never wished this . . . We take ten steps forward with uncovering each mistake.

THE EID CONSPIRACY

Having seized power, the most urgent task confronting the PDPA was the adaptation of its organisation and methods to the new demands placed upon it. It was vital that the party move quickly and confidently to explain its aims to the peasant masses, to enlist their support in the coming struggle against the tribal-feudal elite. The time when survival depended on secrecy was past, but the need for discipline and cohesion was as important as ever. Following the formal reunification of the PDPA in 1977 this was its weakest point. The basic differences between the Khalq and Parcham factions had not been resolved and the events of 27 April 1978 only interrupted the continuing power struggle, but the stakes were now much higher: no longer merely control of the revolutionary party, but control of the revolution itself.

The reluctance with which the PDPA identified itself and Taraki's refusal to reveal details of party organisation or to disclose the identity of members of the Revolutionary Council was a clear indication that problems existed beneath the facade of unity he attempted to maintain, although the first the outside world knew of the bitter conflict proceeding in Kabul was the announcement of the appointment of Babrak Karmal and other senior Parchamite leaders to ambassadorial posts at the end of June and the beginning of July.

Although they were introduced by Amin, it was the military commanders rather than the party leaders who made the radio announcement when the PDPA seized power and the first decree of the new government, promulgated two days later, was issued in the name of the 'Revolutionary Council of the Armed Forces of Afghanistan'. It stated that the revolution had been carried out by 'patriotic officers and soldiers of Afghanistan at the will of the people of Afghanistan'. The Revolutionary Council of the Armed Forces then handed over power to and merged itself with 'the Revolutionary Council of the Democratic Republic of Afghanistan'.[1] Legitimised by the former, shadowy body, the Revolutionary Council then met and elected Taraki Chairman and Prime Minister. Taraki later revealed that there were 35 members of the Revolutionary Council, of whom five were military officers and all were members of the PDPA,[2] but the full list of names was never published.

The composition of the Ministry appointed by the Revolutionary Council at its second meeting, held on 1 May, indicates that the distri-

bution of power was very much in favour of the Khalq.[3] Of the 2.
members, eleven were Khalqis, seven were Parchamites. Watanjar and
Qadir may be regarded as neutral in party factional terms, although in
the immediately ensuing struggle, Watanjar sided with the Khalq while
Qadir joined Babrak Karmal. A question mark hangs over Bareq Shafie
Originally editor of *Khalq*, he went with Babrak Karmal in the 196(
split, but in 1978 he threw in his lot with the Khalq faction once again
His track record as a political survivor was confirmed by his appearance
in Babrak Karmal's Revolutionary Council in January 1980.

Babrak Karmal was formally appointed to the number two position
of Vice-Chairman of the Revolutionary Council, and shared the office
of Deputy Prime Minister with Hafizullah Amin and Aslam Watanjar
respectively Foreign Minister and Minister of Communications. Karma
himself had no specific responsibility and it is not clear what function
he was expected to perform. In fact he took no public part in the affair
of the new government.

The Parchamites were however entrusted with some important
Ministries. Karmal's closest associate, Nur Ahmad Nur was appointed
Minister of Interior, which gave him control over internal security and
the appointment of provincial governors. He had only partial success in
placing Parchamites in key positions. Of the 23 provincial governors he
appointed on 14 May, twelve were replaced on 17 July and two others
sacked in the following three months. The security services however
were under Khalqi control, with Major Daoud Taroon as Chief of Police
and Assadullah Sarwari in charge of AGSA, the security police.

Sultan Ali Kishtmand was appointed Minister of Planning and Sulei
man Laeq to the important post of Radio and Television. Other Parchamite ministers were Anahita Ratebzada, the only woman in the
cabinet whose Ministry, Social Affairs was abolished after her dismissal
Mohammad Rafie in charge of Public Works and Nazimuddin Tahzib in
the potentially sensitive post of Minister of Frontier Affairs, responsible
for relations with the tribes.

It is difficult to trace this phase of the Khalq-Parcham power struggle
with any degree of certainty, although some crucial developments suggest themselves. One such was obviously the Politburo decision to enlarge the Revolutionary Council, announced on 24 May, exactly four
weeks after the PDPA seized power.[4] In this context it should be noted
that *On The Saur Revolution*, the official account of the events of 27
April, of which Amin may be regarded as the author, was published on
22 May, just two days before the Politburo meeting. In it Amin launched
a barely disguised attack on Babrak Karmal not only for his personal

equivocation at a critical point in the operations, but also for attempting to sabotage the party's attempts to seize power. The timing of Amin's attack is important. Coming while Babrak Karmal was still Vice-Chairman of the Revolutionary Council and Deputy Prime Minister it must be regarded as part of the power struggle in which Amin and Karmal were then engaged.

The enlarged Revolutionary Council met for the first time on 12 June and took two controversial decisions. One was to change the national flag and emblem. The other was to declare 23 members of the immediate royal family traitors and deprive them of Afghan citizenship.[5] We have no indication from Babrak Karmal as to his attitude to these decisions. Accusations subsequently levelled by Taraki and Amin, to the effect that his real loyalties lay with the royal family, and Karmal's reversal, in April 1980, of the decision regarding the new flag, imply that his support was something less than wholehearted.

The crunch seems to have come at a meeting of the Politburo on 17 June. It was an unusually long meeting, lasting four and a half hours, and the *Kabul Times* report, never very revealing, was exceptionally terse: 'At the meeting different issues were discussed and appropriate decisions were taken.'[6]

Subsequent statements and actions of the PDPA leaders provide some indication of the issues which concerned the Politburo at its 17 June meeting and of the depth of division within that body. The formation in Pakistan early in June of a counter-revolutionary organisation comprising some of the most powerful reactionary forces in Afghan politics would have ensured that discussion of a strategy to be adopted by the party for mobilising support and combating the counter-revolutionary propaganda portraying the new government as bloody and savagely anti-Islamic would have been high on the agenda. So too would foreign policy, especially in the light of mounting evidence of hostility on the part of Afghanistan's neighbours Iran and Pakistan, and of a tendency in the United States to discount the new regime's commitment to non-alignment. In effect, at issue was the basic strategy underlying the revolutionary policies of the new government.

As a result of this meeting, the Khalq leaders seem finally to have realised that co-operation with the Parchamites was no longer possible and the decision was taken to send the leading Parchamites abroad as ambassadors.[7] None of the three most influential individuals concerned – Babrak Karmal, Nur Ahmad Nur and Anahita Ratebzada – appeared in public between 17 June and their departure from Kabul on 10, 11 and 12 July respectively. Babrak Karmal appears to have spent the

intervening four weeks finalising plans for a coup to remove the Khal
leadership from power.

According to the confession later extracted from Sultan Ali Kisht
mand, he had a meeting with Babrak Karmal at the latter's house abou
ten days before Karmal left for Czechoslovakia.[8] Karmal allegedly tol
him that, 'since the present government was deviating from the path o
socialism' a general uprising should take place under Qadir's leadership
All dissident forces, including any Khalqis willing to support the plan
should join in a 'general united front' and establish a 'People's Demo
cratic Republic of Afghanistan'. In the light of subsequent statement
by Karmal that 'Unfortunately in our country too the Saur Revolutio
was for some time diverted from its right course owing to the influenc
of imperialism through Amin and the Aminis . . .'[9] and of his attempt
to establish such a united front, it would appear that Kishtmand repre
sented Karmal's position accurately.

Karmal had apparently gone out of his way to cultivate Qadir, prom
ising him that after the coup, he would be both President and Defenc
Minister. As commander of the Air Force in the successful operation
of July 1973 and April 1978, Qadir's support was obviously regarde
as essential.

Kishtmand was given the task of organising a mass uprising to co
incide with the Eid holidays, beginning on Monday 4 September at th
end of the holy month of Ramadan. The plan was for Karmal, Nur
Ratebzada, Wakil and Najib to return to Afghanistan before Eid, eithe
directly or through Iran or Pakistan. The Air Force was regarded as th
weak point, and in fact Qadir admitted that he was unable to organis
his part in the coup because 'all of them were either Khalqis or thei
sympathisers'. The failure was not Qadir's alone. Despite the fact tha
Babrak Karmal is frequently presented as the most popular of the PDP/
leaders,[10] he was unable to attract enough support either in the PDPA o
the armed forces to mount a successful challenge to Taraki and Amin

As the Parchamites laid their plans in June and early July the Khalq
leaders set about implementing the decisions of the 17 June Politbur
meeting, one of which was apparently to mount a vigorous public rela
tions campaign, the thrust of which was three-fold.

The first aim was to counteract rebel propaganda that the govern
ment was anti-Islamic, assuring the people that they were free to practis
their religion and that only ulema who opposed the government and it
reform measures would find themselves in trouble. The second was t
reassure national traders that private property was not at risk, and t
encourage them to invest in accordance with government guidelines

'he third was to persuade Afghan lawyers (most of whom had a theo-
ogical background) and medical doctors (most of whom were based in
Kabul) that they should take a socially responsible attitude to their
•rofession, regarding themselves as the servants of the Afghan people
s a whole.

From mid-May Taraki had made a sustained effort to explain govern-
nent policy to tribal leaders brought to Kabul from various parts of the
ountry, and other ministers had delivered speeches explaining policy
n their own areas of responsibility, but after 17 June the momentum
ncreased and included those previously silent. Hafizullah Amin who
ad up to this time confined himself, overtly at least, to his functions
is Foreign Minister — he had made two trips abroad, first to a Non-
ligned Foreign Ministers' Conference in Cuba and then to the UN
Special Session on Disarmament in New York — now openly entered
he domestic fray.

A close analysis of Amin's contribution to the campaign is useful for
he insights it provides into PDPA policy and his own increasingly con-
roversial role in its formation. During this period Taraki's image as
Great Leader', 'Great Teacher' and 'Father of the Nation' was being
established and all ideological innovation and revolutionary analysis
ind policies were attributed to him. Amin played an important part in
building up this image of Taraki and in consequence it is difficult to
establish his own contribution to PDPA ideology or policy, although
this was probably considerable. It is significant that sophisticated and
detailed analysis of the April Revolution and of party ideology was left
to him, and many who knew both men agree that Taraki would have
been intellectually incapable of the theoretical contribution with which
he has been credited.

Amin was concerned to press three points: the independence of the
Afghan revolution; Afghanistan's commitment to non-alignment and its
need for aid 'without strings' from all possible sources; and the government's determination to press ahead with rural reform that would destroy the tribal-feudal authority structure.

In his first major speech inside Afghanistan Amin stressed the unique
character of the Afghan revolution, which he claimed was recognised by
revolutionary scholars in the 'friendly' countries he had visited as 'a new
thesis', providing an example for 'the oppressed of various countries
with economic and political conditions similar to Afghanistan, as the
Great October Revolution is an example [for] the advanced countries
of the world'.[11] Amin's analysis of the April Revolution as providing a
revolutionary model rather than seeking another to follow drew sneers

from self-appointed guardians of Marxist doctrine outside Afghanistan[12] and stunned silence from Soviet theoreticians. Although it was perhap a genuine effort to confront the theoretical problems raised by the PDPA's seizure of power, which certainly placed it outside the revolu tionary mainstream, a more important aspect was Amin's effort to distance the Afghan revolution from the Russian revolution, to empha sise its special national character while at the same time reaffirming it commitment to the establishment of a 'society free of exploitation o individual by individual'.

Ten days later he made a much more explicit declaration regarding the independence of the Afghan revolution: 'I tell you dear colleague . . . the plan of revolution, from the beginning, was only known to ou party leadership and no other person in the world knew about it.'[13] Hi intention was clearly to rebut the counter-revolutionary propaganda increasingly heard in Afghanistan and echoed in the West, that the April Revolution had been engineered by the Soviet Union and that the PDPA regime was merely Moscow's puppet. It was an important point to make in terms of the PDPA campaign for mass support in a country with a long-standing abhorrence of foreign intervention.

It also had important implications for Afghanistan's status as a non aligned state, the second and related point that Amin chose to empha sise, insisting in an interview with a BBC correspondent on 1 July tha relations between the new Afghan government and the Soviet Union were essentially the same as they had been under Zahir Shah and Daoud.[14] The same day he told the Air Force and Air Defence Command tha Afghanistan was interested

> in friendship with all countries that support the Saur Revolution with a spirit of friendship and the utilisation of economic assistance rendered to Afghanistan . . . *with no regard to the socio-economic system of the aid-giving country, provided that the aid is uncon ditional* and in accord with the principle of non-interference in the affairs of one another and respect to national independence.[15]

It was a clear warning to the Soviet Union as well as an appeal to the West. As if for emphasis, Amin made a point of attending the 4 July reception at the American Embassy. It is likely that it was an accurate reading of Amin's signals, rather than shock at his ideological presump tion that accounted for the cool response in the USSR to his claims on behalf of the April Revolution.

The June 17 Politburo meeting also appears to have reached decision

elating to the reforms foreshadowed in *Basic Lines*. While general
eferences to the future appeared in the public statements of several
Khalqi leaders it was left to Amin to make the toughest statement on
he rural reforms, the key to the government's programme.[16] It was also
Amin who issued the sternest warning to the ulema heard so far, indi-
ating the government's growing concern with the use by the regime's
pponents of Islam as a counter-revolutionary weapon. Those who
defended the revolution would be regarded as the 'pupil of our eyes'.
Those who merely 'engaged in worship in accordance with the principles
f Islam and do not interfere in politics' would be revered by all. But
hose who 'under the sacred name of Islam plot against the great Saur
Revolution and misuse the valuable principles of the sacred Islam religion
nd are in the service of enemies of the people' would be considered
raitors and 'we . . . will crush them to the extent that they forget the
lows of Daoud'.[17] While Amin no doubt meant what he said the fact
hat it was he who made the toughest statements was later construed by
is opponents as evidence of his brutality, and probably contributed to
he growing image of him as the party 'strong-man'.

The removal of the top Parchamites not only made it possible for the
PDPA regime to get on with the pressing tasks before it, it also opened
he way for the transformation of the party from the small clandestine
rganisation that had seized power into an instrument of government
nd for the first determined efforts to establish a mass base. Here too
t was not long before Hafizullah Amin emerged as a key figure.

The Politburo, which had met only twice since the revolution, on 24
May and 17 June, began from 1 July to meet regularly, first each week
nd later fortnightly. Politburo meetings were followed by meetings of
he Council of Ministers (or cabinet) which endorsed the decisions of
he Politburo. The Revolutionary Council seems to have suffered a rela-
ive decline in status and although theoretically it was supposed to make
ninisterial appointments, it was the Politburo which, at its meeting on
 July, appointed Watanjar to replace Nur as Minister of Interior, and
Gulabzoi to Watanjar's former post of Communications.[18]

This particular meeting of the Politburo seemed more concerned
owever with organisational matters − not surprising given the crisis
hrough which the party had just passed. The Central Committee was
o be enlarged, suggesting that Taraki was attempting to strengthen the
Khalq position in relation to the remaining Parchamites. Changes were
lso made in the organisation of the Central Committee Secretariat, the
arty's own bureaucracy, reflecting not only the increasing demands
n the party machine but also the changing power balance within the

dominant Khalq faction itself.

After the successful uprising of 27 April, for which Amin had been largely responsible, it was no longer possible to exclude him from the Politburo. Full recognition of his role in the party organisation only came, however, at the 8 July Politburo meeting at which he was appointed Secretary to the Central Committee Secretariat, along with Shah Wali, who had held this position for some time. It was a move designed to improve co-ordination within the party machine, but it had obvious implications for Amin's political career, for it enabled him to exert a formidable influence over the PDPA's organisational structure at a critical stage of its development. There appears to have been a division of labour between Amin and Shah Wali, with Shah Wali taking responsibility for the civilian side and Amin continuing to head the party organisation in the armed forces. Gradually Amin assumed overall responsibility for the Secretariat and with it the entire party machine. Shah Wali, some ten years Amin's junior, seems to have harboured no resentment despite his seniority in the party hierarchy. Not particularly ambitious, he appeared quite relieved to relinquish his position to Amin and the two remained close friends. One former Kabul diplomat recalled: 'Shah Wali was a dour fellow — Hafizullah was the only one who could make him laugh.'

Through July efforts were made to expand the party organisation and strengthen its position in the countryside. Party Committees were gradually established at Province level and, after the shake-out of Provincial Governors on 16 July, many party secretaries also assumed the office of Governor. The party secretary was normally regarded as the ranking official, but in those instances where he served in two capacities as state and party functionary, the potential for development of conflicting loyalties to the Ministry of the Interior (Watanjar) and the Party Secretariat (Amin and Shah Wali) was increased.

The youth organisations, the People's Organisation of Afghan Youth and the Democratic Organisation of Afghan Youth were amalgamated into one People's (Khalq) Organisation of Afghan Youth, (KOAY) under the leadership of Babrak Shinwari. Amin's son Abdur Rahman was appointed to the Central Board of KOAY and later became Deputy President of the organisation which, after the armed forces, was to develop into one of his father's most secure power bases.

The women's organisations were merged in a similar fashion, into one People's Organisation for Afghan Women (KOAW) under the leadership of Dilhara Mahak.

By the second half of August 1978 party organisation was reaching own to woleswali level, and branches of KOAY and KOAW were being organised at province level. 'On 22 July the Politburo called for the establishment of political organs, preparation and organization of party activities in the Armed Forces of the People of Afghanistan . . .'[19]

Immediate responsibility for the implementation of this decision was placed in the hands of the President of the Political Department of the Armed Forces, Mohammad Iqbal, a member of the Central Committee and a close associate of Amin.

Expansion and consolidation of the party organisation was especially important in view of the publication on 12 July of Decree No.6, the first of the agrarian reforms cancelling or reducing a wide range of rural debts, and of the simultaneous initiation of the literacy campaign. Each of these measures struck at the base of the tribal-feudal authority structure and determined opposition could therefore be expected from counter-revolutionary forces in the countryside. Because of the low level of political consciousness among the peasantry and the ideological stranglehold of the rural elite, mass support for the reforms from the peasantry which they were designed to benefit was not a foregone conclusion, and the party required the maximum mobilisation of its resources to carry its message to the people and win their co-operation.

Once again the party was to be distracted from its main task by a renewed attempt by the Parchamites to seize power. Plans for the coup, initiated before Babrak Karmal left Afghanistan, were discovered in mid-August, and the Defence Minister Abdul Qadir, the Chief of the General Staff, Lieutenant-General Shahpur, and the President of the Jamhouriat Hospital Mir Ali Akbar were arrested. Within a week of their arrest the implication of Kishtmand and Rafie was revealed and they too were arrested. Gradually the full extent of the conspiracy, involving Babrak Karmal and the other leading Parchamites exiled with him, became known. It was now clear that the earlier decision to post Karmal and his associates abroad instead of putting them under lock and key where they could do no harm, had been a monumental blunder. Not only that, but they had been sent to important and sensitive posts, including Islamabad, Tehran, Washington and London where they were in positions to do untold damage. It is not known who was responsible for this disastrous decision, but as a senior party leader and as Foreign Minister, Amin must bear a considerable share of the blame. It was a mistake for which he would eventually pay dearly.

The discovery of the conspiracy led to an extensive reorganisation of the upper echelons of the PDPA, and the sacking of many Parchamites and their sympathisers from influential positions in the government,

civil service and armed forces. A Plenum of the PDPA Central Com
mittee formally expelled Babrak Karmal and eight others from the party
on 27 November. Four other members of the Central Committee were
demoted to probationary membership of the party.[20] Bareq Shafie and
Suleiman Laeq 'resigned' from the Politburo, but retained membership
of the Central Committee.

Shafie kept his post as Minister of Information and Culture and was
also given responsibility for Radio and Television when Laeq, regarded
as less trustworthy, was sacked. (He was reportedly arrested, along with
Nazimuddin Tahzib, the former Minister for Frontier Affairs, in March
1979.)[21] Sahib Jan Sahraye, previously Governor of Kunduz was brought
in to take Tahzib's place. Watanjar was appointed Minister of Interior
and Gulabzoi was brought into the cabinet to take over Communica
tions. Panjsheri was transferred to Public Works and the Rector of Kabul
University Abdur Rashid Jalili was appointed Minister of Education.

No new Defence Minister was appointed. Instead, Taraki himself
already (as President) Supreme Commander of the Armed Forces, took
responsibility for the Defence Ministry, appointing Amin to 'assist' him.
His refusal to give Amin responsibility for Defence was the first hint of
his distrust of his protégé. Taraki attempted to head off speculation on
this score in a broadcast to the armed forces in which he made a point
of praising Amin, but at the same time emphasising Amin's subordinate
position.[22] The implication was clear: Amin was not to be permitted to
expand his already extensive power base in the armed forces without
challenge from Taraki.

Although the Khalq emerged victorious within the PDPA, it now had
to deal with attacks both from counter-revolutionary groups and from
the dissident Parchamite left and its foreign sympathisers. Babrak Kar
mal's opportunities for intrigue from his sanctuary in East Europe are
obvious. Less obvious, but scarcely less dangerous, was the opportunity
afforded Nur, Wakil and Baryalai as ambassadors in US, UK and Pakistan
respectively to forge links with the left in those countries. It is a remark
able coincidence that leftist writers outside Afghanistan have generally
accepted the Parchamite line that the only conspiracy in existence was
hatched by the Khalqis (under the *de facto* leadership of Amin) to
remove a blameless Babrak Karmal, and that the implementation of
Amin's plan for self-aggrandisement involved the arrest and execution
of large numbers of Parchamites, with implications of killing on a mass
scale.

Of the existence of a Parchamite-inspired plot in the summer of 1978
there can be little doubt. The subsequent actions of the Parchamite

eaders constitute a prima facie case in this respect. The government's move to protect itself by arresting and executing those involved was a response which any government might be expected to make in similar circumstances. At issue is the extent of the arrests and executions.

Hafizullah Amin reportedly told the Amnesty International delegation visiting Afghanistan in October 1978 that there were 'approximately 100 political prisoners in Afghanistan', but Amnesty estimated that there were four thousand altogether, 'the official figure . . . apparently not including political prisoners *arrested by previous governments* and remaining in detention' i.e., *not Parchamites*. Amnesty then went on to allege:

> Some family members of the accused were arrested in late August 1978, and during the months of July and August 1978 several well-known professors and teachers at Kabul University, particularly in the faculties of medicine and economics, were also reliably reported to have been arrested. These events were accompanied by *hundreds of arrests*, throughout the country, of political workers, alleged to be pro-Parcham, and members of the armed forces reportedly supporting General Qader.[23]

There is an obvious contradiction within the Amnesty report relating to the delegation's estimates of the number of political prisoners and they appear to have found little evidence to support their assertions regarding the 'hundreds of arrests' referred to. The most that can be said is that the government's reaction was tough, signifying its determination not to permit political activity which threatened its existence, but not excessive given the mounting danger of counter-revolution and the suspicion of foreign involvement in the conspiracy, and scarcely the slaughter implied by the regime's critics.

The government's own reticence on the question served it ill. Speculation that the five ringleaders, together with others named as being associated with them, had been summarily executed was allowed to run unchecked, along with rumours that Babrak Karmal and the other ambassadors had obeyed the summons to return home and had then been killed. In the process enormous damage was done to the government's international image.

One of the reasons for official reticence was probably related to the suspicion of external involvement in the conspiracy, especially the suspicion of Soviet involvement. It was later discovered, and the Afghan government probably knew at the time, that when he was recalled from

Prague Babrak Karmal took refuge in East Europe or the Soviet Union
This raises the question of the extent of Soviet involvement in the conspiracy. Observers disagree over the extent to which Moscow took sides
in the dispute which split the PDPA. Before the revolution the leaders
of both factions maintained contact with the Soviet embassy in Kabul
and, although the Parchamite line was more in accordance with Soviet
views regarding the appropriate behaviour for communist parties in third
world countries,[24] it is likely that the USSR tried, at least in the early
stages, to avoid direct involvement.

At the same time, since Moscow is usually well informed about what
goes on within its own or its satellites' borders, the USSR was undoubt-
edly aware of, if not directly involved in Babrak Karmal's plans. When
he eventually gained power he did it with Soviet military support. It is
therefore reasonable to assume that his earlier, unsuccessful manoeuvres
also had Moscow's blessing. In any case, the fact that the USSR gave
the Parchamites protection after the discovery of the Eid Conspiracy
must have made them suspect in Kabul. The Afghan government made
no public protest, but Amin later implied that he at least believed the
USSR was in some way involved in the Eid Conspiracy. Asked, on 9
November by a *Pravda* correspondent: 'Do you have documents and
evidence as to the intervention of foreign sources and circles?' Amin
replied:

> More than you could imagine. We have got sufficient undeniable
> documents and evidence showing that all the anti-khalqi plots and
> instigations are prepared, encouraged and financed in co-operation
> with foreign sources. But we, for the time being, won't disclose the
> names of these countries due to our interest in continued friendship
> with all nations of the world.[25]

In the code phrases that Amin used, 'reaction' or 'regional reaction'
stood for Pakistan or Iran, 'left-extremism' for China, 'imperialism'
for Britain or the USA. Simple 'foreign intervention' referred to the
USSR.[26]

Had the external interference merely referred to Pakistan or Iran
or the US, and had the Kabul regime's relations with the Soviet Union
been as close and friendly as many outside Afghanistan assumed, there
would have been no need for such coyness on the part of the Afghan
leadership. It is perhaps also significant that Tass merely reported, without comment, the arrest of Qadir and Shahpur on 18 August. When the
Plenum of the PDPA Central Committee met on 27 November, expelling

the Parchamites, re-organising the party and confirming Amin's appointment as Secretary of the Central Committee, the Tass report referred simply to discussion of decision on organisational matters, without reference either to the expulsion of Babrak Karmal and his associates, or to Amin's promotion.[27]

Although the Khalq had won this round in the power struggle it was a costly victory. The counter-revolution had been given time to mobilise and plan its strategy, and the savage internal power struggle in the PDPA revealed a vital weakness which the rebels were quick to exploit. How could a party which tore itself apart immediately it seized power expect to govern Afghanistan? Surely it would soon collapse, and the old elite would return to power. The peasants should therefore not rely on the promises of the new government, for they would never be fulfilled.

But perhaps more important was the opportunity afforded the Soviet Union to entangle Afghanistan in a suffocating alliance, within which Moscow could move to establish hegemony over Afghanistan's recalcitrant revolutionary party. The necessity to defend the revolution from attack from this least expected quarter split the PDPA yet again, and led to a new and far more devastating power struggle which racked the party through the summer of 1979.

Notes

1. Armed Forces Council Decree, 29 April 1978. Text, *Kabul Times* (*KT*), 4 May 1978.
2. Press conference, Kabul, 6 May 1978, *KT*, 13 May 1978.
3. The first PDPA Ministry (*KT*, 4 May 1978) was as follows (factional allegiance added):

Nur Mohammad Taraki (Khalq) – Chairman of the Revolutionary Council and Prime Minister
Babrak Karmal (Parcham) – Vice-Chairman of the Revolutionary Council, Deputy Prime Minister
Hafizullah Amin (K) – Deputy Prime Minister and Foreign Minister
Mohammad Aslam Watanjar (No factional allegiance) – Deputy Prime Minister, Communications
Abdul Qadir (No factional allegiance) – Defence
Nur Ahmad Nur (P) – Interior
Shah Wali (K) – Public Health
Saleh Mohammad Zeary (K) – Agriculture
Dastagir Panjsheri (K) – Education
Sultan Ali Kishtmand (P) – Planning
Abdul Karim Misaq (K) – Finance
Hassan Bareq Shafie (P) – Information and Culture
Suleiman Laeq (P) – Radio and Television

Anahita Ratebzada (P) — Social Affairs
Abdul Hakim Sharai Jauzjani (K) — Justice
Mohammad Ismael Danesh (K) —Mines and Industries
Nazimmudin Tahzib (P) — Frontier Affairs
Abdul Qudus Ghorbandi (K) — Commerce
Mahmoud Soma (K) — Higher Education
Mohammad Rafie (P) — Public Works
Mohammad Mansur Hashemi (K) — Water and Power.

4. *KT*, 25 May 1978.
5. Decrees No.4 and No.5, *KT*, 14 June 1978.
6. *KT*, 18 June 1978.
7. Babrak Karmal was sent to Czechoslovakia; Nur Ahmed Nur to the USA;
Abdul Wakil to the UK; Anahita Ratebzada to Yugoslavia; Mahmoud Baryalai
(Babrak Karmal's brother) to Pakistan; Najib to Iran; Faiz Mohammad to Iraq
and Pacha Gul Wafadar to India. Another ambassador who must be suspect was
Raz Mohammad Pakteen, posted to Moscow and, after the Soviet invasion included
in Babrak Karmal's Revolutionary Council.
8. Extracts from the confessions of the conspirators, probably made under
duress, were published in the *Kabul Times* of 23 September 1978, in the form of
facsimiles of the handwriting of the accused. Such confessions are a common
means of discrediting political opponents and since their veracity, even their
authenticity, is often in doubt they are usually quite unreliable as evidence of
guilt, especially as those accused rarely survived to confirm or deny their substance. The alleged 'confessions' of those accused of murdering Taraki on instructions from Amin fall into this category. The case of the Parchamite conspirators
in Afghanistan is different. Not only did they survive, but their subsequent actions
once the opportunity arose, have been generally consistent with those they con-
fessed to planning in the summer of 1978. Although their expulsion from Afghanistan is explained in terms of what they present as Amin's megalomania, at no
stage since their return to power after the Soviet invasion, has any of them denied
the allegations made in September 1978. It is reasonable to assume, therefore,
that the confessions represent a broadly accurate account of the activities of the
Parchamite leaders in the period after the April 1978 revolution.
9. *Kabul New Times*, 8 and 9 January 1980.
10. Generally on the basis of his performance as a member of the Wolesi Jirga
and his group's association with the Daoud coup of 1973. For example, Dupree
has described him as a 'charismatic student leader and a spellbinding orator'
(Louis Dupree, 'Afghanistan Under the Khalq', *Problems of Communism*, July-
August 1979, p. 40). A Pakistani journalist, Feroz Ahmed, editor of *Pakistan
Forum*, described him as 'not only a ranking leader of the party, but a respected,
veteran politician, probably the top-notch parliamentarian in the country'. (Interview, *MERIP Report*, July-August 1980, reprinted in *Intercontinental Press*,
15 Sept. 1980).
11. *KT*, 22 June 1978.
12. See for example Feroz Ahmed, *Intercontinental Press*, 15 Sept. 1980.
13. *KT*, 4 July 1978.
14. *KT*, 1 July 1978.
15. Ibid., emphasis added.
16. '. . . no matter what the cost is we shall do away with the roots of feudalism and imperialism and have resolved to launch the first and most important
project for the advancement and well being of the people . . . namely land reform
in the interests of landless farmers and farmer[s] with meagre landholdings . . .'
KT, 22 June 1978.

17. *KT*, 4 July 1978.
18. *KT*, 9 July 1978.
19. *KT*, 22 July 1978.
20. Those expelled were Babrak Karmal, Nur Ahmad Nur, Sultan Ali Kisht-mand, Abdul Wakil, Anahita Ratebzada, Najib, Mahmoud Baryalai, Abdul Qadir and Mohammad Rafie. Those demoted were Nazimuddin Tahzib, Fida Mohammad Dehnasheen, Sarwar Urish and Majid Sarbulend, *KT*, 28 November, 1978.
21. Amnesty International, *Violations of Human Rights and Fundamental Freedoms in the Democratic Republic of Afghanistan: An Amnesty International Report* (London, September 1979) Appendix B, p. (iii).
22. *KT*, 23 Oct. 1978.
23. Amnesty International, *Report*, September 1979, p. 10, emphasis added.
24. Soviet sources have subsequently indicated that their sympathy was for the Parchamite line. A senior Soviet official, speaking of Moscow's experience with attempts to build socialism in third world countries, said that many moved too slowly, in which case they did not reach their goal at all, while others moved too quickly, and lost the support of the masses. He criticised Amin for moving too quickly (*Der Spiegel*, 28 January, 1980). Another Soviet writer explicitly endorses Babrak Karmal's position:

> Owing to a number of factors, particularly, as Babrak Karmal has noted, the country's general backwardness, insufficient maturity of the People's Democratic Party of Afghanistan, the treachery of Amin who had usurped power and a number of other persons, the period which shortly followed the revolution was marked by deviations in the Party and Government leadership from the principled and correct course.

I. Shchedrov, 'The USSR and Afghanistan: The Firm Foundation of Friendship and Cooperation' *International Affairs* (Moscow), no. 1, 1981, p. 15.
25. *KT*, 14 Nov. 1978.
26. This is illustrated, not only by the above statement, but also by a sharp exchange, again with *Pravda*, after he assumed responsibility for Defence in the late summer of 1979:

> **Pravda** Would you please explain the immediate and important difficulty of the Democratic Republic of Afghanistan?
> **Amin** The interference of foreigners in our internal affairs. (*KT*, 4 Aug. 1979).

27. Moscow, TASS in English, 28 Nov. 1978, *Foreign Broadcast Information Service*, vol. III, 30 Nov. 1978, J(i).

8 A TREATY AND A MURDER: CLOSING THE AMERICAN OPTION

The Afghan-Soviet Friendship Treaty signed in Moscow on 5 December 1978 was prompted by internal developments in Afghanistan rather than by any security considerations. It did not arise from any wish on the part of the Afghan leadership to align itself more closely with the USSR and was in fact a symptom of the increasing strain in that relationship. The recent defeat of Babrak Karmal and the Parchamites was also effectively a defeat for Moscow. The conclusion of the treaty was a means whereby the Khalq leadership could attempt to mollify Afghanistan's powerful and disgruntled neighbour upon whose assistance they remained heavily dependent. But it carried considerable risks in terms of potential damage to Afghanistan's credibility as a member of the non-aligned movement, and in terms of the greater leverage the Soviets would gain in Kabul if Afghanistan's international isolation were to increase. There is some evidence that Hafizullah Amin at least was aware of these dangers and sought to avert them. In so doing he made himself the target of Moscow's special attention.

From the beginning the PDPA government was confronted with a serious dilemma in its foreign relations. It inherited a situation in which Afghanistan was economically and militarily dependent on the Soviet Union.[1] Ideologically it had similar goals to those of the USSR, though the PDPA differed among themselves and with the Soviet Union over how these goals were to be achieved. Although they were Marxists, President Taraki and his Foreign Minister Hafizullah Amin were also nationalists, and wanted to preserve Afghanistan's hard-won independence just as they wanted to establish a society 'void of the exploitation of man by man'.

In the first weeks after the April Revolution Taraki and Amin made a point of reaffirming Afghanistan's commitment to a policy of non-alignment, emphasising their country's need for economic assistance. Asked at his first press conference whether Afghanistan would have a special relationship with the USSR, Taraki replied:

> Our relations with all countries including the Soviet Union and all our neighbours . . . will be based on the extent of their support of our revolutionary government and their help in political and economic

areas . . . We will be non-aligned and our friendship with others will depend on the measure of their help and support to us.[2]

Afghanistan would try to maintain friendly relations with the United States, but again Taraki reiterated the relationship would depend on the political and economic support Afghanistan received from the USA. In his first major policy broadcast on 9 May, Taraki reaffirmed this earlier position.[3]

As Foreign Minister, Amin sought to widen Afghanistan's options as far as possible. Even before the discovery of the Eid conspiracy he had not shown any great enthusiasm for the Russians. In the first three months after the April Revolution he made three trips abroad: to Cuba, in May, for a non-aligned Conference; to New York in June for the UN Disarmament meeting; and to Belgrade in July for another non-aligned Conference.[4] Only on the first occasion did he go via Moscow, where he stayed less than twenty-four hours. He had a brief meeting with Gromyko who had not bothered to go to the airport to greet him. During the discussions, which the joint communique described as 'warm' and 'heartfelt', Amin emphasised Afghanistan's need for economic aid and Gromyko stressed Soviet hopes for the coming UN General Assembly Special Session on Disarmament.[5] Amin took the hint. His speech at the UN explicitly endorsed Soviet proposals.[6] And in August Afghanistan signed 'in rapid succession some 30 aid and co-operation agreements with the Soviet Union'.[7]

At the same time Amin worked consistently to keep open channels of communications to the US, to reassure them of Afghanistan's commitment to non-alignment and to emphasise that Afghanistan needed, and wanted, aid from all sources, including America. While in New York in June 1978 he told *Newsweek* that no change in Afghanistan's relations with the USA was envisaged as a result of the April Revolution.[8] During the same visit he had a meeting with Harold Saunders, the Assistant Secretary of State for Near Eastern and South Asian Affairs. Back in Kabul the following month Amin met the Assistant Secretary of State for Political Affairs, David Newsom, who was passing through on his way to Pakistan. The *New York Times* reported that Taraki and 'a deputy' had asked Newsom that the US increase aid. The US response was that it would not try and compete with the USSR in providing aid to Afghanistan, but the State Department let it be known that it saw the request as indicating Afghanistan's intention to remain non-aligned.[9] This apparent diplomatic success was marred by the fact that even the little aid the US *had* promised was not getting through. Of US $20 million committed for 1978, only $13 million was expected to be spent 'partly because of the political upheaval'.

In several speeches during the summer, Amin attempted to distance the Afghan revolution from the Russian revolution and, in the wake of the discovery of the Eid conspiracy he gave a series of interviews in which he showed himself extremely defensive about relations with the USSR. He emphasised that they pre-dated the April Revolution and that reports that Afghanistan was a Soviet satellite were propaganda spread by Afghanistan's enemies. He insisted that Afghanistan welcomed aid *without strings, from all sources*, especially the United States. This was a theme to which he returned constantly. His most explicit appeal to the United States to help Afghanistan withstand Soviet pressure came in an interview with the *Los Angeles Times* and the *Washington Post* on 25 October, when he said: 'We want the United States of America to *consider realistically the affairs of this region* and further provide us with aid.'[10]

One of the problems confronting Amin in his efforts to attract American aid was ideological. He was a Marxist, committed to radical social and economic reform in Afghanistan and, as a leader of one of the world's least developed countries, to the achievement of certain international socialist goals. With the exception of Tito, the United States has consistently demonstrated its antipathy to communist leaders regardless of their nationalism. Ho Chi Minh was a dramatic case in point. History was therefore against Amin in his efforts to convince the US that support for the Afghan revolution offered the best hope of preventing the expansion of Soviet influence in the region.

His and Taraki's frequently repeated commitment to non-alignment was regarded with scepticism in the West, where the notion that a Third World Marxist regime, particularly one in a country bordering the USSR, might not be a creature of the Soviet Union was scarcely entertained.

An editorial in the *New York Times* published a week after the revolution before the new Afghan leadership had made any public statements, was typical of the Western reaction, and gave a hint of what Kabul could expect. The paper expressed concern that a 'genuine non-aligned government' had fallen to an 'avowedly communist one that is likely to tilt towards Moscow', and went on to anticipate trouble for Pakistan and Iran and bloodshed from tribal resistance. The *New York Times* concluded: 'Outsiders can do little beyond offering sanctuary to those who flee. Countries in the region should be prepared to lend a hand, and the wealthier nations should help them carry the burden.'[11]

The strategic community in the USA also quickly consigned Afghanistan to the Soviet camp. An experienced US analyst of Soviet policies was quoted as saying 'The Great Game is over and the Russians have won it.'[12] This view was shared by both Iran and Pakistan, despite the new Afghan government's attempts to reassure its neighbours. At his first press conference Taraki said that the Pashtunistan question was 'under study' and that Afghanistan wanted a 'peaceful and friendly solution of it with our Pakistani brothers'.[13] The commitment to seek a solution through 'peaceful dialogue' with Pakistan was repeated by Taraki in a broadcast a few days later[14] and by Amin in his speech to the Havana non-aligned conference on 19 May.[15]

Both Iran and Pakistan however delayed recognition of the new regime for more than a week (6 and 5 May respectively), an indication that relations would not be easy. A 'high Iranian official' told the *New York Times*:

> Tehran felt that Mr Taraki's declaration of non-alignment was absurd, in view of the dominant role the Russians were playing in Kabul and in light of Mr Taraki's role as head of the Communist Party of Afghanistan.

Speaking of Iranian intervention in Oman, he went on to warn of the possibility of military intervention in Afghanistan.[16]

Pakistan's reaction to the new Afghan government was also hostile, although it seems likely that the government was exaggerating its fears in order to persuade the United States to increase military aid. A high-ranking Pakistani official told the *New York Times*: 'For all practical purposes, the Soviet Union now has a border with Pakistan . . . The United States must realize that there has been a historic readjustment in this part of the world and act accordingly . . .'[17]

The conclusion of a Friendship Treaty with the Soviet Union providing for military co-operation was scarcely calculated to improve this situation. American officials insist that the conclusion of the treaty made no difference to American perceptions of Afghan non-alignment, that as far as they were concerned, Afghanistan ceased to be non-aligned when the PDPA seized power. However the statement, in a US government publication, that the 'Khalq regime had decided to align more closely with the Soviets and on December 5, 1978, signed a new friendship treaty with Moscow', suggests that Washington's perceptions of Afghanistan's position *were* modified as a result of the signing of the treaty.[18]

Amin does seem to have had reservations on this score, and he certainly displayed an equivocal attitude to the treaty. It was negotiated quickly, in no more than a fortnight, probably on Soviet initiative. Certainly the conclusion of such a treaty formed part of the USSR's overall strategy for the construction of a system of 'collective security' in Asia and the Soviet-Afghan treaty was modelled closely on other Soviet Friendship Treaties with third world countries. Moscow's use of a Friendship Treaty in an attempt to shore up its position following the defeat of its protégés in a client state finds a precedent in the signing of the Soviet-Egyptian Treaty in May 1971, just after President Sadat had successfully moved against the pro-Moscow faction of Ali Sabri.

Rumours that something like this was being contemplated began circulating in Kabul in mid-November but, when Amin was asked in an interview if Afghanistan hoped to sign a Friendship Treaty with the USSR he replied by referring to the Treaty signed in 1921 which he said had been renewed several times, implying that nothing more was contemplated.[19] Amin took an unusually low profile throughout the entire proceedings. When Taraki left for the Soviet Union accompanied by a large delegation including the entire PDPA Politburo, Amin was listed simply as the first among those accompanying him. A source who was close to Amin at the time has said that Taraki, who had a strong sense of self-importance and liked making extravagant gestures, grandly agreed in principle to the main provisions of the treaty, saying 'You can work out the details with Hafizullah.'[20] It is difficult to see what detail was left to be worked out, since the Afghan treaty is almost a carbon copy of that concluded between the USSR and Ethiopia a few days before.[21] The negotiations received no coverage in either the Afghan or the Soviet media, although both devoted considerable space to the visit and the signing of the Treaty. Taraki naturally received most attention, though one would have expected Amin as Deputy Prime Minister and Foreign Minister to have taken a somewhat more prominent public role. In fact he was virtually ignored in Soviet reports.

It is not clear whether Amin's reservations amounted to outright opposition to the treaty which was overruled by Taraki or whether they were overcome by his own ebullient self-confidence and seemingly unquenchable optimism that, whatever the difficulties, he would somehow surmount them. Perhaps the truth lies somewhere between. Certainly his relationship with Taraki and with the Russians deteriorated after the signing of the treaty, and comments made by Selig Harrison, who interviewed

Amin twice in 1978, suggest that there was plenty of optimism:

> I found him a formidable strongly nationalistic figure who was clearly
> not prepared to play the role of supine puppet. His confident atti-
> tude, reflected in numerous off-the-record comments, was that he
> knew how to handle the Russians, who needed him as much or more
> than he needed them . . .[22]

In any case Amin continued to downplay the December 1978 Treaty
by linking it to the 1921 Treaty and arguing that it did not really change
things very much.[23] The USSR had been a major supplier of economic
and military assistance to Afghanistan for 25 years and could have continued providing financial support for the PDPA reform programmes
and military assistance to combat the (at that stage) extremely limited
counter-revolutionary violence initiated by the Peshawar-based rebel
groups, without any such new treaty arrangement. It did perhaps provide an additional deterrent against attack from Pakistan, or from Iran
which had already implicitly threatened as much. Subsequently Pakistan's President Zia ul-Haq admitted that the existence of the treaty
was a consideration preventing him from aiding the rebels as much as he
would have liked, though how important a consideration is not known.[24]

Amin's optimism that problems arising from the signing of the treaty
would be manageable had some foundation. Despite repeated evidence
of its hostility to the Afghan revolution the United States had assigned
one of its most competent and knowledgeable diplomats to its Embassy
in Kabul. Adolph Dubs's appointment was announced on 1 June 1978
and he presented his credentials on 12 July. His previous experience in
Moscow from 1972 to 1974 and then as Deputy Assistant Secretary for
Near Eastern and South Asian Affairs from 1975 meant that he was
especially well-equipped for the Kabul post. Although US officials have
insisted that Dubs's appointment was purely accidental, it appeared that
the United States was taking the new Afghanistan very seriously indeed.

Of special significance was the good working relationship soon established between Dubs and Amin. Abrasive, arrogant and extremely proud,
Amin had a difficult relationship with many influential foreign ambassadors in Kabul. 'If he made an advance to someone and was rebuffed,
he wouldn't try again, he'd just go back into his shell', recalled one
diplomat who had known him well. With Dubs it was different. Although
official Americans deny it, other observers agree that the two men liked
and respected each other. During his brief tour Dubs is reported to have
called on Amin some fourteen times,[25] and in the same period three

senior American officials visited Afghanistan and had talks with Amin
— Newsom, Miklos and, as late as 13 January 1979, Thomas P. Thorn-
ton from Brzezinski's staff. A month later the ambassador was murdered.
The assassination provided the *coup de grâce* to Amin's efforts to maintain relations with the US and signalled the beginning of a savage political
attack on Amin himself.

The incident is still surrounded by a good deal of mystery. The ambassador's death has never been satisfactorily explained and his killers
have never been identified, despite the fact that at least one was taken
alive. No person or group claimed responsibility, which suggests it was
no ordinary terrorist operation. There are discrepancies between the
Afghan and American accounts and both parties have been evasive on
certain issues.

The crisis began shortly before 9 a.m. on Wednesday 14 February,
when Dubs's car was stopped on the way to the Embassy by a man
dressed in police uniform who said he had instructions to search the
car. When the ambassador agreed, the man drew a gun and ordered the
chauffeur not to move. Three others appeared, one of whom was also
armed. The four terrorists got into the car and ordered the chauffeur to
drive to the nearby Kabul Hotel where Dubs was taken and held hostage
in Room 117 on the second floor. The chauffeur was told by the kidnappers to inform the Embassy.

It ended approximately four hours later when Afghan police, claiming that the terrorists had refused a further extension of the deadline
and intended to kill the ambassador launched an assault on the room.
Dubs was killed along with three of the kidnappers (two according to
the Americans). Another terrorist was taken alive, but was killed (or
died) shortly after.

The circumstances of the abduction itself are not altogether clear.
Amin held the Americans largely responsible for allowing the incident
to occur. Afghan authorities had, some months before, suggested that a
police escort be provided for the ambassador's car, he said, and even the
ambassador's chauffeur had said that his guards had told the ambassador
his car was being followed, yet the Americans took no precautionary
measures.[26] American sources deny having received any such offer of
protection, or that the ambassador's car was being followed.[27]

For security reasons the ambassador's chauffeur varied his route each
day when taking Dubs to and from the Embassy. How then did the
kidnappers know where to wait on the morning of 14 February? The
American report does not raise this question, and instead seeks to implicate the Afghan authorities. It notes that 'an abduction of this nature

would appear to have entailed considerable risk', since it occurred within sight of three locations where Afghan police are normally stationed, and at the time at least one police officer was standing across the street. 'The abduction occurred with relative ease, and without any apparent interference from the host country authorities.'

Why did the ambassador, or his chauffeur, stop the car on request and open the doors to allow a police search when, as Amin correctly pointed out, he had complete diplomatic immunity and could legitimately have refused both requests? Americans have explained this in terms of Dubs's desire not to antagonise the local authorities. The report claims that the ambassador *might* on an earlier occasion have permitted two searches of his vehicle in one evening and, if this was so (the report does not claim that it was) it might have 'permitted the kidnappers to proceed with their plans unrestricted'.[28]

The Americans complained in particular that they were excluded from decision making regarding the handling of the crisis, that their frequently stated and clearly understood requests for caution were ignored, and that senior Afghan government officials were unavailable when contacted by US embassy personnel. In particular they held Hafizullah Amin responsible. But there was apparently considerable conflict within the Afghan government, much of it revealed in the American report itself. Amin's role is by no means obvious.

Although the Americans claim that they were unable to contact senior Afghan officials, the report states that the Chief of Police, Sayed Daoud Taroon, who was in charge of the operation, told US officials that 'the DRA had no intention of breaking into the room by force and thereby possibly jeopardizing the safety of the Ambassador'. They received similar assurances from another senior official, the Deputy Foreign Minister Shah Mohammad Dost. While Dost was a Parchamite, Taroon was Amin's man, and assurances coming from him may be regarded as coming from Amin himself.

However, it appears that plans for an assault on Room 117 were in train quite early, although there is some confusion regarding the timing. The official Afghan report claims that between 9.30 and 10 a.m. 'The American Embassy was "contacted" and requested to send a representative to act as an interpreter and convey the government's assault intentions to the ambassador.'[29] However, the Embassy official at the hotel (presumably Bruce Flatin) did not receive the request until approximately 11.40 a.m. The Afghan report also claimed that at 10.30 a.m. security personnel were assigned to attack the terrorists, although it was not until 11.20 a.m. that the Americans at the hotel noticed preparations for an assault. At 12.10 p.m. they were told that a decision to storm Room 117 had been taken *on the orders of the Prime Minister*, i.e., Taraki.[30]

The US response was to accuse the Afghan government of bad faith, but the fact that the Afghan report claimed that plans for the assault were being made relatively early while Taroon was assuring them, until late in the morning that no such action was planned suggests that there was a serious conflict within the Afghan government, and that Taroon, while theoretically in charge of operations, was overruled. In this connection it is worth noting that Taroon was never seen at the hotel himself; that shortly before the assault a Soviet official who had been closeted with Taroon for 'at least one hour and forty minutes' was seen leaving by an American waiting at Taroon's office; and that the order for the attack came from Taraki.

Another aspect of the assault remains puzzling. The Afghan authorities requested the American Embassy official, Bruce Flatin, to speak to the ambassador in German and warn him that an attack was imminent and that he should either get out of the bedroom area on the excuse of going to the bathroom, or else lie on the floor. Despite the fact that preparations for the assault had been observed half an hour before and that Flatin recognised that 'the message obviously meant the authorities were poised to strike' he refused to relay the instructions which might have saved Dubs's life.

Further mystery surrounds the demands of the kidnappers, their identity and even their number. The Americans were not told directly of the kidnappers' demands although in the course of the morning they received information that they had asked for the release of three prisoners, 'Wahez, Majid and Faizant'. Later that afternoon, after the ambassador's death, Amin went to the airport to bid farewell to the Iraqi Foreign Minister and afterwards gave an informal briefing to the foreign ambassadors present, confirming that the terrorists had demanded the release of three prisoners, though he did not name them. However, Amin later said that they had asked for the release of only one prisoner, Bahruddin Bahes, who he described as 'an extreme leftist adventurist' which he defined as a combination of 'extreme leftist' and 'narrow-minded nationalist'.[31] Although he disclaimed any knowledge of the identity of the terrorists, he said that one had an accent that sounded as if it came from Badakhshan. This was a clear attempt to implicate the pro-Chinese Settem-i-Melli (National Oppression Party) in the operation. Bahes could not be handed over, Amin said, because he was no longer in custody, having escaped at the time of the April Revolution.

Afghan and American sources differ over the number of kidnappers and their condition after the assault. The Afghan government claimed that three terrorists were found dead in the room with the ambassador and a fourth died of his wounds shortly after. The US report claims that only two terrorists, both dead, were taken from the room and that a third who had been captured shortly after 9 a.m. had been held elsewhere in the hotel and was later taken from the hotel 'alive and relatively unharmed'. He was later identified, along with the other two, when American officials were given an opportunity to view the bodies of the four terrorists that evening. The fourth body could not be identified by Embassy officials at all. Americans complain that they were given no opportunity to interrogate the surviving kidnapper and that the Afghan government 'has provided no evidence that any effort on their part has been made to locate or identify others who may have been involved'. Amin later revealed that some arrests had been made at the hotel, but those involved had been found to have no connection with the terrorists and released.[32]

The implication is that the Afghan authorities were well aware of the identity of the kidnappers but chose not to disclose it, attempting instead to lay the blame on Settem-i-Melli. The attempt lacks credibility for a variety of reasons. Had the kidnappers been as close to Bahes as Amin claimed, they would surely have been aware of his whereabouts. And since Settem-i-Melli had broken with the PDPA in the 1960s there was no reason not to accuse them directly, and certainly no reason to silence the wounded terrorist so quickly, permanently and apparently deliberately. The kidnapping of the American ambassador by Settem-i-Melli is also unlikely in view of its pro-Chinese and anti-Russian leanings. The choice of Settem-i-Melli as the culprit appears a convenient ploy to divert attention from the real beneficiaries of the kidnapping and murder of the US Ambassador: pro-Soviet elements in Afghanistan and the USSR itself.[33]

There is also some mystery regarding the weapons involved. US experts determined that the ambassador died as a result of bullet wounds inflicted by .25 and .22 calibre weapons. The Americans identified the .25, but not the .22, among the weapons listed by the Afghan government as being in the possession of the kidnappers. They complain that they were not permitted to examine the weapons, although Amin told them he had given specific instructions that they should be allowed to do so and to photograph them, and that Shah Mohammad Dost passed this message on. Amin claimed that US officials did not avail themselves of the opportunity offered. The US asserts that no such offer was received.

It is possible that Dost, the committed Parchamite, failed to carry out
Amin's instructions. It would not be the last time he withheld full co-
operation from the Foreign Minister.

A question mark hangs over Amin's role in the entire proceedings,
from his alleged unavailability to and lack of co-operation with American
embassy officials on the morning of the kidnapping to his disappearance
from public view for four days (until after the ambassador's body had
been flown home) when he emerged to face a hostile and sceptical
foreign press corps. The fact that the kidnappers were never publicly
identified or their demands satisfactorily explained, and that they chose
as their victim the United States' Ambassador suggests that Amin was
their target, and their intention was to put pressure on him in some
way. The only people who stood to gain from the incident were Amin's
enemies both inside and outside Afghanistan, who might have wished to
isolate and discredit him, and to undermine any potential Afghan-US
rapprochement.

Much has been made of Amin's 'unavailability', but US officials become angry and evasive when asked for precise details about who was
refused what, where and by whom. It is certainly not true that they had
no access to top Afghan officials: they saw both Taroon, who was supposed to be in charge of the operation, and Dost, the Deputy Foreign
Minister.[34]

That there was conflict within the Afghan government over the
strategy to be adopted and panic among the American Embassy staff
is not Amin's responsibility. The Americans were not the only ones
excluded from the decision making process. The decision not to delay
the assault on Room 117 accords with known Soviet strategy in similar
circumstances and suggests that Soviet advisers persuaded Taraki to
overrule Taroon. It merely testifies to the relative weakness of Amin's
position at the time. If the outcome embarrassed him, so much the
better for them.

In strict protocol terms, the Afghan government probably did all that
was required by sending telegrams of condolence; flying flags at half
mast; having the Deputy Foreign Minister take a wreath to the Embassy
and a Minister, Bareq Shafie sign the condolence book; and by having
Dost and Bareq Shafie go to the airport when the ambassador's coffin
was flown out. Apparently it was not enough: the US wanted a scape-
goat. One American official suggested that if Amin had had Taroon
sacked it might have made amends. The US never admitted that the
actions of its own personnel, including Dubs himself, contributed to the
tragedy but Amin clearly indicated that he regarded the Americans as a

east partially responsible. It was the nearest he ever came to defending himself.

One of his opponents' most brilliant manoeuvres was to place Amin in a position where he was forced publicly to accept responsibility for the bungled rescue attempt. In what must have been one of the most difficult press conferences he ever gave, Amin defended the government's action as an attempt, up to the last moment, to save Dubs's life. By saying that Taroon had been in charge of the operation, and had reported directly to him, he assumed personal responsibility for what had happened. Further, he stated explicitly that Soviet officials had had no part in the decision or its execution, thereby absolving them from any share of the blame. The effect of the press conference was to make Amin appear a liar and a hypocrite, yet he had little choice but to act as he did.

There was already considerable tension between Amin and Taraki over other issues. Amin had antagonised Moscow and his relationship with Dubs had left him dangerously exposed. The pro-Soviet clique that was forming around Taraki, including Watanjar, Mazdooryar, Sarwari and Gulabzoi was waiting for an opportunity to move against him. Any attempt to defend himself over the handling of the Dubs affair would have involved criticism of Taraki and the Russians, and, given the delicacy of his position, that was a luxury Amin could not afford.

The most he could do to salvage something from the wreckage of his diplomatic initiative was to appeal to the United States not to allow the incident to damage the relationship. He did this first, indirectly, through an editorial in the *Kabul Times* on the morning after the kidnapping:

> The terrorists and the enemies of the people of DRA by committing such an inhumane and cruel act may think they would disturb or damage the ties between the two friendly nations . . . The people and government of the DRA and the USA are fully aware of the acts of their enemies. They know that such provocative acts will not undermine the friendly relations between the two nations . . .[35]

Amin followed this up in his press conference with a more direct appeal, although his usual optimism was tinged with desperation: 'The US is a world superpower and I am sure nothing could influence its leaders to change their minds . . .'[36]

In the intervening period he had not simply been unavailable to the Americans, he had disappeared completely from public view. There is no parallel with his snubbing of the Soviet Ambassador later in the year

when he went about normal public appearances, simply avoiding those
involving the Soviet Embassy. It is arguable that a special display of
regret might perhaps have mollified the Americans, but it would almost
certainly have been interpreted by others as an undue inclination in their
direction. Again, his position was too precarious for him to run the risk.

Whether this was an error of judgement on his part is a matter for
debate. Certainly his behaviour at the time appears to have done irrepar-
able damage to his relations with the Americans, and they cite his handling of Dubs's kidnapping as one of the principal barriers to any co-
operation at a later date. At the time US officials were unwilling to
acknowledge the extent of their own responsibility for the ambassador's
death and sought to lay the blame entirely on the Afghan government.
Later, Amin's alleged indifference became a convenient excuse for the
United States' failure to respond to his appeals for assistance in the face
of a mounting Soviet threat.

The immediate consequences were unmistakable. The United States
suspended all aid programmes and refused to send another ambassador.
Bruce Amstutz, bitterly antagonistic towards Amin, was left in charge,
and the black propaganda emanating from the US Embassy increased.
For Amin, the American option was closed.

Notes

1. For an account of the development of this relationship see Louis Dupree,
Afghanistan (Princeton University Press, Princeton, 1980).
2. Press conference, 6 May 1978, *Kabul Times* (*KT*), 13 May 1978.
3. Democratic Republic of Afghanistan, *Basic Lines of Revolutionary Duties
of the Government of Democratic Republic of Afghanistan* (Government Printing
Press, Kabul, 1978).
4. Among those at the airport to receive him was the recently appointed
Afghan Ambassador, Dr Anahita Ratebzada. It must have been a memorable
meeting!
5. For the text of the Joint Communique, see *KT*, 20 May 1978.
6. For the text of Amin's UN speech, see *KT*, 8 June 1978.
7. *New York Times*, 4 Aug. 1978, p. 4.
8. *Newsweek*, 3 July 1978.
9. *New York Times*, 4 Aug. 1978, p. 4.
10. *KT*, 28 Oct. 1978 (emphasis added).
11. *New York Times*, 5 May 1978, p. 28.
12. See Drew Middleton, 'How Afghans Fit Into Soviet Global Strategy', *New
York Times*, 24 June 1978, p. 5, for report of a high level NATO symposium on
the changed strategic environment.
13. Press conference, 6 May 1978.
14. *Basic Lines*, pp. 33-4.
15. *KT*, 21 May 1978.
16. Nicholas Gage, 'Iran Fears Threat From Afghans to the Oil Passage Route'

in the Gulf', *New York Times*, 20 May 1978, p. 4.

17. William Borders, 'New Afghan Regime Worries Pakistanis', *New York Times*, 20 May 1978, p. 4.

18. United States International Communication Agency, *The Global Significance of the Occupation of Afghanistan by the USSR* (n.d.), p. 3.

19. Interview with *US News and World Report*, *KT*, 20 Nov. 1978.

20. Conversation with the author, December 1980.

21. For text of the Soviet-Afghan Friendship Treaty, see *Soviet News* (London), 6 February 1979.

22. 'Did Moscow Fear an Afghan Tito?', *New York Times*, 13 Jan. 1980, p. E.23.

23. *KT*, 21 Feb. 1979.

24. *Nawa-i-Waqt*, 22 March 1979, in *Urdu Press Summary* (Australian Embassy, Islamabad).

25. Information obtained in several interviews in India and Pakistan, December 980-January 1981.

26. Press conference, 19 February, *KT*, 21 Feb. 1979.

27. 'Kidnapping of U.S. Ambassador Dubs', Summary of report of investigation Prepared by US State Department, *Vikrant* (Delhi), May 1980, pp. 44-53.

28. A further point raised in the US report, intended to suggest complicity on the part of Afghan authorities was the kidnappers' choice of the Kabul Hotel as a place to hold their hostage, because it was then under heavy security due to the visit of the Iraqi delegation which was staying there. They also query the choice of a room upon which such an easy assault could be made. It could equally be argued that a hotel where foreigners were present would be more likely to inhibit violent reaction on the part of the authorities and a good view of the approaches to the room would be essential from the point of view of the kidnappers.

29. Cited in USICA, *Occupation of Afghanistan*. The Afghan report did not name an author, but the Americans assumed it to have been written by Taroon. This may not have been the case.

30. For some reason the American report attempts to cast doubt on the source of the decision by placing the words 'Prime Minister' in inverted commas.

31. Press conference, 19 February, *KT*, 21 Feb. 1979.

32. Ibid.

33. The US report makes no allegations regarding the identity of the terrorists but in private conversation American officials accept the explanation that they were Settem-i-Melli, which they describe, accurately enough, as a small Shi'i organisation with leftist sympathies, though they omit mention of China. Why they should choose to believe one of the most incredible of Amin's statements while professing to disbelieve everything else he said remains a mystery. Another question which American sources fail to answer is why, if the intention was to put pressure on a fanatically pro-Soviet regime to release political prisoners, the kidnappers selected an American as their victim? Surely they got the wrong ambassador? US officials attribute this 'mistake' to 'the generally chaotic situation existing in Kabul at the time', although I found no evidence of such chaos when I visited the city the following month.

34. The assertion, by a senior American diplomat in a conversation with the author, that 'If an ambassador is kidnapped you (i.e. the Foreign Minister) drop everything' is questionable. Would the Secretary of State drop everything in the event of the kidnapping of an Afghan Ambassador? He would most probably do what Amin did: place the operation in the hands of the competent authorities, the police, with instructions that he be kept informed.

35. *KT*, 15 Feb. 1979. The editor of the *Kabul Times* Kazem Ahang was a supporter of Amin, and the latter was able to use the editorial columns of the newspaper as a mouthpiece when necessary.

36. *KT*, 21 Feb. 1979.

9 THE QUESTION OF LEADERSHIP

The tension between Taraki and Amin, first hinted at in August 197 when Taraki refused to give Amin full responsibility for Defence grad ally became public through the early months of 1979. They differe not over ideology, but over the conduct of day-to-day administratio and the relationship between the Party and the government. The con flict arose directly from the personality cult that had been allowed t develop around Taraki. Although Amin himself had contributed t building it, he was the first to realise its potential danger and to soun a warning. He immediately ran up against Taraki's very considerabl ego, for the PDPA General-Secretary, President and Prime Minister ha begun to believe the extravagant praise that had been heaped upon hin In the circumstances it was a comparatively simple matter for less figures in the party, jealous of Amin's ability and ambitious for the own advancement, to manipulate Taraki and turn what should hav been serious consideration of the role of the party leadership into ye another savage struggle for power.

Riven by factionalism from its inception, the PDPA had never deve oped a tradition of collective leadership. Taraki, well-liked and respecte probably seemed a harmless enough choice as the first General-Secretary When Amin returned from the United States and became involved i party activity, he brought to the PDPA an outstanding intellectual an organisational ability that it had until then lacked, and which Tara was quick to recognise and use.

In 1977, however, Taraki sacrificed Amin in order to accommodat the Parchamites in a reunited PDPA. It is likely that Amin's distrus of Taraki had its origins in this experience, for there was no guarante that Taraki would not at some future date once more display the sam lamentable weakness in the face of pressure from the Parchamites an their foreign patrons. As it turned out any apprehensions Amin migl have had on this score were fully justified. Twice more, in March an September 1979, Taraki formed an alliance with the pro-Soviet factio in the PDPA in an attempt to destroy Amin.

Why, if he was aware of Taraki's weakness, did Amin participat in the development of the personality cult around him after the Apr 1978 revolution? An explanation might be found in the party's de perate need to present at least a façade of unity. Given the fundament

156

isagreement between the Khalq and Parcham factions and the growing
nbitions of the military clique headed by Watanjar, genuine collective
adership was out of the question. Competent enough to lead a small
andestine party, Taraki did not have the qualities required for leader-
 up of a revolutionary government. At the same time there did not
ppear to be any viable alternative: Amin certainly had the ability, but
e did not at that stage command sufficient support. The PDPA there-
re sought to solve the problem by presenting Taraki as something
e clearly was not — a brilliant revolutionary leader. Every successful
initiative that had been taken, up to and including the April Revolution,
as attributed to Taraki. It was a short-sighted policy, for the object of
ll this adulation could not live up to the image. In putting him on a
edestal his party colleagues placed him beyond criticism. In so doing
ney created a monster.

Further evidence that all was not well between Taraki and Amin
ame at the end of December when Taraki made an attack on Amin
efore a carefully chosen audience: a group of army officers, Amin's
lost important constituency.

> The students we have trained in our party have cooperated with their
> party according to their talent and capacity . . . Our Comrade Amin
> is one of the most brilliant students of our school who has taken
> part in every regard. *There is no doubt that other friends have also
> taken part.* Comparatively I should say that whatever plan I have
> given Comrade Hafizullah Amin he has put it into action very well.
> I am satisfied with him and the party is pleased with him.[1]

araki was in effect telling them that whatever Amin had done, had
een done on his, Taraki's, instructions and however important Amin's
ole may have appeared, he was merely one among many. Amin there-
ore had no special claim to leadership or loyalty.

Amin responded four days later with unprecedented criticism of
araki's leadership:

> The other creativity of Comrade Noor Mohammad Taraki was recog-
> nition of the fighting members of the party and always keeping track
> of their continuous work, a pious attitude towards them, never
> adopting a destructive attitude and always attaching great value to
> constructive possibilities . . . *He was not [a] dogmatist in party pro-
> cedures.* He used to determine the course of activities of the party
> according to the prevailing conditions thus steering the party to

[the] victorious Saur Revolution.

Our great leader always put together different forms of struggl. He never gave way to the possibility of [the] development of [an] attitude of submission in the party. *He always controlled every form of adventurism in the party. He always studied issues dialectically...*

The inference was clear. Amin was accusing Taraki of dogmatism, of failing to give due recognition to the contribution of longstanding and loyal party members, of not paying sufficient attention to prevailing conditions and of allowing himself to be influenced by adventuristic elements in the party. It was a plea for consultation and for caution. A month later he reminded an audience of high-level university and Higher Education Ministry staff that even before the foundation of the PDPA there were patriots who struggled for the liberation of the Afghan people. Eventually, inspired by Taraki, 'Together with our comrades we realised that the only way for real deliverance of the people of Afghanistan was the establishment of a new type of party.'[3] Credit for the formation of the PDPA and its successful seizure of power did not belong to Taraki alone.

Then, on 21 February, in the wake of the Dubs murder, and on the eve of the visit to Afghanistan of a high powered Soviet economic delegation, Amin gave the inaugural address at the opening of the Academy of Sciences of Afghanistan.[4] It was a prestigious occasion, and Amin took advantage of it to make a detailed and explicit statement of his position on several important issues.

Once again he emphasised the independence of the 'glorious Saur Revolution' which 'triumphed in its Afghan form' and 'surprised our friends and enemies both throughout the world'. It did so 'without any financial and material aid of any country or any source in the world'. He reminded his audience of the early clashes with the Parchamites:

Though the party was dealt great blows from inside and outside through plots of the enemies of the people, due to the fact that the loyal and true members of the party had occupied their places in the ramparts of the class struggle these plots failed to hamper the growth or triumph of our party.

Amin then declared that, owing to the special conditions prevailing in Afghanistan it had been possible, through the April Revolution to 'directly change the most important part of the suprastructure, that is the government, from the feudal into the proletarian and not into ourgeois or national democratic one . . .'

What appears at first glance to be an extravagant ideological boast
vas in reality a defence of the role of the PDPA against those who
ought to impose on it a different strategy. By asserting that the April
Revolution had transformed the state structure from feudal to pro-
:tarian thereby by-passing the national democratic phase, Amin was
xplicitly rejecting the ideological necessity for the PDPA to share
ower with other political groups. In so doing he was merely reaffirm-
ng what had been the Khalqi leadership's position all along, but it did
epresent a theoretical modification of the party's endorsement of the
.ational democratic revolution contained in the 1966 manifesto and by
mplication in *Basic Lines*. It is unlikely that Amin's insistence on the
roletarian nature of the Afghan state was designed, as some writers
ave suggested, to appeal to the Russians.[5] It was rather a renewed
ffort to resist continuing Soviet pressure on the PDPA to modify its
osition and bring it more into line with Soviet preconceptions and
'archamite proclivities.[6]

Finally Amin recalled the leading role of the armed forces (and, by
mplication, himself) in the revolution:

In the great Saur Revolution in spite of the fact that it triumphed
according to the general and particular laws of the epoch making
ideology of the working class the army played the major role of the
proletariat, that is the powerful centre of the victory of revolution.
The Army, as a result of the regular work of the PDPA, had been
[transformed] to a khalqi army equipped with scientific ideology of
the working class and organised in the People's Democratic Party of
Afghanistan, the vanguard of the working class of the country.

That Amin felt the need to reassert the independence of the Afghan
evolution from the Soviet Union, to renew the attack on the Parcham-
tes (and in particular the suggestion that the PDPA should relinquish
ts monopoly on political power) and, perhaps more important, to re-
ssert his own claims to leadership suggests that he was under pressure
on these points.

A week later Ivan Arkhipov, Vice-Chairman of the Soviet Council
of Ministers arrived for a two day visit timed to coincide with the 58th
inniversary of the original Soviet-Afghan Friendship Treaty of 1921. At
he end of the visit Amin and Arkhipov signed what was described as a
broad-based economic cooperation accord'. Considering that Arkhipov
vas the most senior Soviet official to visit Afghanistan since the April

1978 revolution, and that the Soviet Union had committed itself t
contribute more than US $1000 million to the new Five Year Pla
scheduled to commence with the new Afghan budgetary year on 2
March — a fact only disclosed by Amin at a press conference nearly
month later[7] — Arkhipov's visit was a low-key affair.

The ceremonial aspects of the visit were kept to a minimum: Ami
hosted a dinner for his guest, but the *Kabul Times* did not publish an
speeches. It did devote one editorial to Afghan-Soviet relations, empha
sising the 1921 Treaty rather than the more recent one, and making n
mention at all of Arkhipov or the economic co-operation accord.[8] Th
Soviet media were equally restrained in their references. No joint com
munique was issued, and few details of the agreement were made public
The general impression created was that the negotiations had not bee
plain sailing and that both sides were less than satisfied with the results
A clue to one of the problems was revealed by Amin in an interviev
with *Der Spiegel* on 8 March: the Federal Republic of Germany, alon
with Japan, Britain and Canada had written off credits extended t
Afghanistan. No such gesture had been forthcoming from Afghanistan'
largest creditor, the Soviet Union, although Amin expressed the hop
that Moscow would one day take similar action.[9]

Meanwhile speculation that a serious rift had developed betwee
Taraki and Amin over policy matters was beginning to appear in th
foreign press.[10] Taraki dismissed it as propaganda spread by Afghan
istan's enemies: 'I tell them that we are like flesh and nail and flesl
and nail cannot be separated from each other.'[11] Within days howeve
Taraki's actions would belie his words. The temporary collapse of th
Herat garrison in mid-March together with the mounting violence in th
east that came with the melting snow provided the pretext for Taraki'
move against Amin, in the form of a major government reorganisatio
at the end of March and the beginning of April.

The uprising in Herat was the first serious challenge to PDPA autho
rity. It is often represented as a revolt against the government's 'com
munist' measures and the presence of Soviet advisers, but the revolutior
in Iran and the deteriorating relationship between Afghanistan and Irar
were more important contributing factors. Herat has close historical
cultural and economic links with Iran. The population is predominantly
Dari speaking and Shi'i Muslim. Ethnically the inhabitants are Farsewan
and historically the western province of Herat has frequently formed
part of an Iranian empire. Herat itself is traditionally an important
trading centre, and more recently many Afghan workers crossed into
Iran in pursuit of the higher wages being offered there.

Because much of this emigrant labour was illegal it is impossible to
rrive at a completely accurate figure for the numbers of people involved
r the amount of remittances they sent back. One source estimated that
etween 100,000 and 300,000 people were involved. Another claimed
hat at the height of the Iranian boom Afghan workers were remitting
etween 1.2 million and 1.4 million US dollars per day. Many were
gricultural workers, leaving Afghanistan in March and returning in
)ctober (with implications for the Afghan harvest, for in some areas,
specially around Herat, much of the wheat crop could not be harvested
or lack of manpower). More important, the Iranian economic boom
fter 1973 attracted skilled Afghan workers, particularly to the con-
truction industry — skilled manpower that Afghanistan needed itself
ut for which low Afghan wages could not compete.[12]

With the collapse of the Iranian economy as a result of the growing
unrest which led to the overthrow of the Shah in February 1979, these
vorkers drifted back into Afghanistan. While some were readily absorbed
nto the workforce many found themselves without work or means of
upport.[13] The government, while acknowledging the importance of
•roviding employment for young Afghans[14] tried to minimise the im-
nediate impact of the returning workers by keeping them moving back
o their home villages. Despite the government's efforts, there was con-
iderable dislocation in Herat.

Whether the Afghan workers were expelled by the new Iranian
uthorities or returned of their own accord because there was no longer
ny employment in Iran is not clear. A tense situation was made worse
•y reports that some three thousand Afghan nationals had been killed
n Iran, for which the Afghan government sought an explanation from
ehran.[15] At the same time repeated calls from Ayatollah Shariatmadari
over Iranian radio and television for support of the Afghan rebels only
ncreased Kabul's suspicion of Iranian involvement.[16]

The first hint of trouble was a communiqué issued in Peshawar on
!0 March by the Afghan Jamaat-i-Islami claiming that 'religious oppon-
:nts of the pro-Communist regime' had attacked and wounded the
3overnor of Herat on 5 March. After publication of the Jamaat-i-Islami
:ommuniqué, Sigbhatullah Mujaddidi of the so-called 'National Libera-
ion Front' moved swiftly to order a general uprising of his followers
ind a jihad against the Kabul government. He claimed later that the
ighting in Herat was a response to his call.[17]

On the night of 17 March heavy fighting was reported in the city of
Herat. The government informed embassies that communications be-
ween Kabul and Herat had been cut.[18] On 19 March the government

issued a statement accusing Iran of instigating the rebellion, referring to
Iran's decision to expel 7,000 Afghan citizens:

> In fact these were not citizens of Afghanistan, but were Iranian sol
> diers in disguise . . . about 4,000 managed to settle in Herat city and
> its vicinity in the name of Afghan citizens with the help of the Con
> sulate of Iran and organised disorders there.[19]

Reference was made to Shariatmadari's statements, seen as an attempt
to set Afghan Shi'is and Sunnis against each other. The Afghan govern
ment statement was an expression of the view held in some government
and diplomatic circles in Kabul that the uprising had been touched off
by returning Afghan workers recruited and trained much earlier on the
instructions of the Shah.[20]

Whether Iranian trained guerrillas, or individually armed unemployed
malcontents, workers returning from Iran seem to have been a key factor
in the violence. The problem was compounded by the inability of the
commander of the Herat garrison, a young man with no previous ex
perience in the command of such a large force, to cope with the mutiny
that ensued.

Reports reached Kabul that the targets of the violence in Herat were
Soviet advisers, sought out and slain in particularly horrible circum
stances. The source of these rumours was apparently the Iranian consu
in Herat who maintained radio contact with agents in Kabul who in
turn relayed the 'information' to the US embassy, from where it was
disseminated to the expatriate community and the foreign press corps
The most commonly quoted figure was forty Soviet dead, the highes
four hundred.[21] Officially the Afghan government acknowledged the
death of only one Soviet adviser[22] but unofficially government sources
said that nine Russians had been killed.

Less generally known is the fact that a UN vehicle, painted an un
mistakable, vivid blue, was destroyed by crowds shouting not only
'Death to Taraki' and 'Death to Russia' (as commonly reported), but
'Death to Farangis' (i.e. foreigners), suggesting that there was a signifi
cant element of common xenophobia involved.[23] Despite the claims of
the counter-revolutionary leaders in Peshawar, there was little evidence
of co-ordination of opposition activity. The central role of the Iranian
consul was recognised and he was expelled soon after. The government
retaining control of the nearby airbase at Shindand was able to reasser
control over Herat without much difficulty. By 25 March communica
tions had been re-established and calm restored.[24]

Coincidentally with the worst of the violence in Herat, the Revolu-
onary Council met to ratify the Afghan-Soviet Friendship Treaty,
pprove the first year of the new Five Year Plan and the budget for the
oming Afghan year: a formality since these matters had already been
onsidered and approved by the Politburo and the Council of Ministers.
Iowever the Revolutionary Council was also presented with a series of
roposals relating to the regulation of the affairs of the armed forces,
riminal investigation and proceedings and amendment of the laws relat-
ig to the functions of the Revolutionary Council itself. This was com-
letely new, and while the official report stated that 'after deliberation
nd discussion all articles were voted upon and unanimously approved
ne by one with some amendments in a democratic manner',[25] that
oes not seem to have been the end of the matter. The Revolutionary
'ouncil met again the following day and approved the provisions for
he budget and the first year of the Five Year Plan, but the govern-
ental reorganisation was apparently not so easily dealt with. Taraki
id, however, appoint Aslam Watanjar Chief of the General Staff and
her Jan Mazdooryar (formerly commander of the 4th Armoured Divi-
ion, Kabul) as Minister of Interior.

It is not clear to what extent the proposals for the reorganisation of
he government machinery were related to events in Herat or whether
hey would have taken place anyway. Certainly the atmosphere of crisis
vhich resulted gave Watanjar, the ambitious young Deputy Prime Minis-
er and Minister of Interior an opportunity to make a bid for power.
Vatanjar and his associates Mazdooryar and Gulabzoi represented a
'ounger generation, radicalised but not committed. The oldest of them
vas only 33 and none were ranking members of the PDPA.[26] Observers
oted that Watanjar's acquaintance with Marxist theory was sketchy in
he extreme and it was apparent that he had joined the Khalq less out
f conviction than ambition. These three, impatient, ambitious and
aïve, were easy prey for the wily Soviet Ambassador, Alexander Pusa-
ov, anxious to find a means of striking at Amin.[27] Together they put
ressure on Taraki, by now apparently convinced that he really was the
great genius leader' and increasingly distrustful of his erstwhile protégé.

Whether Amin realised at this stage how effectively he was being
utmanoeuvred is not clear, although it seems he did not, for it was
nly after the reorganisation had taken place that he made public his
lissatisfaction with the situation.[28] On 26 March the Politburo and
'ouncil of Ministers finally approved the changes to the laws regulating
he Revolutionary Council, as well as the provisions for the establish-
nent of the Homeland Higher Defence Council which was to take overall

responsibility for security matters. On 27 March the new measures were ratified by the Revolutionary Council, and this time there were no hitches. Taraki presented the changes as another step towards democracy which would be served by the strengthening of the executive, benefit he claimed would flow from the separation of the offices of President and Prime Minister. In appointing Amin to this post, Taraki told the Revolutionary Council:

> As one of our slogans is 'to everyone according to his capacity and work', therefore as a result of past performances and services he has won our greater trust and assurances. I have full confidence in him and in the light of this confidence I entrust him with this job . . .[2]

Taraki's praise of Amin was, as usual, back-handed. Amin's appointment as Prime Minister has been regarded by many analysts as signifying an increase in his power at Taraki's expense. In fact the reverse was the case: Taraki had manoeuvred Amin into a position where he had the prestigious-sounding title of Prime Minister, while real power remained in Taraki's own hands.

The law regulating the operations of the Revolutionary Council set out the powers of the Prime Minister as distinct from those of the President. An examination of the new law reveals that Taraki, as President, intended to surrender very little of his power. While the Prime Minister had power to appoint his deputy and other ministers, he himself was appointed by the President, who had to approve ministerial appointments and dismissals. Furthermore, while the government as a whole (i.e. the Prime Minister and Council of Ministers) was collectively responsible to the Revolutionary Council and the President, individual ministers were 'directly responsible before the President of the Revolutionary Council' in relation to the performance of their duties.[30] These provisions effectively limited the power of the Prime Minister, reducing the functions of the office to minor administrative matters.

The Council of Ministers was to be responsible for financial, planning and budgetary matters, for the conduct of foreign policy, and for 'consolidation of order and public security', in practical terms the responsibility of the Minister of the Interior.

In the context of March 1979, security overlapped with national defence, and responsibility in this regard was placed firmly in the hands of the President and the newly established Homeland Higher Defence Council, of which the President was Chairman. It was in the HHDC that the alignment of forces against Amin, who was appointed Vice-Chairman of the new body, emerged most clearly. The other members were Aslam Watanjar, the newly appointed Defence Minister; Sher Jan Mazdooryar, now Interior Minister; Mohammad Iqbal, President of Political Affairs of the Armed Forces; Major Yaqub, Chief of the General Staff; Colonel Ghulam Sakhi, Commander of Air Defence; Lieutenant-Colonel Nazar Mohammad, Commander of the Air Force; and Assadullah Sarwari, Chief of AGSA (the security police).

The arrangement whereby Taraki himself took responsibility for Defence with Amin 'assisting' was now institutionalised with Taraki as Chairman and Amin as Vice-Chairman of the HHDC. By formalising and extending the decision-making process to include several other individuals Taraki strengthened his position considerably *vis-à-vis* Amin. In addition, the appointment of a Defence Minister meant that Amin no longer had direct access to or authority over the military. In fact, as Vice-Chairman of the HHDC he had no specific power or function at all.

Certain ministerial appointments made at the end of March suggest that Amin had been outmanoeuvred here also. The key ministries of Defence and Interior were in the hands of two of his opponents, Watanjar and Mazdooryar. This meant that Watanjar was in a position to challenge Amin's power base in the armed forces. Mazdooryar now had responsibility for provincial appointments as well as for the security functions of the Interior Ministry. Even AGSA, which was a department of the Prime Ministry and theoretically under Amin's direction, was headed by a Taraki man, Assadullah Sarwari.[31]

Although the government reorganisation had been a severe blow, Amin had strategically placed allies. The Chief of the General Staff, Major Yaqub, was his brother-in-law, and Iqbal, the man in charge of the Political Department of the Armed Forces was a close supporter. Sayed Daoud Taroon, who died saving Amin's life the following September was then Security Chief in the Ministry of Interior. His appointment to the HHDC in mid-April redressed the balance a little in Amin's favour and his subsequent appointment as aide-de-camp to Taraki was of vital importance. In addition, Amin managed to bring two close supporters into the Council of Ministers: Mohammad Sediq Alemyar as Minister of Planning and Khayal Mohammad Katawazi as Minister of Information and Culture. Early in May Faqir Mohammad Faqir, who had been closely associated with Amin in the planning and execution of the seizure of power in April 1978 was appointed Deputy Minister of Interior.

Even so, Amin was very much on the defensive when General Alexei Yepishev, the Soviet First Deputy Minister of Defence and President of

Political Affairs of the Army and Navy arrived in Kabul on 5 April.[3]
The number of Soviet casualties in the recent violence in Herat and th
extent of political disaffection within the Afghan armed forces wer
taken by many foreign observers to explain Yepishev's visit, while a
the same time the visit, and particularly its duration, was taken as con
firmation of these assessments of the situation.[33] This circular reasonin
is unsatisfactory particularly as it turned out that both the estimates o
Soviet casualties and of the political unreliability of the Afghan arme
forces were exaggerated.

The number of Soviet advisers in Afghanistan at that time was ver
small. Even US estimates put the number at only 3,000 with 1,000 i
military roles. Other sources suggested that there were around 2,00
Russians in Afghanistan altogether, and Amin, as late as July 1979 sai
that there were between 1,300 and 1,400.[34] The security and deploy
ment of less than 1,000 men would hardly have warranted the attentio
of such a senior official as Yepishev. In any case, that is a *military* prob
lem, and not one with which Yepishev, whose function was purel
political, would have been expected to deal.

It is also difficult to see why it was necessary to send Yepishev t
deal with political problems in the Afghan armed forces when Amin ha
already demonstrated his capability in this regard. The mutiny in Hera
was dealt with quickly and effectively, as was a later one in Jalalabad i
April. Furthermore, Amin's political control over the armed forces an
their loyalty to him were to be demonstrated dramatically the followin
September when the attempt to oust him failed. In order to remov
him the Russians eventually had to send in a sizeable force of their owr

It is more likely especially in the light of Taraki's recent move agains
him, and the scarcely concealed Soviet disapproval of him, that it wa
the extent of Amin's control over the armed forces, and not the lack o
it, that prompted Yepishev's visit and kept him in Kabul for a week
During that time he had very little to do with Amin.[35] The most seriou
working session in which Yepishev was engaged was his meeting witl
Taraki on 7 April. The Soviet delegation was not listed, but Pusano
was present. For the Afghan side, apart from Taraki, Mohammad Iqbal
technically Yepishev's opposite number, and Yaqub, the CGS, took par
in the talks. Amin was conspicuous by his absence, the more notabl
since he was the Party Secretary ultimately responsible for the arme
forces, a position in the Soviet Union held by Brezhnev himself.

It is not clear what concessions, if any, Amin was forced to make a
a result of Yepishev's visit. There were no important changes of person
nel: Yaqub remained CGS and Iqbal remained in charge of politica

ffairs in the armed forces. The only noteworthy changes took place in araki's office: Vassily Safronchuk, listed as counsellor at the Soviet embassy, but believed to be the ranking Soviet functionary in Kabul, moved into an office in the Presidential Palace. He was followed by Major Taroon who, as aide-de-camp to the President was well placed o guard Amin's back. It appeared that General Yepishev, believed by many to have masterminded the Soviet invasion of Czechoslovakia in 968, had met his match.

Meanwhile the full implications of Taraki's constitutional sleight of hand were becoming evident. In the first half of April the Council of Ministers, of which Amin as *Lomray Wazir* (Prime or First Minister) was normally the head, met twice, on the eighth and fifteenth. But there was no obvious change from the situation that had existed previously. Taraki took the chair, Zeary reported on the land reforms and some minor economic decisions were taken. If the Lomray Wazir was there his presence was not noted. These first two meetings set the pattern for the following months: as long as Taraki remained President, he took charge of meetings of the Council of Ministers and Amin *was never mentioned*.

Also in the first half of April, the Politburo met, once, on the seventh. It discussed the slogans for the first anniversary of the April Revolution and approved the establishment of an Institute for Party Education.[36] Again a pattern was set: so long as Taraki remained in power he sought to deprive the Politburo of its major policy making role and to confine it to consideration of purely party matters.

Amin first voiced a public protest on 16 April when he warned against sectarianism in the party:

Our homeland's enemies, the enemies of the working class movement all over the world are trying to penetrate into the PDPA leadership and above all woo the working class party leader but the people of Afghanistan and the PDPA both take great pride in the fact that the PDPA leader and its General-Secretary enjoys a great personality and a strong character, far reaching fame and popularity which render him impossible to woo . . .[37]

A week later, after Taraki had presented party membership cards to the Politburo members, Amin, replying to Taraki's address, again called for party unity and issued a direct warning to Taraki: 'The role of leader is never in accord with a personality cult . . . The prestige and popularity of leaders among the people has no common aspect with a personality cult.'[38]

It seems Amin was not alone in his concern at the recent trend of events. In an article entitled 'Taraki's Theory of Popular Revolution' Zeary emphasised the importance of choosing from a 'class viewpoint the party leadership from among genuine, brave and pious people with good social standing so that the masses would trust them . . .', as well as the need to 'ensure in this leadership the unity of ideology and action and *act collectively* so that party members may be able to continue their struggle with certainty . . .'[39]

Taraki chose to disregard these warnings. Denying that he was in any way the object of a personality cult he later told a group of foreign journalists that the people were so grateful to him that they put his picture everywhere. As for Amin's suggestion that 'some people are making efforts to influence you', he denied that Amin had ever said it.[40]

Although his position in the government was seriously weakened from the end of March, Amin emerged from Taraki's assault on him with his power base in the party intact. But it was some months before he managed to reassert himself, and then only after the revolution had been seriously damaged. Taraki soon showed himself incapable of exercising the power he had accumulated and Watanjar and the other young turks he had gathered around him were unable to cope with the mounting threat from counter-revolutionary forces which developed through the summer months.

Notes

1. *Kabul Times* (*KT*), 27 Dec. 1978, emphasis added.

2. *KT*, 3 Jan. 1979, emphasis added. Amin also chose his platform well: he was speaking at a function celebrating the fourteenth anniversary of the founding congress of the PDPA.

3. *KT*, 3 Feb. 1979.

4. *KT*, 22 Feb. 1979. Saur was the month in the Afghan calendar when the Revolution took place.

5. See for example Fred Halliday, 'War and Revolution in Afghanistan', *New Left Review*, no. 119, Jan-Feb. 1980, p. 32. Although Halliday correctly interprets Amin's argument as defending the PDPA's right not to surrender any political power to other groups, he misrepresents Amin's position on the role of the peasantry who Halliday claims are 'demonstratively excluded from a leading place in the revolution'. There was no independent progressive peasant organisation outside the PDPA and, to the extent that the peasantry had been radicalised (which was much greater than Halliday acknowledges) it had been a result of the efforts of the cadres trained by Amin in the 1950s and 1960s and sent out into the rural areas. Amin repeatedly stressed the importance the PDPA placed on the organisation of the peasants, not only in co-operatives but in the Committees for Defence of the Revolution established from the end of 1978 in an effort to

nobilise the support of the Afghan masses, in particular the peasants: see, for example, his press conference, *KT*, 24 May 1979.

6. That a disagreement on this issue existed is revealed in an article published in the Soviet monthly *International Affairs*, which appears to be a direct reply to Amin: 'The national-democratic revolution was successfully carried through on April 27, 1978, as a result of revolutionary action by the Afghan army supported by the broad masses. It was headed by the People's Democratic Party of Afghanistan (PDPA) which is, as its documents record, "a party of the working class".' L. Mironov and G. Polyakov, 'Afghanistan: The Beginning of a New Life', *International Affairs* (Moscow), no. 3, 1979, pp. 46-7.) In specifically characterising the Afghan revolution as 'national democratic' and denying the PDPA's claims to be the 'vanguard' of the working class, describing it merely as 'a party of the working class', the Soviet analysts were openly repudiating Amin's thesis.

7. *KT*, 7 April 1979.

8. *KT*, 27 March 1979.

9. *Der Spiegel*, 19 March 1979. It is perhaps worth noting that the *Kabul Times* report (10 March 1979) makes no mention of Amin's complaint.

10. *Jasarat*, 23 February 1979 in *Urdu Press Summary* (*UPS*), Australian Embassy, Islamabad; *Financial Times* (London), 22 February 1979.

11. *KT*, 11 March 1979.

12. Information obtained in Kabul, March 1979.

13. UN sources reported that, in contrast with previous years, there was no problem recruiting labour for UN projects in the spring of 1979 (conversation with the author, Kabul, March 1979).

14. Hafizullah Amin, press conference, *KT*, 3 March 1979.

15. *KT*, 17 March 1979.

16. *New York Times*, 23 March 1979, p. 12.

17. *Hindustan Times*, 12 March 1979 and *Times of India*, 12 March 1979, Institute for Defence Studies and Analysis, *News Review on South Asia and Indian Ocean* (Delhi) March 1979, p. 995; *The Statesman*, 23 March 1979, *News Review*, April 1979, pp. 84-5.

18. *Morning News* (Karachi), 18 March 1979, quoting a BBC report, and *The Statesman*, 23 March 1979, *News Review*, March 1979, p. 85.

19. *KT*, 19 March 1979.

20. Interview, Kabul, March 1979.

21. One of the fascinating aspects of life in Kabul in the second half of March 1979 was attempting to keep track of and trace to their source the rumours abounding relating to events in Herat. There was an atmosphere of near panic among the European expatriate community engendered by the stories spread by the American embassy which many people accepted without question.

22. Hafizullah Amin, *KT*, 4 April 1979.

23. Senior UN sources, Kabul, March 1979.

24. The Governor and Provincial Party Secretary for Herat, Nazifullah Nahzat was transferred to Ghazni, another important post, which suggests that he was not held responsible for the situation that arose in Herat. He was replaced, early in April, by Eng. Abdul Hai Yatim, who also held the positions of Provincial Party Secretary and Military Commander.

25. *KT*, 18 March 1979.

26. Mazdooryar was 33, Watanjar was 32 and Gulabzoi was only 28.

27. Nicknamed 'the Czar' by members of the government and the diplomatic corps alike, Pusanov's activities at the end of March are perhaps significant: on 28 March he called on Mazdooryar and Zeary (*KT*, 29 March 1979), and on 29 March he called on Watanjar, at that stage still CGS (*KT*, 31 March 1979). He did not, however, bother to call on the newly appointed Prime Minister.

28. Observers in Kabul noted however that during this period Amin was showing physical signs of being under considerable strain.

29. *KT*, 28 March 1979.

30. For text of the amended law, see *KT*, 31 March 1979.

31. According to one report it was Assadullah Sarwari who first drew a gun on Amin on 14 September (*Der Spiegel*, 7 January 1980) although this may have been another of 'King Kong's' idle boasts. Nevertheless Sarwari did acquire a reputation for brutality and seems to have been responsible for many of the excesses which so damaged the government's reputation. For a firsthand account of some of his exploits, see Louis Dupree, *Red Flag Over the Hindu Kush, Part V: Repressions, or Security Through Terror. Purges I-IV* (American Universities Field Staff Reports, Asia Series, 1980, No.28) and *Red Flag Over the Hindu Kush, Part VI: Repressions, or Security Through Terror. Purges IV-VI* (American Universities Field Staff Reports Service, Asia Series, 1980, No.29).

32. *KT*, 7 April 1979.

33. Richard Burt, 'Heavy Russian Toll in Afghanistan Seen', *New York Times*, 13 April 1979, p. 4.

34. *KT*, 7 July 1979.

35. Amin had only one meeting with Yepishev, and it was clearly no more than a courtesy call. For the rest he appears to have avoided the social functions associated with the visiting Soviet delegation.

36. *KT*, 8 April 1979.

37. *KT*, 19 April 1979.

38. *KT*, 23 April 1979.

39. *KT*, 22 April 1979, emphasis added.

40. *KT*, 3 May 1979. If Halliday is correct in stating that towards the end of the summer, the President 'was kept increasingly out of contact with visiting journalists' ('War and Revolution', p. 30) the sheer inanity of Taraki's 3 May press conference would appear to provide ample justification.

THE SUMMER OF DISCONTENT

The new factionalism afflicting the PDPA left it ill prepared to face the intensified counter-revolutionary campaign which began in mid-March and grew more serious as the summer progressed. The government's military response was slow and disorganised. The Homeland Higher Defence Council, established to co-ordinate defence strategy, does not appear to have been effective and the Politburo decision to set up a national defence organisation was not implemented. Eventually it became clear that so long as the counter-revolution received outside support a military solution was impossible, but there was no agreement on the diplomatic strategy to be pursued. These problems were worsened by Taraki's increasing physical incapacity and the renewed attempts by the USSR to foist its own strategy on the Kabul government.

The principal areas of counter-revolutionary activity were the border provinces of Paktya, Nangarhar, Kunar and Badakhshan, combined with an attempt to subvert the predominantly Shi'i Hazara population. Sporadic terrorist attacks were mounted in other provinces as well, a particular problem area being the Panjsher valley north of Kabul. The counter-revolutionary campaign was not co-ordinated and different organisation were active in different areas. Throughout they had the moral, material and financial assistance of Pakistan, the conservative Arab Gulf states, Iran, China and the United States, as well as the Western media as a whole.

The campaign of terror and intimidation was mostly the work of two groups, the Jamaat-i-Islami led by Burhanuddin Rabbani, a graduate of the Faculty of Theology of Kabul University, and the Hizb-i-Islami led by Gulbuddin Hekmatyar, a former student of engineering, also from Kabul University. The Hizb-i-Islami had been organising resistance to Daoud for several years with the connivance of the Pakistan government and had not only the best terrorist network inside Afghanistan, but mounted the most elaborate public relations operation outside: the most extravagant rebel claims reported were usually based on Hizb-i-Islami press statements. Rabbani too had an extensive terrorist network inside Afghanistan, where he had gone underground in opposition to Daoud after the 1973 coup. Prepared to co-operate with other groups as Hekmatyar was not, Rabbani left for Peshawar to found a counter-revolutionary coalition calling itself the National Liberation Front in

171

June 1978. Rabbani later withdrew the Jamaat-i-Islami from the Front when leadership of the coalition was taken over in October by Sigbhatullah Mujaddidi.[1]

Mujaddidi was also a theologian who had opposed Daoud. After 1973 he taught in Saudi Arabia and then became director of the Islamic Centre in Copenhagen. He was a close relative of Mohammad Ibrahim Mujaddidi, the Hazrat of Shor Bazaar and Afghanistan's most influential religious figure, eventually arrested by the Afghan government in January 1979. The Mujaddidi family derived their religious authority from their claim to descent from the prophet Mohammad. They had consistently placed this authority at the disposal of the most reactionary groups in Afghan society and been rewarded with lands and honours. In 1978 they were among the wealthiest landowners in Afghanistan. The National Liberation Front had no organisation inside Afghanistan and its activities were confined to international political posturing.

One ally of Mujaddidi did have a small regional following in Afghanistan: Mohammad Ghulam Nabi, another mullah, and leader of the Harakat-i-Inqilab-i-Islami, boasted that his group had begun its antigovernment activity within fifteen days of the April 1978 revolution, though it had in fact been active in the Panjsher valley long before. Apart from the Panjsher valley which gave the rebels important access to Badakhshan through the Anjuman pass, there were three other areas traditionally hostile to the central government where the rebels achieved some success. These were Nuristan, in the north of the Kunar valley; the three provinces of the Hazarajat: Ghor, Uruzgan and Bamyan; and the Khost area of Paktya.

Of these three the rebel campaign in Paktya was potentially the most dangerous. It was led by Syed Ahmed Gailani's National Islamic and Revolutionary Council established some six months after the revolution. The Gailani family, comparatively recent settlers in Afghanistan claimed religious authority on the basis of their alleged descent from a highly revered Arab saint. Like the Mujaddidis they had placed this authority at the disposal of the former royal family and been richly rewarded. Their regional power base was in the area of Nangarhar and Paktya south of Jalalabad, and it was in this region that Gailani attempted to carve out a base of operations for himself.

Although Gailani also had Saudi contacts his most important foreign association was with the United States. The US already perceived the Afghan revolution in cold war terms as a victory for the USSR, but the fall of the Shah of Iran in February 1979 deprived it of its greatest regional ally and was therefore an intolerable blow. While some in

Washington like the Secretary of State Cyrus Vance urged caution, others including the President's National Security Adviser Zbigniew Brzezinski wanted to 'sow shit' in Russia's backyard.[2] Consequently when Syed Ahmed Gailani's representative Zia Nassry, an Afghan-born US citizen, arrived in Washington early in March 1979 he was received warmly if discreetly, returning jubilant to Peshawar with guarantees that the Afghan rebels would 'soon be receiving a lot of help from America'.[3]

Part of Gailani's strategy was to form an alliance with the Hazara tribes of the central uplands and through them the Hazara community in Kabul.[4] The Hazaras were easy game for opponents of the PDPA. Impoverished as a result of Abdur Rahman's policies of the 1890s they had suffered subsequently at the hands of successive Pashtun-dominated (and therefore Sunni Muslim) Kabul governments. They were reluctant to believe that the PDPA would be any different, and their anti-Kabul sentiments were easily manipulated both by the aggressive Shi'i religious oligarchy which came to power in Iran in February and by the counter-revolutionary parties in Peshawar. The Hazarajat itself, remote and isolated, was not especially important in strategic terms, but there was a large Hazara community in Kabul maintaining close links with fellow tribesmen in the highlands. Deprived of their lands and thereby their livelihood by Abdur Rahman, many Hazaras had drifted to the capital where they had gradually established a virtual monopoly over Kabul's bakeries and wood-fuel distribution. If the counter-revolution could form an effective alliance with the Hazaras, the one controlling important grain and wood producing areas in Nangarhar and Paktya and the other controlling bread and wood supplies in Kabul the headquarters of the revolution could be slowly strangled.

None of this — neither Gailani's ambitious plan, nor the insurgency that developed in the Kunar valley and parts of the Kabul valley in Nangahar — would have been possible without the active assistance of the martial law regime in Pakistan. Pakistan officially denied that it did more than offer 'humanitarian' assistance to the refugees who crossed the 'porous' border into Pakistan's tribal areas. The evidence suggests that Pakistan in fact did much more.

Its first important contribution was the provision of a platform from which the counter-revolution could mount its propaganda campaign, and a sanctuary from which it could organise its guerrilla activities. The Afghan politicians were able to issue press statements and hold press conferences not just in Peshawar but in Lahore and Islamabad as well. The Pakistani media, carefully controlled, gave publicity to the rebels' press statements. Given the martial law regime's ability to silence Pakistani politicians if and when it deemed this necessary, demonstrated by the periodic arrests of Bhutto supporters, it is clear that the propaganda campaign had Islamabad's blessing.

Pakistan claimed with some justification that it could not prevent refugees from entering Pakistan from Afghanistan across a mountainous, sometimes undemarcated border with dozens of uncharted passes. It also claimed (with less justification) that it was unable to control what went on in the tribal territories which, though an integral part of Pakistan, were formally administered by the local tribes according to tribal law, and where the Pakistani Political Agent was once described as 'half-ambassador and half-governor'.[5] If the tribes on the Pakistan side of the border wished to assist fellow tribesmen on the Afghan side in their jihad against the PDPA Pakistani officials claimed that there was nothing Islamabad could do to prevent them.[6] This overlooked the considerable power available to the government by virtue of its financial contribution to the tribes,[7] a power which it made no attempt to exercise in order to inhibit the attacks on Afghanistan by locally organised tribal *lashkars* (armies). Islamabad seemed rather to be encouraging them. The Pakistan government offered four rupees per day subsistence to the Afghan 'refugees' as 'humanitarian aid'. Although the sum being paid amounting to about US $145 annually was roughly equivalent to Afghanistan's average per capita income (and was certainly more than the annual income of many of the rural population) Pakistan strenuously denied that it was encouraging the Afghan border tribes to join the rebels. Pakistan also claimed that in the first year after the revolution it spent approximately US $65 million maintaining the refugees. Even assuming that there had been 80,000 refugees for the whole year (which there were not) this means that an additional US $53.4 million was spent over and above the daily subsidy, a large sum especially when compared with Islamabad's expenditure of approximately US $24.0 million in the tribal areas as a whole in 1976-7.[8]

While some tribes resisted Islamabad's blandishments, others succumbed and allowed the rebels to establish guerrilla bases on their territory. The most important of these were at Miram Shah in the North Waziristan Agency and at Parachinar in the Kurram Agency. From these two it was possible to launch a pincer operation through the Khost area of Paktya directed towards the provincial capital of Gardez. Other important bases were located in the Mohmand Agency, bordering Nangarhar; the Bajaur Agency, bordering Kunar; and Chitral, bordering the Nuristan region of Kunar Province and Badakhshan. Pakistan denied the existence of guerrilla 'bases', but, however they were described, the fact emained that guerrilla operations against Afghanistan were carried out from these areas of Pakistan.

The evidence also suggests that Pakistan's road and rail system was used to transport arms to the rebels. The Afghan rebels denied that they received any outside aid at all, and maintained that the only weapons they had were World War I style British .303s and replicas of Chinese, Soviet and other weapons manufactured in the village gun factories in Pakistan's North-West Frontier Province, or Soviet weapons captured from Afghan forces. The village factories, while noted for their ingenuity and craftsmanship were not geared to mass production, they rarely employed more than a dozen men and it took a fortnight to complete one weapon. They could scarcely have supplied the tribal invasion force which attacked Afghanistan in the spring and summer of 1979. While the Afghan army no doubt lost some weapons through defeat or desertions, reports of its disintegration were exaggerated.[9] The scale of the fighting and the arms caches discovered by the Afghan government suggests that the weapons were supplied to a large extent from outside, from China and from Egypt which had a large stockpile of Soviet weaponry.[10]

It is difficult to trace the exact course of the fighting because of the element of fantasy surrounding reports from counter-revolutionary sources and the blanket of silence thrown over the entire situation by the Kabul government, but the claims made by the rebels, even if exaggerated, give some indication of the intensity and location of their activities, generally confirmed both by the government's statements relating to military action as well as the scope and direction of its efforts to counter rebel propaganda.

The Afghan government first protested to Pakistan on 9 April about an alleged attack two days before, and warned against further interference.[11] The newly formed Homeland Higher Defence Council, dominated by Taraki and Watanjar, met on 14 April but does not appear to have been particularly effective in producing a co-ordinated defence policy.[12] At the end of April Taraki appeared more preoccupied with celebrating the first anniversary of the Revolution than in confronting the threat to its survival. The rebels reported that they met little resistance in their initial drive into Paktya.[13]

Deprived of his major role in policy making, Hafizullah Amin as Party Secretary in charge of the PDPA's central organisation turned his attention to building up the party machine and strengthening its mass base. Formal party membership was established only in April with the distribution of membership cards first to the Politburo and then to the Central Committee. This was followed by distribution of party cards to the Kabul City Committee (of which Amin's son-in-law Assadullah was First Deputy Secretary) and so on down the line. Emphasis on the development of primary party organisations signalled a rapid expansion of membership, estimated by Amin to be 'more than 100,000' at the end of August.[14] Steps were also taken to establish 'advisory groups' or party cells within the various ministries, as they had earlier been set up in the armed forces. The Party Secretariat itself, which had grown in an *ad hoc* fashion in response to the demands placed upon it, was reorganised and expanded.

During this period Amin joined Taraki in a belated effort to regain the propaganda initiative through an intensive campaign of meetings with tribal elders, beginning at the end of April and continuing for the next three months, gradually tapering off at the end of July. Although they met groups from most provinces, some names recurred suggesting that these were the more troublesome areas: the Jaji, Tira and Mangal Afridi of Paktya,[15] the Shinwari, Mohmand and Bajaur elders of Nangarhar and Kunar; the Waziri, including the Shi'i Turi Khel Waziri from North Waziristan and the Masoods from South Waziristan. It is no coincidence that these were the areas where the counter-revolutionary offensive was concentrated, or that these tribal groups had members either living on the Pakistan side of the Durand line, or moving back and forth across it.

The government declared an amnesty on 6 May for those tribesmen who had been 'misled' by counter-revolutionary propaganda, urging them to return to their homes. The amnesty was renewed on 21 May and again on 10 June. The government claimed that it received a favourable response, but according to BBC reports, this was disputed by the rebels who described it as 'a mischievous trick to confuse and divide' the Afghan refugees in Pakistan and Iran.[16] Senior party leaders travelled to the provinces to carry the government message personally: Jauzjani to Balkh, Hashemi to Badakhshan and Faqir to Khost in Paktya. Mohammad Zarif, Governor of Kandahar and a reliable Amin supporter was transferred to the Governorship of Nangarhar on 24 July.

The broad thrust of Taraki's and Amin's speeches during this period was similar, although there were important differences of emphasis. They stressed the benefits to the rural population of the PDPA reforms, reminding them that the Khalq had delivered when others had only made promises, but refrained from introducing greater ideological content into their speeches.

Instead of merely asserting that they respected Islam they now declared the government's measures to be fully in accordance with the requirements of Islamic law and challenged the counter-revolutionary leaders to cease spreading malicious rumours about the persecution of believers and the desecration of mosques and to point out, if they could, where any of the government's reforms was contrary to the teaching of the Shariat.

While both Taraki and Amin made a point of offering prayers on important religious occasions, Amin also made at least one explicit attempt to identify himself as a Muslim by recalling an incident which took place when he was a member of parliament:

> ... one of the Maulawis who is now absconding, stood up in front of all the deputies and while mentioning me said that I was not abiding by the sacred religion of Islam. I went to him and told him 'esteemed Maulawi Sahib, I am abiding by the lofty values of Islam every day, why do you level such accusations against me?' Maulawi Sahib while staring at me said, 'I did not know that you were Hafizullah Amin.'[17]

They also made efforts to refute the accusations of several leading Iranian Ayatollahs that Afghan Shi'is were being persecuted by emphasising that for the first time in Afghanistan Shi'is had real freedom of worship, since the domination of the Sunni religious establishment had been broken. Related to this was the issue of nationalities and Taraki and Amin drew attention to their commitment to the promotion of minority languages and culture in contrast to the treatment of their minorities by the governments in Tehran and Islamabad.[18]

The Afghan leaders also showed restraint in accusing foreign governments of supporting the counter-revolution, preferring instead to describe the support as coming from 'reactionary circles' in Pakistan and 'religious fanatics' in Iran, thereby leaving the way open for a hoped-for change in the policy of the regimes in Islamabad and Tehran.

From early June they began to claim that the Afghan revolution had the support of 'Muslim toilers' not only among national groups within Afghanistan, but also of Sind, Punjab, Azerbaijan, Kurdistan and Khuzistan as well. There was some substance in this claim. The leaders of the Afghan counter-revolution were not universally welcomed in Pakistan. They received important support from Mufti Mahmood, leader of the Pakistan National Alliance, the loose coalition of political parties which had united to bring down the Pakistan People's Party government of Zulfiqar Ali Bhutto, and which now supported the martial law administration of General Zia ul-Haq. Zia himself was also personally sympathetic to the Afghan politicians who gathered in Peshawar, although he was astute enough to realise that he could not give them open support not only for fear of a confrontation with the USSR[19] but also because of the considerable sympathy for the Afghan revolution within Pakistan, especially in the still formidable PPP. Opposition to Zia's *de facto* support of the counter-revolution from Pakistani political groups became more outspoken as the violence mounted and the dangerous implications for Pakistan became clearer.[20]

In Iran too there was a hint that Tehran and Qum did not altogether agree on Afghanistan. On 17 July the Iranian Foreign Minister, Dr Ebrahim Yazdi told a press conference that there was no connection between the Iranian government and the Afghan counter-revolution, but he did confirm 'the possibility of the existence of a link between Iran's revolutionary organisation and the [counter-revolutionary] movement in Afghanistan'.[21]

While both Taraki and Amin were reluctant to name the foreign powers supporting the counter-revolution, Amin showed greater caution in this respect. Taraki eventually openly criticised Pakistan and also, obliquely in references to 'left extremism' and the activities of American imperialism in Vietnam, China and the United States.[22] Amin instead focused his attacks on British imperialism and the BBC, a shrewd move since it allowed him to play down American and Chinese involvement, and to appeal to a tribal audience for whom Britain was the traditional enemy of Afghan independence. In making the BBC his main target Amin was neither paranoid nor dishonest for in its foreign language broadcasts to Afghanistan and Pakistan, the BBC's reporting of events in Afghanistan since the 1978 revolution had been at best irresponsible, and was often mischievous.[23] Although Amin later also listed Radio Peking and the Voice of America along with the Pakistani, Iranian and West German radios as sources of hostile propaganda, and identified rials, rupees, American dollars and pounds sterling as the currencies in which the rebels were paid, he never openly accused the governments involved, and in particular bent over backwards to avoid making hostile references to China and the United States.

The Afghan leaders' caution contrasted markedly with the public position taken by the USSR, which openly accused Pakistan along with China, the US and Egypt of aiding the rebels.[24] While an accurate enough representation of the situation, the strident tone adopted by the Soviet media suggested that the USSR was pushing Afghanistan towards an open confrontation with the governments of Pakistan, China and the United States that the Afghan leadership, and in particular Hafizullah Amin, wished at that stage to avoid.

Kabul's military response to the counter-revolutionary thrust was slow and only partially effective. On 10 May the government issued a statement accusing Pakistan of aggression and again on 5 June protested the incursion of 'armed militiamen' (as Kabul described the tribal *lashkars*) from Chitral, Mohmand and Waziristan. This protest was followed by reports of heavy fighting in these areas on 7 and 11 June. Pakistan merely rejected the protests and levelled counter-accusations that Afghanistan was violating Pakistan's airspace.

The same month counter-revolutionary agitation among the Shi'i population came to a head. At the end of May Amin met the leaders of the Shi'i community in Kabul in an attempt to reassure them and win their support.[25] A section of the Shi'i leadership was apparently unimpressed, and ready to respond to a call from one of Iran's prominent religious figures, Ayatollah Haj Sayeed Hasan Tabataba'i on 21 June, inciting his 'Afghan brethren' to 'continue their resistance'.[26] Two days later serious rioting broke out in the Shi'i Hazara quarter of Kabul city following a demonstration by about 200 people in the bazaar area and attempts by counter-revolutionary groups to seize police stations. It was the first major incident in the capital since the April 1978 revolution. Light tanks took up positions near public buildings and gunfire continued until 2 p.m. Police set up road blocks and carried out house to house searches, arresting several Shi'i leaders. Helicopters later dropped leaflets saying that the violence which was blamed on Iranian intervention had been suppressed, but calling on people to remain vigilant. Casualties do not appear to have been heavy: the BBC only reported eleven deaths including a Soviet officer while the highest unofficial estimate was 'over a hundred' dead.[27] The small size of the demonstration suggests that the dissident Shi'i leadership did not have wide popular support and the prompt and decisive action on the part of the government effectively nipped in the bud any counter-revolutionary attempt to use Kabul's Hazara community to undermine the government's position in the capital. Although the government had headed off a situation with potential for far greater bloodshed and violence than actually occurred its relations with the Shi'i community suffered as a result and the Hazarajat remained in sullen revolt.

The results of its military action in the eastern provinces were equally ambivalent. The counter-revolutionary thrust to capture Gardez and with it control of Paktya Province had been defeated as had attempts to seize the provincial capital of Kunar, Assadabad. But it was clear that so long as the rebels enjoyed sanctuary and support outside Afghanistan the government would not be able to secure the border areas against persistent guerrilla raids.

One consequence of the counter-revolutionary offensive was the increase in the Soviet military presence in Afghanistan although considering its outspoken public posture Soviet military aid was less than generous. From April some additional military equipment was supplied but for the military campaign against the rebels the only important Soviet contribution was the delivery of a few recently developed Mi-24 helicopter gunships. With the equipment came more Soviet military personnel. American sources estimated that by June 1979 the number of Soviet advisers had risen from 1,000 to between 1,500 and 2,000 and that by the beginning of August there were altogether 3,000 Soviet military advisers in Afghanistan. In addition the US claimed that early in July a Soviet airborne battalion of 400 men was stationed at Bagram airport north of Kabul, the first Soviet combat troops to be deployed in the country. US intelligence sources also asserted that Soviet advisers were attached as far down the command structure as company level, possibly even platoon level.[28] Even if American estimates of the number of Soviet military personnel in Afghanistan were not exaggerated (and official Afghan sources insisted that they were) this did not amount to an inordinately large Soviet presence.[29] It did, however, signify an important increase in that presence, which together with Soviet efforts to penetrate the command structure of the Afghan armed forces, carried serious implications for the independence of the Afghan reovlution, making it increasingly difficult to retain control of important levers of power in Afghan hands and to counter rebel propaganda that the government in Kabul was the creature of the Soviet Union.

By midsummer other problems were becoming acute. Taraki, though only sixty-two, had the appearance and demeanour of a much older man. His had not been an easy life and he did not enjoy good health. In addition, before the revolution both he and Amin had been known as heavy drinkers. Amin, with characteristic self-discipline became more abstemious after the PDPA came to power but Taraki continued to drink heavily as the pressures mounted. His physical capacity to cope with the responsibilities of his office was increasingly open to question.[30]

The personality cult was no solution. The display of huge photographs of Taraki on public buildings, in processions and in the press where they were also distorted, and the extravagant but somehow pathetic birthday celebrations held for the 'Great Leader' on 14 July were no substitute for effective leadership. Having made his disapproval of the situation clear in April, Amin gradually disassociated himself from Taraki. On 4 May, in what was ostensibly an extravagant profession of loyalty Amin made it clear that it was Taraki who took all the policy decisions and therefore by implication bore all the responsibility for the deteriorating situation.[31] Thereafter Amin's speeches contained only the most perfunctory references to Taraki and sometimes none at all.

Amin's disquiet was apparently shared by other PDPA leaders and matters came to a head at the Politburo meeting of 28 July when the whole question of leadership was aired. The *Kabul Times* report noted:

> ... discussions took place on [the] realisation [of] collective leadership in the party organisations as soon as possible and on realisation of the principle of criticism and self-criticism and complete and democratic discussion in the party meetings and a resolution was passed unanimously in this connection by the Politburo.[32]

Following the row in the Politburo Taraki agreed to changes in the cabinet. Amin regained his former position as Minister of Defence 'assisting' Taraki, relegating Watanjar to his former job as Minister of Interior. Mazdooryar became Minister of Frontier Affairs; but Saheb Jan Sahrayi was retained as minister without portfolio. Amin relinquished the Foreign Ministry to Shah Wali who was also appointed Deputy Prime Minister; Zeary took over Public Health and Jalili assumed responsibility for Agriculture and Land Reforms. Mohammad Salem Masudi, then serving as Ambassador to Bulgaria, was brought into the cabinet as Minister for Education.

It was the first defeat for the pro-Soviet Watanjar clique, but it was by no means decisive. Watanjar and Mazdooryar still held important positions, as did Gulabzoi and Sarwari. In forcing the issue in the Politburo on 28 July Amin regained some of his former power and demonstrated the strength of his support in the Party's top policy-making body, but his position was far from secure. The mutiny in the garrison at Bala Hissar on 5 August, though quickly suppressed, was an indication that his return to power would not go unchallenged.

Amin's re-emergence brought greater coherence and direction to the government's policy making. One of the first and most important steps was the convening of a jirga of the Jamiatul Ulama, a meeting of senior religious leaders loyal to the government, who issued a *fatwa* or directive to the effect that the PDPA was governing in accordance with Islam and obedience to the government was therefore a religious obligation for all Muslims.[33] A few days later the Jamiatul Ulama issued another fatwa declaring the Ikhwan-ul-Muslimin (i.e., the religious parties in Peshawar opposing the government) to be anti-Islamic and the killing of Ikhwan thereby an obligation under Islam.[34] This was the most vigorous action so far undertaken to mobilise Islam in support of the government, and turn the religious weapon back on the counter-revolutionaries. In another move designed to control the terrorist activities of the Peshawar-based parties, Amin appointed his brother Abdullah, Security Chief for the four northern provinces of Samangan, Balkh, Takhar and Kunduz.[35]

Another long overdue measure was the approval on 26 August of provisions for the establishment of special revolutionary courts to try those accused of treason against the revolution. This had been a long-standing issue between Amin and Taraki and Taraki's disregard of the principles and requirements of justice was one of Amin's main criticisms of his predecessor when he eventually assumed the Presidency the following month.[36]

The most serious problem confronting Amin during this period, including the counter-revolutionary insurgency, was Afghanistan's relationship with the Soviet Union which as it had developed by August 1979 carried dangers for the Afghan revolution. For Moscow too there were problems and risks inherent in support of the PDPA regime. Although the PDPA had come to power independently of the USSR, this was not universally accepted, especially in the regions. Moreover the policies undertaken by the new government were bound to provoke violent counter-revolutionary opposition as soon as it was realised that, unlike previous Afghan governments, the Khalq kept its promises to the people. An unwilling supporter of a government over which it had so far failed to establish control, the USSR was portrayed as the instigator of regional instability. With the Strategic Arms Limitation Treaty, regarded as especially important in Moscow, at a crucial stage of negotiation, this was not the image that the USSR would have chosen to present.[37] It was therefore as important for Moscow as for the PDPA to bring the rebellion to an end as quickly as possible. A military solution alone was clearly out of the question but the USSR, still committed to the concept of the national front as envisaged by the Parchamites, was not prepared to endorse Amin's strategy which combined a hard-hitting military campaign against the rebels with a diplomatic effort to persuade Pakistan, China and the US to withdraw support from them.

In July and August 1979 this last appeared a hopeless task. The US Congress had just suspended all aid to Afghanistan on the pretext of the Afghan government's failure to apologise for the assassination of Ambassador Dubs. The Afghans responded by requesting the US to reduce its embassy staff in Kabul to a level more in keeping with the minimal functions they were now called on to perform. The US com-lied, but announced that the embassy staff was being reduced because f the deteriorating security situation in Afghanistan. Despite these rovocations, Amin merely expressed regret at the 'destructive nature' f the American announcement.[38]

Afghanistan encountered similar problems with China which also cut ts already small aid programme and with customary cynicism seized he opportunity to embarrass the USSR by echoing the counter-revolu- ionary propaganda that the April Revolution was a Soviet plot to urther Russia's expansionist ambitions.[39] In the slanging match that eveloped between Moscow and Peking the Afghan Revolution seemed o be no more than a bone over which two querulous dogs wrangled. In n official statement issued on 27 June, the Afghan government took eking to task on this issue, but made no reference to the more serious ccusations levelled at China by the USSR.[40] At the end of July the hinese were also requested, though with less publicity, to reduce the ize of their mission in Kabul. Even so, Amin continued to resist the fforts of foreign journalists to provoke him into openly accusing China nd the United States of aiding the rebels.[41] Instead, in an address to Vorld Peace Congress delegates meeting in Kabul at the end of August, Amin made a clear and unequivocal appeal for Chinese friendship.[42]

Such manoeuvres would scarcely have been welcomed in Moscow. Amin's uncompromising commitment to Afghanistan's independence nd his consistent determination to back his own judgement had already narked him out as a difficult personality from the Russians' point of iew. His re-emergence at the end of July at the expense of the pro- Soviet faction of Aslam Watanjar, and after he appeared to have been lefeated a few months earlier, must have been an unpleasant surprise or Moscow.

For Amin's part, he was clearly deeply concerned not merely at the ncreased Soviet presence in Afghanistan but more especially at the nanner in which the USSR sought to make use of that presence. On 7 July he warned: 'Those who boast of friendship with us, they can eally be our friend when they respect our independence, our soil and ur prideful traditions.'[43] At the same time he sought to reassure the JSSR that his commitment to a close relationship with the Soviet Union vas not in question:

Any person and any element who harms the friendship between Afghanistan and the Soviet Union will be considered the enemy of the country, enemy of our people and enemy of our revolution. We will not allow anybody in Afghanistan to act against the friendship of Afghanistan and the Soviet Union.[44]

Amin was too much of a realist to imagine that the PDPA coul
survive without Soviet assistance, and in any case too good a socialis
to wish to see relations with the USSR deteriorate further. His reserva
tions related to the form of that assistance and the extent of Afgha
control. Subsequent claims that Amin asked for military aid on severa
occasions and was refused by Moscow, before his alleged request i
December 1979, are consistent with the interpretation of Amin's pos
tion which sees him as seeking Soviet military aid, but not necessaril
prepared to accept it on the terms offered by Moscow. He was in effec
pleading with the USSR to understand the situation in Afghanistan, an
to let the Afghan government work out its own solution. It was on th
question of the appropriate solution that Amin and the Russians differe
as they had done all along.

In mid-August the USSR sent General Pavlovsky, the Commander
the Soviet Ground Forces, to investigate the situation in Afghanistar
Unlike that of General Yepishev, Pavlovsky's visit was given no publicity
and it is not clear on whose initiative he came or if in fact he was a
uninvited guest. A few days after Pavlovsky's arrival and in the sam
speech in which he expressed a desire for friendship with China, Ami
again hinted at his reservations about the Soviet role in Afghanistan b
likening it to the assistance promised the short-lived Hungarian sociali
republic by Lenin in 1919.[45]

It is not clear when the USSR decided that Amin had to go, but
was probably some time in August 1979. Moscow was anxious as befor
to ease Babrak Karmal back into power in Kabul, and given the hostilit
between Karmal and Amin, it was clear that Amin would first have
be removed. The increasing tension towards the end of August probabl
suggested to Moscow that the time was ripe.

The opportunity presented itself when Taraki stopped in Moscow c
9 September on his way home from the Non-aligned Summit in Havan
He met the Soviet Foreign Minister Andrei Gromyko and also, r
portedly, Babrak Karmal. The fact that Shah Wali, the Foreign Minist
but also a loyal supporter of Amin, was excluded from the discussio
suggested that some plot against Amin was in preparation, and certain
served as a warning.

Taraki however planned to give Amin little time to react. Within
hour of his return to Kabul on 11 September he called a meeting of t
Council of Ministers, ostensibly to report on the Havana Summit. It
likely that instead he put before the ministers the plan worked out

Moscow, and attempted to dismiss Amin. It was a miscalculation on Taraki's part. Amin had already shown that he had the support of the Politburo at the end of July; he now demonstrated that he had the support of the Council of Ministers as well. Whatever reservations they may have had about him and his style of leadership, they were clearly not prepared to accept Babrak Karmal with all the implications of Soviet dominance that such acceptance would have entailed. The only ones who supported Taraki were Watanjar, Mazdooryar and Gulabzoi, together with the AGSA chief, Sarwari.

The crisis came to a head on Friday 14 September, although the actual details are obscure.[46] It appears that Amin, as Prime Minister, tried to sack the three ministers who had supported Taraki in trying to oust him and that Taraki as President withheld his approval. One version of events has a quarrel developing from this confrontation, which took place in the presence of the Soviet Ambassador, and which led to an exchange of gunfire in which Taraki's aide-de-camp, Sayed Daoud Taroon died protecting Amin and in which Taraki was fatally wounded. Another version, later leaked by Amin himself, claims that Taraki summoned him to a meeting of the Revolutionary Council, and that, suspecting a trap, he demurred, only agreeing to obey the summons after receiving a phone call from the Soviet Ambassador guaranteeing him safe conduct. Still suspicious Amin went to the Presidential Palace but with a heavily armed bodyguard. When he entered the room, Taraki's supporters opened fire, in the presence of the Soviet Ambassador, killing Taroon who threw himself in front of Amin. Taraki was fatally wounded and died three weeks later.[47] The common elements in each version are Taraki's plot to get rid of Amin, the involvement of Ambassador Pusanov, and Taroon's action which saved Amin's life. Watanjar, Mazdooryar, Gulabzoi and Sarwari — the 'Gang of Four' — disappeared, apparently under the protection of the Soviet Embassy.

On 16 September Amin formally took over as Secretary-General of the PDPA, and President of the Revolutionary Council. The fact that, apart from replacing the three Ministers and the AGSA chief who defected, he made no changes in the Council of Ministers is a clear indication that he had their support,[48] but the circumstances under which he assumed the Presidency could have left him in no doubt as to the extent of Soviet hostility towards him.

Notes

1. Most of the information on the Afghan counter-revolutionary groups was collected during field trips to Pakistan in 1979 and 1980-1. See Beverley M. Male, 'Afghanistan: Rebels Without Policies', *The Bulletin* (Sydney), 27 Feb. 1981 and 'Afghanistan' in Mohammad Ayoob (ed.), *The Politics of Islamic Reassertion* (Croom Helm, London, 1981); Azmat Hayat Khan, 'Afghan Groups Based in Peshawar', *Central Asia* (Peshawar University), Summer 1980; and Andreas Kohlschuetter, 'The Day of the Kabul Rising (& after)', *Encounter*, Aug-Sept. 1980.

2. Kuldip Nayar, *Report on Afghanistan* (Allied Publishers, New Delhi, 1981), p. 32.

3. Conversation with the author, April 1979. Among the people Nassry saw in Washington were Senators Church and Javits of the powerful Senate Foreign Relations Committee and Ron Lorton, then desk officer in charge of Afghanistan in the State Department, now in the US Embassy in Islamabad. *New York Post*, 5 March 1979; Iona Andronov, *Literaturnaya Gazeta*, 14 March 1979, in *Current Digest of the Soviet Press*, vol. XXXI, no. 11, 11 April 1979.

4. At the end of May the rebels claimed control of Ghor, Bamyan and Uruzgan (BBC, reported in *Nawa-i-Waqt*, 28 May 1979, in *Urdu Press Summary* (*UPS*) Australian Embassy, Islamabad) and in the first week of June, Gailani's followers claimed to have full control of communications routes between Uruzgan and Ghazni (*Nawa-i-Waqt*, 6 June 1979, *UPS*). Although the rebels never gained control of the provincial capitals, they were able to create enough of a security problem to make it impossible for the government to carry out a UN sponsored demographic survey of the Hazarajat planned for the summer of 1979.

5. J. Spain, *The Way of the Pathans* (Oxford University Press, Karachi, 1972 cited in Akbar S. Ahmed, *Social and Economic Change in the Tribal Areas* (Oxfo University Press, Karachi, 1977), p. 43.

6. Conversations with the author, 1980-1.

7. A substantial proportion of this contribution was paid direct to tribal chiefs, see Ahmed, *Social and Economic Change*, p. 48.

8. Information obtained from various sources in Pakistan in 1980-1. See also Ahmed, *Social and Economic Change*, p. 61. I have assumed an approximate conversion rate of 10 Pakistani rupees to the US dollar.

9. The Western media portrait of the Afghan tribesman under arms is a fascinating one. If he is fighting with the rebels he is a highly skilled and courageous guerrilla soldier, trained to arms and warfare from childhood. But once he puts on an Afghan army uniform he becomes a cowardly bumbling incompetent. It is also remarkable that the 80,000 strong Afghan army (International Institute of Strategic Studies, *Military Balance 1979-80*, September 1979) melted away to 50,000 (*New York Times*, 23 Dec. 1979, p. 10) just before the Soviet invasion only to have miraculously reconstituted itself to 80,000 in the wake of the Soviet attack according to 'diplomatic sources' in New Delhi (Michael Richardson, *Sydney Morning Herald*, 3 Jan. 1980) so that it could again 'melt away' to between 30,000 and 40,000 (*Military Balance, 1980-1*) by the late summer of 1980. Intelligence sources admit that they have no way of knowing the extent to which the Afghan armed forces are affected by defections.

10. Information relating to Pakistani involvement in support of the counter-revolution was obtained in conversations with a wide variety of individuals in India, Pakistan and Afghanistan in 1979 and 1980-1. They have been supported, predictably, in some detail by the Afghan government, see DRA *Undeclared War Armed Intervention and Other Forms of Interference in the Internal Affairs of the Democratic Republic of Afghanistan* (Information Department, DRA Minist

of Foreign Affairs, Kabul, 1980). For a less partisan account see Hani Baloch, 'How Pakistan Destabilised Afghanistan', *Link*, 23 March 1980 and Robert Trumball, 'Command Chain of Afghan Revolt is a Network of Exiles in Pakistan', *New York Times*, 16 April 1979, pp. 1, 8.

11. *Kabul Times (KT)*, 9 April 1979. Pakistan responded with the counter-accusation that Afghan aircraft had strafed a house in Chitral on 10 April (*Jang*, 11 April 1979, *UPS*).

12. The HHDC met only seven times after its establishment on 4 April, at irregular and increasingly long intervals. In June and July, with counter-revolutionary violence at its height, it met only twice, on 5 June and 3 July. After Amin resumed responsibility for Defence, it met on 4 and 30 August. Once he became President, he abandoned it altogether.

13. *Jang*, 5 June 1979, *UPS*.

14. Interview 30 Aug. 1979, *KT*, 6 Sept. 1979. In his efforts to recruit new members Amin made use of the traditional basis of many Afghan political alliances – kinship and tribal ties – to strengthen the party. He was especially successful among the Shinwari and the Katawazi (a Ghilzai sub-tribe), most of whom became PDPA supporters loyal to Amin.

15. A British observer wrote in 1908

> The Afridi of today, though professedly a Muhammadan, has really no religion at all. He is, to a great extent, ignorant of the tenets and doctrines of the creed he professes, and even if he knew them, would in no way be restrained by them in pursuit of his purpose. (H.W. Bellew, *The Races of Afghanistan* (Calcutta, 1908, reprinted by Sheikh Mubarak Ali, Lahore, 1976), p. 82.)

Bellew also told of a mullah from Peshawar who settled among the Tira Afridi and felt it incumbent upon him to point out to them the merit to be derived from pilgrimages made to sacred shrines of saints and martyrs to the faith. The Tira Afridi were impressed, but were confronted with a problem for there were no saints' tombs in their territory. They solved the problem by killing the mullah and erecting a shrine over his grave (ibid., p. 83). Ahmed, (*Social and Economic Change*, p. 58) also testified to the problems encountered by the Pakistan government with the Tira Afridi, though he was optimistic that they would eventually accept the idea of a road. The problem confronting Taraki and Amin was therefore neither new nor unique.

16. *Nawa-i-Waqt*, 10 May 1979, *UPS*.

17. *KT*, 23 May 1979.

18. On 14 June Amin told a group of elders from Badakhshan that the oppression of Abdur Rahman (more than any other ruler responsible for the repression of non-Pashtun, non-Sunni minorities) was a thing of the past: 'No such tyranny can recur here.' *KT*, 7 June 1979.

19. *Nawa-i-Waqt*, 22 March 1979, *UPS*.

20. The first protest came from Begum Nasim Wali Khan, wife of Khan Abdul Wali Khan, and leader of the National Democratic Party, a powerful force on the Frontier (*Jang*, 30 Jan. 1979, *UPS*). She was supported by a group of twelve leading Pakistani socialists (*Musawat*, 2 Feb. 1979, *UPS*) and by spokesmen for the Pakistan People's Party, whose leader Zulfiqar Ali Bhutto was then under sentence of death after a blatantly political trial. Opposition gradually extended to the more conservative groups, including the Tehrik-i-Istiqlal, led by former air force chief Asghar Khan (*Nawa-i-Waqt*, 24 May 1979, *UPS*) and even to Abdul Quayum Khan, whose right wing Quaid-i-Azam Muslim League had in other respects been a loyal supporter of the PNA (*Nawa-i-Waqt*, 4 June 1979, *UPS*). On 5 June a

former PPP Governor of NWFP called on the Government to send the Afghan refugees back (*Tameer*, 5 June 1979, *UPS*) and was endorsed by both the PPP leader in NWFP, Aftab Sherpao (*Tameer*, 7 June 1979, *UPS*) and Benazir Bhutto (ibid., 26 June 1979).

21. Tehran home service, 17 July 1979, BBC *Summary of World Broadcasts* (*SWB*), ME/6171/A/9, 19 July 1979.

22. *KT*, 15 July, 19 July and 30 July 1979.

23. Because of the extent of its foreign language broadcasts, the size of its audience and its wide (though not necessarily deserved) reputation for veracity, the BBC was a powerful ally of the counter-revolution. Although the BBC is particularly sensitive to this kind of criticism, the author was told by officials of the foreign language broadcasting division of the BBC in May 1979 that specific complaints of misleading reporting would be investigated by the organisation itself, but that transcripts of foreign language broadcasts would under no circum stances be made available to the public. This would surely be a simple way of refuting such criticism if it were unjustified. Reports in the Pakistani press based on BBC broadcasts suggest that in many cases there was ample justification. Som examples include the report of the execution of 170 opponents of the regime including the Hazrat of Shor Bazaar (BBC, reported in *Nawa-i-Waqt*, 29 Jan. 197 *UPS*) which were later denied by a member of the Hazrat's own family (*Jang*, 6 Feb. 1979, *UPS*); BBC reports of rebel claims that the amnesty offer was a trick (*Jang*, 10 May 1979, *UPS*); BBC reports that as a result of fighting near Kabul Taraki and Amin had sent their families to Moscow (*Jang*, 5 June 1979, *UPS*), later found to be untrue but never acknowledged as such by the BBC (Mrs Tarak had visited Moscow for medical treatment); the BBC report that Muslim guerrilla were fast advancing towards Kabul and their occupation of Kabul airport was on a matter of time (*Jang*, 27 October, 1979, *UPS*), also untrue. The repercussions these reports when heard inside Afghanistan can easily be imagined. The BBC itself provides an excellent monitoring service of other country's broadcasts: perhaps somebody should monitor the BBC.

24. For example, I. Alexandrov, 'Reactionary Schemes Against Democratic Afghanistan', *Pravda*, 19 March 1979, extract, *Soviet News*, 27 March 1979; A. Petrov, 'A Rebuff to the Revolution's Enemies', *Pravda*, 10 April 1979, abstract in *Current Digest of the Soviet Press*, vol. XXXI, no. 5, 9 May 1979; Yu. Glukho 'Intrigues Against Afghanistan', *Pravda*, 23 May 1979, text in *CDSP*, vol. XXXI, no. 21, 20 June 1979.

25. See especially Part 2 of the text of his speech, *KT*, 3 June 1979.

26. Tehran home service, 21 June 1979, BBC, *SWB*, ME/6148/A/6, 22 June 1979. The Western media preferred to attribute the initiation of the violence to the arrest of intellectuals at Kabul University (BBC, quoted by *Nawa-i-Waqt*, 26 June 1979, *UPS* and *New York Times*, 28 June 1979, p. 3). The rector of Kabul University, Aziz Rahman Sayeedi later denied these reports stating that the two academics concerned, Ghalam Ghaus Shaurdari and Abdul Rahul Amin were stil teaching at the university. (Prague radio, 31 July 1979, BBC, *SWB*, ME/6184/A. 3 August 1979). The Western media did not bother to give coverage to Sayeedi' statement.

27. BBC, quoted by *Nawa-i-Waqt*, 26 June 1979, *UPS*, and *The Statesman* (India) 25 June 1979 in Institute for Defence Studies Analyses, *News Review on South Asia and Indian Ocean* (*News Review*), July 1979, pp. 349-50.

28. United States International Communication Agency, *The Global Signifi-cance of the Occupation of Afghanistan by the USSR*, 1980; Patrick J. Garrity, 'The Soviet Military Stake in Afghanistan: 1956-1979', *Royal United Services Institute Journal* (*RUSI*), September 1980.

29. At the time there were an estimated 30,000 Cubans in Angola and 30,00

dvisers, either Cuban or Warsaw pact, in Ethiopia. Michael T. Kaufman, 'Afghan Guerrillas Boast of Success in Struggle Against Soviet Backed Regime', *New York Times*, 14 Aug. 1979. It is perhaps also worth noting that 'By 1976 it was reckoned that the majority of the 24,000 Americans in Iran were defence and defence-elated. This number was expected to reach between 50,000 and 60,000 by 1980, largely as a result of purchases of arms from the US', Robert Graham, *Iran: the Illusion of Power* (Croom Helm, London, 1978), pp. 176-7.

30. This assessment of Taraki was communicated to the author in conversations with several persons who had had the opportunity of observing the President at close quarters over varying periods. It appears to have been one of the underlying factors in the developing quarrel between Taraki and Amin and explains Amin's alleged outburst (according to one 'eye-witness' account) during the fatal confrontation on 14 September, when Amin called Taraki an incompetent old wreck and called on him to resign (*Der Spiegel*, 7 Jan. 1980).

31. *KT*, 4 May 1979.

32. *KT*, 29 July 1979.

33. *KT*, 11 Aug. 1979.

34. *KT*, 15 Aug. 1979.

35. *KT*, 12 Aug. 1979.

36. *KT*, 27 Aug. 1979.

37. The problems for the USSR were illustrated by a strongly worded speech by the US Presidential National Security Adviser Zbigniew Brzezinski on American global military power. Although designed primarily to mollify internal opposition to SALT II it contained a clear warning to Moscow: 'The US pursued prudent policies during some recent upheavals the consequences of which were not of indifference to us and we expect others similarly to abstain from intervention and from efforts to impose alien doctrines on deeply religious and nationally conscious peoples.' Zbigniew Brzezinski, 'American Power and Global Change', (text) United States International Communication Agency, *East Asia and Pacific Wireless File*, 2 August 1979; see also report of interview of a senior Soviet official with *Der Spiegel*, 28 Jan. 1980.

38. *New York Times*, 23 July 1979, p. 1, *Bangkok Post*, 24 July 1979, *KT*, 28 July 1979, and Amin interview, 30 July, text *KT*, 4 Aug. 1979.

39. See for example NCNA, 9 April 1979, BBC, *SWB*, FE/6089/C/1, 10 April 1979; Peking home service, 16 April, ibid., FE/6096/C/1, 20 April 1979; NCNA, 31 May, ibid., FE/6129/C/1, 31 May 1979 and Peking Radio, 15 June, ibid., FE/6145/C1/1, 19 June 1979.

40. *KT*, 28 June 1979.

41. Interview 14 Aug. 1979, text *KT*, 18 Aug. 1979.

42. 'We are desirous of having friendship with China according to the general laws of the epoch-making ideology of the working class. But unfortunately the Peking radio reflects the other extreme contrary to our good wishes', *KT*, 24 Aug. 1979.

43. *KT*, 21 July 1979.

44. *KT*, 23 July 1979.

45. *KT*, 24 Aug. 1979.

46. Versions of the September 14 affair appear in Della Denman, 'Afhgan Leader's Position Shaky', *Guardian Weekly*, 4 Nov. 1979; *Der Spiegel*, 7 Jan. 1980; S.P. Sinha, *Afghanistan in Revolt* (Hescht Publication House, Zurich, 1980) extract in *Der Spiegel*, 14 July 1980; Kuldip Nayar, *Report on Afghanistan*, pp. 38-9. Though differing in some details, these reports agree on the essentials and can be corroborated in many respects in public sources. Only Kuldip Nayar, claiming that Taroon was shot in cold blood before Amin's arrival at the House of the People, departs to any significant extent from the commonly accepted version.

Nayar cites 'diplomatic sources' as the basis for his story, but none of those to whom the present author spoke put forward the Nayar version.

47. Babrak Karmal's regime subsequently claimed that Taraki had been deposed and later strangled on Amin's instructions, although the confessions of those involved, published in the *Kabul New Times*, 21 and 23 Jan. 1980 are imprecise on important points of detail. One, for example, was unable to recall whether the alleged order was given on 8 or 9 October, 1979. All those involved have subsequently been executed, so the allegations cannot be verified. On 10 Jan. 1980 the *Kabul New Times* also published a letter written by Mrs Taraki to President Carter in which she accused Amin of illegally seizing power, killing her husband (she gave no details) and throwing the family into jail. One exception appears to have been Taraki's sister-in-law who was photographed seated next to Mrs Amin at the President's reception celebrating the anniversary of the Russian Revolution (*KT*, 7 Nov. 1979). Mrs Amin, in contrast, has not survived either to defend her husband or to level accusations at his murderers.

48. There is some doubt about the position of Dastagir Panjsheri who left for 'medical treatment' in the USSR soon after Amin became President (*KT*, 22 Sept. 1979) returning to Kabul a few days before the final Soviet coup and subsequently assuming a prominent position in the Karmal regime. If there was a rift between him and Amin (whom he hated, according to Kuldip Nayar, *Report on Afghanistan*, pp. 4-5) then Amin gave no indication of it. Panjsheri, at least formally, retained his position in the Politburo, although Amin's appointment of *two* new Politburo members in October may be significant. Panjsheri also retained his post as Minister for Public Works, although his functions as Minister were effectively taken over by the Deputy Minister, Eng. Saleh Mohammad Peroz, an Amin supporter who was promoted to full Central Committee membership in October.

11 THE END GAME

For Hafizullah Amin the satisfaction of finally taking up the reins of office must have been overshadowed by a sense of great personal grief and betrayal. It had been a weekend of unprecedented blood-letting. The previous year the Parchamites had been exiled and the Eid conspirators discovered and arrested without bloodshed, and that was an old feud. The split within the Khalq, traditionally close knit, was comparatively new and although relations between Amin and Taraki had been bad and growing worse for several months, it must have come as a shock to Amin to realise that Taraki had been prepared to condone a plot to kill him, and that the Soviet ambassador had been a party to it. Now Taraki lay critically injured and Major Taroon, one of Amin's oldest and most loyal supporters was dead, his body riddled with bullets that had been meant for Amin himself.

Watanjar and his three accomplices had escaped, but Amin moved tanks to strategic points in the city and arrested as many of their associates as could be found in order to forestall any subsequent attempt by them to seize power. He was quickly able to consolidate his position and it soon became clear that he had the backing of the armed forces as well as the party. He had to cope with only one serious mutiny, in the 7th Infantry Division at Rishkur on 15-16 October.[1]

Made increasingly wary by the events of the last few months Amin drew his close supporters around him. Faqir Mohammad Faqir, Deputy Minister of Interior was brought back from his extended visit to Paktya where he had been de facto governor, and appointed to fill Watanjar's position as Interior Minister. Mohammad Zarif who as governor of Nangarhar had effectively contained the counter-revolution in that province was appointed Minister of Communications.[2] Saheb Jan Sahrayi got back his old job as Minister of Frontier Affairs and Babrak Shinwari, formerly President of KOAY, was appointed Deputy Minister. The new President of KOAY was Dr Ghani Wasiq, but Amin appointed his son Abdur Rahman Deputy President.

In his first address to the nation as President, Amin announced that the name of the security police would be changed and guaranteed that in future the organisation 'would never perform any unjust act and will not put anyone in jail without reason . . .'[3] The following day he told the employees of the organisation that '. . . a mere change of name will

191

not be enough. We should change its total nature . . ."[4] The man appointed to head the organisation, now known as KAM was soon replaced by Amin's son-in-law Assadullah who was also Secretary of the Kabul City Party Committee and a member of the Central Committee of the PDPA: the security apparatus would never again be allowed to fall into unreliable hands.

Amin lost no time in having his election as Secretary-General of the PDPA and President of the Revolutionary Council endorsed by the religious establishment in a statement published by the Jamiatul Ulama on 20 September.[5] The following day, after normal Friday prayers, ulema in Kabul met, endorsed the Jamiatul Ulama statement and called for obedience to Amin 'who himself is a Muslim and is born in a religious Muslim family . . .'[6] In the next few days ulema from most parts of Afghanistan issued statements couched in similar terms. In having himself declared a Muslim, a step Taraki had never been prepared to take, Amin demonstrated his determination to cut the ground from under the counter-revolutionary propaganda campaign which condemned the Kabul government as 'atheist'. He followed this up with the time-tested strategy of putting loyal ulema on the government payroll and issuing instructions that mosques throughout the country were to be cleaned up and painted, a high visibility gesture designed to counter rebel propaganda accusing the PDPA regime of desecrating mosques.

Amin also sought to identify himself with the tribal ethos, not a new position for him. His rhetoric had always been more calculated to appeal to the Pashtun pride and sense of history than had that of Taraki and his emphasis on the red of the DRA flag representing the blood of tribal ancestors shed to maintain Afghanistan's independence was an acknowledgement of the power of this rallying cry. He also revealed himself, in one speech to tribal elders, unusually defensive about his Western style of dress, arguing that he wore a necktie because this was appropriate to the office of Foreign Minister which he then held.[7] Once he became President he issued a biography of himself which, as well as studiously avoiding any reference to Taraki, included photographs of himself in Pashtun dress.[8]

While aware of the need to present a modified image to Afghanistan's predominantly conservative rural population, Amin was also alive to the necessity of making the machinery of government work effectively. One of his most important moves and the commitment by which he himself set greatest store was the establishment of collective leadership, the promise that 'from now on there will be no one-man government . . .'

espite his adoption of a somewhat caliphal style, not only in the amiatul Ulama directive to obey him personally, but in the issue of the rst few decrees in his own name, the evidence suggests that he was far ore prepared to delegate than his predecessor.

From the start he set a cracking pace for his ministers. Cabinet eetings under Taraki had rarely lasted more than three hours. Under min the norm was four-and-a-half to five hours. At the first working ssion of the Council of Ministers after he became President, Amin drew the attention of the members of the Council to their grave duties' nd the need to improve the conduct of affairs in the various minis- ries.[9] Three days later the Council held a special meeting to catch up with the backlog of work. One of the main subjects discussed was the uidelines for the implementation of the new Five Year Plan. Almost three months earlier Amin had drawn attention to existing problems nd called for a more flexible approach to planning in order to avoid rrors[10] but it was only now that he was able to elicit a positive res- ponse. The following day a hitherto dormant Economic Commission net under the chairmanship of Shah Wali, the Deputy Prime Minister, nd agreed that it should henceforth meet regularly in the interests of mproved financial administration. The Economic Commission, which was in effect a high-powered subcommittee of the Council of Ministers, ncluding the Ministers of Public Health, Finance, Mines and Industries, Planning and Commerce, became one of the most active organs of overnment.[11]

Another of Amin's early initiatives was the establishment of a commission to draft a constitution for the Democratic Republic of Afghanistan. Although nearly eighteen months had passed since the April 1978 revolution, Taraki had seemed willing to postpone indefi- nitely the question of a constitution. On 24 September, a week after his election to the General-Secretaryship of the PDPA, Amin put before the Politburo a proposal for the establishment of a Constitution Drafting Commission. On 10 October the 58 member Commission, divided into seven working committees, and comprising a wide cross- section of Afghan society, was approved by a special session of the Revolutionary Council and its inaugural session opened by Amin, who laid down the broad guidelines on which it was to work. The views and proposals of various groups were to be solicited in the preparation of the document.[12]

The drawing up of a constitution was only one of the objectives encompassed by the new slogan 'Security, Legality and Justice' on which Amin laid so much emphasis. It is this aspect of his brief presidency which is perhaps most controversial. In his address to the nation on 17 September Amin pledged that a team would be appointed immediately to release any people imprisoned without reason, and his second decree of 23 September established an Extraordinary Revolutionary Court to provide a vehicle for the justice he sought to implement. Many of those imprisoned in the preceding months were released and their release reported daily in the Kabul press. On 6 October he issued another decree commuting the death sentences passed on two of the Eid conspirators, Qadir and Kishtmand to 15 year gaol terms, and reducing the 20 year prison sentence awarded Rafie to 12 years.[13]

On 22 October Amin convened a Plenum of the PDPA Central Committee, in part to ratify the measures he had undertaken since he assumed the General-Secretaryship of the party, but more especially to ratify changes in the party organisation itself. The Central Committee had not been regularly consulted under Taraki's leadership. It had in fact met only once, on 27 November 1978 and had not reconvened until it met to elect Amin in September 1979. It was proposed that the Central Committee should meet more frequently, and on a regular basis. The Plenum also approved amendments to the PDPA charter, proposed by the Politburo, the details of which were not published.

There were important changes in the membership of both the Politburo and the Central Committee itself. Jauzjani was promoted to full Politburo membership to fill the vacancy left by the death of Taraki announced on 9 October, and an additional member, Abdurrashid Jalili was elected, bringing total Politburo membership to eight. Changes in the Central Committee were more drastic, with the addition of twelve new full members and seven new alternate members. Most of them were close supporters of Amin, reflecting his determination to reinforce his position in the central organs of the party. Suleiman Laeq, sacked from the Politburo the previous November, was expelled from membership of the Central Committee.

Changes were also made in the Secretariat, with the election of Hashemi, Alemyar and Gul Nawaz. Under Amin's leadership the role of the Secretariat was upgraded, and formal meetings of this group came to play an important part in the day-to-day functioning of the PDPA through November and December.[14]

The Central Committee Plenum was followed on 23 and 24 October with meetings of the Revolutionary Council, which Amin also appears to have planned to revitalise. The meeting on 10 October had been a brief and formal session to approve the appointment of the Constitutional Commission. These later sessions of the Revolutionary Council

pear to have been convened in order to ratify other measures under-
ken by the government since Amin's election to the Presidency. An
mportant move was the appointment of the members of the Politburo
the Presidium of the Revolutionary Council, a measure designed to
irther integrate party and government organs and thereby overcome
ie administrative problems of the previous months which had arisen
om lack of co-ordination. The Revolutionary Council was also called
n to amend Article 11 of Decree No. 3, introduced by Taraki the
revious March when he separated the offices of President and Prime
finister, to bring the law regulating the Revolutionary Council and
overnment into line with Amin's decision to revert to the previous
rrangement whereby both offices were held by the same individual.

Amin also presented to the Revolutionary Council the new ten-year
ocio-economic plan, with revised targets for the first Five Year Plan.
he Soviet Union (which had finally agreed to reschedule Afghanistan's
ebt) and other socialist countries were to contribute 66 per cent of
ie finance during the first five years, a measure of Afghanistan's heavy
ependence on the USSR.[15]

One of Amin's most important initiatives was the establishment of a
Tational Organisation for the Defence of the Revolution (NODR).
lthough the Politburo had decided to set up such an organisation at
ie end of June, Taraki had taken no further action. At the end of
eptember Amin appointed a steering committee under the chairman-
nip of Jauzjani, and including Alemyar, Katawazi, Assadullah Amin
nd Peroz to set up the basic organisation and prepare for the first
lenary session of the NODR which eventually met on 5 December.
he aim of the NODR was to co-ordinate the activities of the various
roups and organisations which had been established to mobilise mass
upport for the government. It was in effect a broad national front, as
hat concept was interpreted by the Khalq. The object was not to draw
ther political groups into a power-sharing arrangement with the PDPA
ut rather to encourage other classes and social groups to participate
n the revolutionary process under PDPA leadership.[16]

As well as turning his formidable organisational skills to the estab-
shment of a workable and working revolutionary administration and
oing over to the offensive in the propaganda campaign against the
ounter-revolutionaries, Amin also launched a vigorous military
ampaign against them at the end of October. Early in his presidency
e had renewed the government's amnesty offer to those tribesmen
vho had joined the rebels. His military strategy involved a massive
hrust into Ghazni and Paktya in order to break the back of the most

formidable of the counter-revolutionary forces, those of Syed Ahmed
Gailani and to regain control of the countryside of both provinces
before the onset of winter inhibited military activity, leaving the rebel
in a dominant position in these regions for the duration of the cold
weather. Another important objective was to secure control of timber
producing areas and the roads to Kabul so that vital wood supplies
got through before the capital slowly froze under the first winter snow
which usually fell in November.

Amin's military campaign was largely successful. Although the
Western media were reluctant to admit it, sections of the Indian press
were more frank:

> The rebels were pushed out of Paktia to the hills bordering Pakistan
> . . . Another offensive, supported by tanks, was mounted at Ghazni
> about 150 km. south of Kabul, and successfully completed . . . As i
> in confirmation of the completion of the operation, Kabul television
> put out a programme in which scores of trucks laden with wood
> from Paktia were shown arriving . . .[17]

This assessment was endorsed by members of the Gailani group, in
conversations with London *Times* reporter Stephen Taylor: 'They say
that they have learnt a lesson from the recent government offensive in
Paktia in which they suffered serious reverses . . .'[18]

The same group also obliquely acknowledged that the government's
renewed amnesty was beginning to show positive results: 'The Afghan
rebel leader said that the Russians had been "buying" loyalty of some o
the warlike tribes in the Khyber pass area and had turned them against
the Moslem forces that rebelled against the Amin government . . .'[19]

Counter-revolutionary organisation was also apparently breaking
down elsewhere. A British television cameraman, Nick Downey, who
spent the last four months of 1979 with rebels in Kunar province
supposedly one of the key centres of the insurgency, reported that the
rebels were 'leaderless, bitterly divided and fought mainly for loot'.[20]

Although the rebels were still able to mount guerrilla raids from
Pakistan territory these reports suggest that Amin had arrested the
government's retreat. Even US sources subsequently acknowledged that
in December 1979 'We did not believe Amin was in any danger from
the rebels.'[21] The reports also underline the rebels' dependence on sanc
tuary in Pakistan and the importance for them of continued tension
between Pakistan and Afghanistan.

One of Amin's first priorities as President was to disentangle the web

Afghan-Pakistan diplomacy and attempt to improve relations which ad steadily deteriorated since the 1978 revolution. Relations were aditionally uneasy on account of the Pashtunistan issue. In the langu-e of the Pashtunistan dispute Amin's and Taraki's statements calling r a peaceful solution to the 'only political problem' between the two ountries suggested that they did not intend to push the issue, an npression reinforced by the low key treatment of Pashtunistan Day, 1 August, in 1978 and 1979. From Pakistan's point of view, however, ay mention of the dispute, the existence of which Pakistan formally fuses to recognise, was regarded as a hostile act.

Early statements by Pakistani officials revealed Islamabad's hostility the new regime in Kabul, and this was confirmed as the Afghan unter-revolutionaries were permitted to organise and operate from akistan territory within weeks of the Afghan revolution. Pakistan's fusal to permit Afghan transit trade with India to pass through akistan overland and Afghanistan's refusal to support Pakistan's bid join the Non-Aligned Movement provided further confirmation of e increasingly difficult relationship between the two.

High level diplomatic contacts were few and unproductive. In June 978 Hafizullah Amin met Agha Shahi, Foreign Affairs Adviser to the akistan President, at the United Nations. While the meeting appeared micable, with both evincing a desire for a settlement of differences, gha Shahi encountered some criticism from conservative circles in akistan on his return. In September that year General Zia paid a brief nofficial visit to Kabul en route to Iran. While Taraki accepted an vitation to pay a return visit to Pakistan, no date was set and Amin let be known privately that he considered Zia's visit useless.[22]

As the tension mounted through the summer of 1979 the situation vas exacerbated by the personalities of two key figures, Pakistan's mbassador to Kabul, Riaz Piracha and Afghanistan's Deputy Foreign linister, Shah Mohammad Dost. A highly skilled and experienced iplomat, Piracha was bitterly anti-communist and temperamentally nsuited to the tensions of a 'front-line' embassy and the role of rouble-shooter. His relations with Amin were especially bad. In terms f Afghan-Pakistan relations his appointment to Kabul had unfortu-ate repercussions. His withdrawal after Amin became President was nevitable and his subsequent appointment to an influential position n the Foreign Ministry in Islamabad was scarcely calculated to improve he situation.

On the Afghan side the decision to send Shah Mohammad Dost to slamabad in June was equally unfortunate. A Parchamite, Dost had

little incentive to take any action which would strengthen Amin's position and relieve the problems of the Khalqi regime.[23]

Through July and August an incident relating to a Pakistani diplomatic officer who, according to Afghan authorities was a spy who
defected but who, according to Pakistani official sources was kidnapped, drugged and then made to appear on Kabul television denoun-
cing the Pakistan government, brought relations to a new low. According to Pakistani sources, Taraki attempted to place the blame for the
incident on Amin whom he claimed he could not control, and who had
arranged the 'kidnapping' without his knowledge.[24] Whatever the truth
of the matter the incident demonstrates the extreme tension existing
between Islamabad and Kabul. Taraki's attempt to discredit Amin in his
dealings with the Pakistanis also illustrates the extent to which relations
between the two men had deteriorated.

Another factor complicating relations between Afghanistan and
Pakistan was the divergence of opinion in Pakistani official circles
regarding Amin. One group, who appear to have had the ear of the
President, saw Amin as a 'hardliner' and believed that Pakistan's
interests would be best served by dealing directly with Taraki. This
strategy culminated in talks between General Zia and Taraki at the
Non-Aligned Summit in Havana in September, during which some kind
of agreement appears to have been reached. Taraki's replacement by
Amin a few days later was therefore a blow to Pakistani diplomacy
and General Zia openly expressed his disappointment.[25]

Another group within Pakistan saw Amin as a Marxist purist who
realised that the nationalist claims inherent in the Pashtunistan question
were incompatible with the more important demands of proletarian
internationalism. They believed that he was therefore more likely to
accept a settlement of the border dispute as part of an overall agreement including some action by Islamabad to curb the activities of the
counter-revolutionaries operating inside Pakistan. They also believed
that Amin was committed to maintaining the independence of the
Afghan revolution against Soviet intervention, and argued that his
overtures to Pakistan, both before and after he became President were
genuine and should be taken seriously. They were however in a
minority and were unable to convince Pakistan's decision-makers, who
continued to regard Amin with suspicion as a 'hardliner'.

At the same time there was a degree of ambivalence in Amin's own
position. Both he and Taraki were committed to ending Pashtun dominance in Afghanistan and frequently cited 'narrow-minded nationalism'
as one of the enemies of the revolution, but in his efforts to appeal to

the tribesmen Amin's rhetoric was much less restrained than that of Taraki who on one occasion referred to 'the people of Afghanistan and other Pashtuns and Baluchis' thereby explicitly acknowledging that these people were not Afghans. However, when challenged by a Pakistani journalist, Amin denied that his reference to 'our people' living between the Abasin (Indus) and the Oxus represented a territorial claim to that part of Pakistan west of the Indus, saying that he merely meant that the people involved, many of them nomads, were free to regard Afghanistan as their home.[26]

Another problem for the 'Afghan lobby' in Islamabad was Amin's open alignment with the anti-Zia forces in Pakistan. Like many others, Amin appears to have believed that General Zia would not long survive the execution of Bhutto and he sought to supplement his so far unproductive diplomacy with a direct appeal to the Pakistani opposition. While he denied that his references to support for the Afghan revolution from the 'toiling Muslims' of Pakistan amounted to an attempt to export revolution, which he described as a 'traitorous act', when asked by the correspondent of the PPP paper *Masawat* if he had any message for the Pakistani people he replied that he sent them messages at least twice a week.[27] At the same time there were reports that a number of Pakistani leftists, including Murtaza Bhutto, son of the executed Pakistani leader were in Kabul and in contact with the Afghan government.[28] Amin seems to have pinned his hopes on the replacement of General Zia's government with one more sympathetic to the Afghan revolution. In consequence Zia's decision of 16 October to suspend all political activity in Pakistan and postpone indefinitely the elections scheduled to take place at the end of 1979 was a critical blow to Amin.

It is likely therefore that it was his ideological commitment to socialism rather than his position on Pashtunistan that caused ruling circles in Pakistan to regard him as a 'hardliner' and to withhold cooperation. The argument that Amin was Pakistan's best hope of keeping the Russians north of the Oxus and that it was therefore in Pakistan's interest to help him consolidate his position carried little weight in Islamabad in the autumn of 1979.

Once he became President, Amin also sought to re-open communications with the United States. He had consistently sought to impress upon the Americans Afghanistan's need of economic assistance, not merely in absolute terms but also as a means of reducing Afghanistan's increasingly heavy dependence on the USSR and gaining greater room for manoeuvre. This policy received a severe setback with the murder of Adolph Dubs, and relations worsened through the summer of 1979.

Amin now attempted to reverse this trend. Shah Wali arrived in New York for the UN Session on 27 September and the same evening had discreet meeting with Newsom and Saunders. This time the American responded positively: early in October Archer Blood, the Deputy Chief of Mission in New Delhi, was sent to Kabul, ostensibly to relieve Bruce Amstutz who was to go on leave, but actually to conduct negotiation with Amin. Blood remained in Kabul for four weeks.

It is not clear what each sought from the other, but the United States was well aware of the growing tension in Amin's relations with the USSR and may have tried to take advantage of this. What better way to do so than to repeat the diplomatic coup that had drawn Egypt into the American orbit in the early 1970s? The indications are that Afghan-US negotiations did not progress very far. Whatever the temptations of substantial US economic aid, it is unlikely that Amin was prepared to follow the example of President Sadat. The Egyptian President had not only expelled Soviet military advisers and abrogated the Egyptian-Soviet Friendship Treaty, he had also aligned Egyptian foreign policy with the requirements of the US State Department and abandoning any pretensions to the establishment of socialism in Egypt had opened his country's economy to the depredations of foreign investors whose goals were more usually quick profits than the development of the Egyptian economic infrastructure. While Amin might have welcomed the development of a situation – the end to counter-revolutionary intervention from Pakistan – which would have enabled him to consolidate the revolution and thus gradually scale down the Soviet military presence as well as providing an opportunity to balance Soviet economic aid with aid from other sources, he at no stage indicated that he was prepared to terminate Afghanistan's military or economic relations with the USSR. He consistently emphasised that aid should be 'without strings'. Given his commitment to socialism, he would have been most unlikely to accede to American demands that he abandon or modify this goal. That this was the case was later confirmed by Archer Blood's comment that Amin 'wanted American aid all right. But he was not prepared to offer anything in return'.[29] It was clear that the United States was no more receptive than Pakistan to Amin's argument that strong, independent and socialist Afghanistan under his leadership constituted their best guarantee against their fears of Soviet expansion.

The American failure to respond to Amin's appeal was and has since been enveloped in a smokescreen relating to his alleged violations of human rights. On 23 July 1979 the State Department issued a statement alleging mass arrests and executions, based on reports that could not be and never have been substantiated. The publication by Amnesty International of its equally flimsy report just three days after Amin assumed the Presidency served to bolster the American propaganda campaign, and Amin received little credit for establishing the machinery which brought the Eid conspirators to trial, or for commuting the sentences on three of them.[30]

Amin had consistently refused to accept Western definitions of what constituted human rights violations and pointed up the hypocrisy of the Western position. With the devasting candour that left so many foreign journalists nonplussed, he told a press conference in July 1979 that there were indeed political prisoners in Afghanistan, although not as many as foreign sources claimed, 'because this is a revolutionary government. Every revolutionary government has its enemies and its friends.'[31] The following week he told an audience of senior academics and education officials that the government had every right to deprive the feudals and agents of imperialism' of the right to political activity because, 'If the right to political struggle is given to oppressive feudals and imperialistic exploiters in Afghanistan to re-instate the feudal system or a puppet regime of the imperialists, this is harmful to the revolution. It is a betrayal of the people . . .'[32] Lest anyone remain in doubt he told the *New York Times* correspondent that 'human rights should be studied separately from the point of view of the toilers, exploiters and oppressors' and that from the point of view of the toilers Afghanistan's human rights record was one of the best in the world.[33] He later denounced the Amnesty International report as malicious propaganda, repeating his assurance that the cases of all prisoners would be investigated by the commission he had established, and that 'no one will remain untried'.[34]

Nevertheless the American media campaign against the Afghan government continued, giving prominence to sensational stories even while admitting that they could not be confirmed.[35] Official American sources were equally irresponsible. The *Country Reports on Human Rights Practices for 1979* published by the US Congress in February 1980 repeated most of the accusations made by critics of the PDPA over the previous year, and even included Babrak Karmal's assertion 'that "tens of thousands" of Afghans were executed under former President Amin'. The American report contained sweeping generalisations from 'reliable sources' but was unable to provide evidence of specific instances of atrocities which could be documented or checked. Perhaps the most revealing aspect of the report, demonstrating American priorities in terms of human rights, was that in the six pages devoted to Afghanistan, only one was given over to consideration of the PDPA record (to which the US Congress gave grudging approval) in such basic aspects of human rights as provision of food, shelter, health care and education. The table showing US aid to Afghanistan revealed that the pitiful US $21.6 million offered in 1977 had been cut by more than half to $10.6 million in 1979.[36]

While Amin's diplomatic initiatives regarding Pakistan and the United States encountered difficulties, it was his relationship with the USSR that proved his greatest problem. Two of Amin's most notable characteristics were his tremendous self-confidence and his apparently unquenchable (if not always justified) optimism. He may well have believed that he had finally demonstrated to the Russians that his position in the party and in the armed forces was so strong that efforts to remove him were fruitless and that they would therefore be obliged to accept and deal with him.[37] It is also possible that his judgement was not entirely mistaken. Had it not been for the seizure of the American hostages in Tehran which raised the level of tension in the region and caused the USSR to react to what it perceived as an unacceptably threatening situation, Amin would probably have survived.

Although the Russians had made no secret of their aversion to his leadership, it is not clear at what point and for what reasons they decided that his continuation in office constituted a sufficient threat to their interests to justify military intervention to remove him, with all the costs that this involved in terms of their global and regional relationships.

There was probably a combination of factors contributing to the Soviet decision. The report of General Pavlovsky, who returned to Moscow in mid-October after a two month stay in Afghanistan is widely believed to have been critical in influencing the final Soviet decision to move against Amin. It is also widely believed that his report stressed the unreliability of the Afghan army, and that the USSR in consequence intervened to save an unpopular Marxist regime from destruction.[38] It is more likely that Pavlovsky reported, as did other observers, that Amin's military and political offensive promised to be effective and that if the Afghan armed forces were 'unreliable' it was from the Soviet rather than the Afghan point of view.

While Amin did not, after he became President, publicly criticise the USSR, on 6 October Shah Wali briefed a meeting of ambassadors in Kabul on the events of 14 September, including the role of the Soviet Ambassador, Pusanov, upon whose recall Amin insisted. Given Pusanov's knowledge of and long-time involvement in Afghan politics not least of which was the 14 September affair Amin may well have judged that it was time for 'The Czar' to leave. It was possibly also a serious mistake: Pusanov in Kabul was clearly hostile but his activities could be monitored at least to some extent. Pusanov in Moscow, in a position to exert direct influence on Soviet policy-makers, was infinitely more dangerous. The situation was potentially more serious since the Soviet Embassy in Kabul made no secret of Moscow's doubts of Amin's commitment to socialism, which meant in effect that it doubted his willingness to serve the interests of the USSR.[39]

Apart from Pavlovsky and Pusanov, Babrak Karmal was also in a position to lobby Soviet policy-makers who had already shown themselves sympathetic to his views. The later inclusion in Babrak Karmal's Central Committee and Cabinet of the then Afghan Ambassador in Moscow, Raz Mohammad Pakteen must also cast doubts on his loyalty to his government in his capacity as ambassador.

Soon after Pusanov left Kabul the Tehran hostage crisis broke. The day after the seizure of the US Embassy, Iran cancelled its treaties with both the US and the USSR. This meant that the USSR no longer had the treaty right to put troops into Iran should the latter be used as a base for aggression against the USSR. In the light of American responses to the hostage crisis this was a matter of grave concern for Moscow. Although the US initially played down the possibility of military action, on 20 November President Carter ordered an additional six naval vessels, including the aircraft carrier Kitty Hawk, to reinforce the US fleet already in the Persian Gulf and Arabian Sea. This second fleet was due to reach the region by the end of November. The same day the US indicated that it had not ruled out the use of military force to solve the hostage crisis.[40] The build up of US forces in the region, and the increasingly belligerent tone of US statements together with the unpredictability of US reactions in the face of its humiliation by the Iranians created a situation which when viewed from Moscow, traditionally nervous of hostilities on its borders, was fraught with danger.

In the light of the growing regional crisis the USSR reportedly asked Amin, at the end of November, for base facilities at Shindand, in Herat near the Iranian border. Unwilling to agree to a further escalation in the Soviet military presence in Afghanistan which was not only unlikely to contribute to the security of his government, but would in all probability further antagonise opposition groups and be construed as a provocative act by Iran and the United States, Amin refused.[41] At the same time the KGB, operating in Badakhshan, reportedly captured documents revealing Amin's contacts with the Chinese and the

Americans.[42] The significance of Archer Blood's presence in Kabul in October could hardly have escaped the attention of the Soviet govern ment, and Soviet diplomatic sources have subsequently confirmed Moscow's suspicions of Amin's contacts with China and the US.[43]

In the light of these reports it seems likely that the Soviet decision to intervene in force dates from the end of November. Available evi dence also suggests that it was from about this time that Amin himself realised the extent of his predicament. In his speech inaugurating the NODR on 5 December he attempted to reassure the Soviets, giving fulsome and uncharacteristic praise of their assistance to Afghanistan, adding:

> I deem it necessary to state these facts here because efforts are being made through (the) hostile imperialistic propaganda machine to arouse suspicions about the DRA-USSR relations, distorting the facts about the character of the aid we have been receiving from the Soviet Union.[44]

He also renewed his efforts to convince Pakistan of the seriousness of the situation. General Zia ul-Haq later revealed that from early December Amin sent him frantic messages seeking an immediate meeting.[45] Although Zia refused to go to Kabul, Pakistan finally agreed to set a date for Agha Shahi's long-planned and oft-postponed visit. While the choice of 22 December suggests that Pakistan still did not share Amin's sense of urgency, Pakistani officials have indicated that the main stumbling block was US refusal to take the situation seriously. Until the US made a move there was little Pakistan could do on its own.[46]

Obviously menacing Soviet military preparations apparently began around 7 December. On 21 December US officials revealed that in the previous two weeks more than 30,000 Soviet troops had been placed on alert near the Afghan border and that three battalions of armoured and airborne troops had been flown to an airbase near Kabul. US officials drew an analogy with Soviet preparations for the invasion of Czechoslovakia in 1968.[47] The following day Washington announced that several times in recent days it had expressed its concern to the USSR over the Soviet military build-up, warning that it 'threatened Afghanistan's traditional role in the region as a buffer between the Soviet Union and the pro-Western countries in the Persian Gulf and the Middle East'.[48] The US may finally have seen Amin's point, but it was a case of too little too late.

On 20 December Amin moved his residence and his operational headquarters from the House of the People in central Kabul to Daru-laman on the south-western outskirts of the city. From this time Amin's own movements and the details of the Soviet operation are lost in a mass of conflicting reports. After 19 December Amin made no verifiable public appearances.[49] The Agha Shahi visit planned for 22 December was cancelled because a snowstorm closed Kabul airport. On 23-4 December the massive Soviet airlift into Kabul took place and Amin was reportedly killed on 27 December. One interesting aspect of the whole affair is that no one appears willing to accept responsibility for his death, preferring to place the blame for the murder elsewhere.[50] Whether responsibility lies with Russians or Afghans, it was the large-scale Soviet intervention that made his overthrow possible. The original claim that it was Amin himself who requested the Soviet intervention is no longer advanced even by the USSR which simply claims that it was invited by the Afghan government without specifying which Afghan government.[51]

In the end a set of imponderables remains. What was it that alarmed the USSR so much that it found it necessary to intervene in Afghanistan with such force as to destroy Hafizullah Amin and the Khalq regime? Amin was in no danger from the counter-revolutionary forces or from a military coup. In any case, had the latter possibility existed it could only have benefited the Soviet Union. The most likely instigator would have been Watanjar and he was Moscow's man. It could hardly have benefited the counter-revolutionaries, towards whom the Afghan armed forces had demonstrated their aversion twice before, in 1973 and 1978. Had Amin been as weak and unpopular as is often suggested, it would have been a comparatively simple matter to remove him and install Babrak Karmal who could then if necessary have invoked the 1978 Treaty quite openly himself.

Amin's refusal to give the Russians a base at Shindand, while no doubt annoying for Moscow is not the stuff of which invasions are made. At the same time, given Amin's commitment both to socialism and Afghan independence it is most unlikely that he was preparing to preside over the imperialist dismemberment of Afghanistan as Babrak Karmal's regime later asserted, or that he was preparing to follow the example of Egypt's Sadat and sell out his vision of a socialist Afghanistan in return for American dollars. But in the context of late November and December 1979, the fear that he might do so, combined with their longstanding distrust and disapproval of his policies, might well have persuaded Moscow that the risks of intervention would in the long run be lower than the risk of losing their remaining regional foothold in Afghanistan. The Soviet intervention in Afghanistan was most likely the consequence of multiple miscalculations.

There are other questions surrounding the events of the last week of December 1979. Why, with the party and the armed forces behind him did Amin not make some attempt to resist the Soviet attack? He may not have been able to prevent the USSR achieving its goal, but he could have made victory much more costly for them. He could also have escaped from Kabul and continued to provide leadership for Khalqi opposition to the occupation force. His apparent paralysis in the face of the Soviet build-up is sometimes attributed to panic, but his political track-record was that of an optimistic and ingenious survivor cool-headed and capable in a crisis. He was not a man to panic. It is possible that he was killed or incapacitated on or soon after 20 December, although diplomatic observers in Kabul at the time believe that he was active in his role as President until 26-7 December.

A more likely explanation of his seeming inactivity in the last few days may be found in the conflict between his convictions as a social ist and his cultural identity as a Pashtun. A realist, he probably recog nised that any attempt to resist the Soviet invasion would have been to decimate the Afghan armed forces and the party, the backbone of the Khalq. But to have fled, however justifiable, even essential, in terms of his own assertion only a few months earlier that 'one should live to struggle' would have been totally at odds with the Pashtun ethic which equates survival through flight with dishonour.

In the event he withdrew to Darulaman with a small personal guard who resisted their attackers, hopelessly, for several hours, fighting to the death among the ruins of the lightly fortified residence. Of the fate of Hafizullah Amin himself little is known, neither how he died nor who killed him, although the fact of his death seems not to be in doubt In choosing to sacrifice himself and his personal guard he averted wider bloodshed and, perhaps more important for the future of Afghanistan he saved the Khalq from utter destruction. He also remained true to the Pashtun tradition that requires its heroes to die facing the enemy.

Notes

1. Those arrested were described by the government as members of an 'anti-revolutionary clique' under the leadership of Ghulam Mohammad Farhad, leader of Afghan Millat, *Kabul Times* (*KT*), 16 Oct. 1979, *New York Times*, 20 Oct. 1979, p. 5. A spokesman for Afghan Millat also claimed credit for organising the mutiny in a conversation with the author in Peshawar in January 1981. However,

a senior US diplomat told the author that Afghan Millat had had nothing to do with the mutiny which had been the work of Afghan officers opposed to Amin and that he had only survived because Soviet military advisers had helped quell the uprising. The American was unable to offer any explanation for this curious Soviet behaviour in the light of their previous and subsequent activities.

2. Mohammad Omar Saghari, the Governor of Samangan was transferred to Badakhshan, which had been without a governor for some months although it was the end of October before Hashemi was able to return from his long stay in Faizabad to resume full-time duties as a member of the Council of Ministers. New governors were also appointed to Paktya (Usman), Nangarhar (Sardar Mohammad) and Samangan (Karim Nanjo), *KT*, 20 Sept. 1979.

3. *KT*, 18 Sept. 1979.

4. *KT*, 22 Sept. 1979. After the April Revolution the organisation had been named the Afghanistan de Gatto Satonki Idara (Administration for the Protection of Afghanistan's Interests), known as AGSA. The name was changed by Amin to De Kargarano Astekhbarati Moassessa (Workers' Intelligence Agency), referred to as KAM.

5. They declared that 'obeying his orders and instructions as the brave chief ruler of the Islamic society of Afghanistan is *Farz* (obligation) to every patriot and Muslim of Afghanistan according to the provision of the sacred verse of the Holy Koran which says Obey God, his Prophet and your rulers. Any disobedience to his instructions is against God's will and Islamic teachings . . .' (*KT*, 20 Sept. 1979).

6. *KT*, 22 Sept. 1979.

7. *KT*, 7 June 1979.

8. Democratic Republic of Afghanistan, Ministry of Information and Culture, *Comrade Hafizullah Amin's Short Biography* (Publications Department, Afghanistan Publicity Bureau, Government Publishing House, Kabul, 16 Sept. 1979). One of these photographs, said to be taken on the day of his marriage, showed him riding a horse, with his brother walking beside him carrying a rifle, and may well have been genuine. Two others showing him announcing the revolution in April 1978 were almost certainly reconstructed after the event as a half-hearted public relations exercise: after the revolution Amin was never seen in public wearing anything other than an elegantly tailored three-piece suit.

9. *KT*, 20 Sept. 1979.

10. *KT*, 23 Sept. 1979, Kabul radio in Dari, 24 Sept. 1979, BBC, *Summary of World Broadcasts* (*SWB*), FE/6231/C/2, 28 Sept. 1979; *KT*, 1 July 1979.

11. *KT*, 24 Sept. 1979.

12. *KT*, 16 Oct. 1979. Initially Amin hoped that the Commission would complete its task in time for the fifteenth anniversary of the founding of the PDPA on 1 January 1980, but this was an over-ambitious target and his advisers persuaded him that the second anniversary of the revolution, in April 1980, would be a more realistic date for the presentation of the new constitution. Interview with French journalist, 29 Oct. 1979, text, *KT*, 4 Nov. 1979.

13. Kabul radio in Dari, 6 Oct. 1979, BBC, *SWB*, FE/6240/C2/1, 9 Oct. 1979

14. For report of PDPA Central Committee Plenum, see *KT*, 23 Oct. 1979. A full list of Politburo members as such was never published, although they were from time to time identified, see for example *KT*, 6 Dec. 1979. At this time the Politburo probably numbered eight: Amin, as Secretary-General, Shah Wali, Misaq, Zeary, Panjsheri, Soma, Jauzjani and Jalili. The Agence France Presse report broadcast by Karachi radio to the effect that a new 80 member Politburo had been appointed (BBC, *SWB*, FE/6256/C/2, 24 Oct. 1979) appears to be unfounded. It may perhaps have referred to the Central Committee, and if so

probably included full and alternate members, although again no complete list
was published by the Afghan government. New full members of the Central
Committee were Faqir Mohammad Faqir, Saleh Mohammad Peroz, Gul Nawaz,
Assadullah Amin, Lt. Col. Mohammad Yaqub (the Chief of General Staff), Omar
Saghari, Mir Ahmad Gerbuz, Ahmad Shah, Mohammad Salem Masoodi, Guldad
and Khanmir Ghafari, Nazifullah Nahzat, Hassan Gul Wafa Kargar, Bashir
Basharyar and Fateh Gul Mohammad.

15. For a report of the Revolutionary Council meeting, see *KT*, 24 and 25
Oct. 1979.

16. The leading role of the PDPA was demonstrated by the election of Amin
as President and the inclusion of Politburo and several Central Committee
members in the presidium of the first plenary session of the NODR. Other groups
represented included Workers' Unions, Agricultural Co-operatives, Assisting Funds,
KOAY and KOAW, the Jamaitul Ulama, local Committees for the Defence of the
Revolution, faculty members of Kabul University, students, teachers, writers,
artists and national traders. A 35 member Central Council was appointed with
Abdul Ahad Wolesi, a member of the Central Committee and former Governor
of Balkh as Vice-President. *KT*, 6 Dec. 1979.

17. *Indian Express*, 11 November 1979; see also however AFP correspondent
Jean-Francois Le Mounier, 8 Nov. 1979, BBC, *SWB*, FE/6268/C1/2, 10 Nov.
1979.

18. Stephen Taylor, 'Afghan Rebels Waiting for Their Own Ayatollah', *The
Times*, 20 Nov. 1979.

19. Zia Khan Nassry, interview. Drew Middleton, 'Soviet Display of Flexibility',
New York Times, 28 Dec. 1979. Nassry himself is something of an enigma. An
Afghan-born US citizen his personal card gave his business address as Khiber
International Marketing Consultant, New York. But a check of the New York
telephone directory reveals no such entry. In conversation with the author in
April 1979 he made it clear that his contacts were with the Waziri tribes and soon
after the government's successful offensive in Paktya he apparently broke with
Gailani and joined forces with a Waziri leader from Paktya. Sometime during 1980
he disappeared. Soviet and Afghan sources imply Nassry had CIA connections. In
conversations with the author in late 1980 and early 1981 American diplomatic
and Voice of America personnel, Afghan exiles and Pakistani officials went out of
their way to attempt to discredit Nassry, describing him as a 'crook' and 'a complete fraud' who had taken in many Western journalists, including an old and
experienced *New York Times* correspondent. Both American and Afghan sources
claimed that Nassry had been killed inside Afghanistan by other Afghan rebels
who had 'seen through him'. When asked in what way Nassry had shown himself
to be 'a crook and a fraud', these sources were unable to give precise replies.
Pakistani authorities make no comment on his whereabouts, merely stating that
he was expelled from Pakistan. When the author asked how being a crook and a
fraud (if indeed he was) distinguished Nassry in any way from other Afghan
counter-revolutionary politicians in Pakistan, she was told: 'He went round saying
too many of the wrong things.' In 1981 he was arrested and imprisoned in Tehran
by the Iranian authorities who claimed he was a CIA agent.

20. *The Times*, 31 Dec. 1979.

21. Conversation with the author, 1980. That this was indeed the American
assessment of the situation in Afghanistan in late 1979, was confirmed by other
diplomatic sources.

22. Diplomatic sources. See also *KT*, 8 June 1978; *Dawn*, 7 June 1978,
Nawa-i-Waqt, 10 June 1978 (*Urdu Press Summary*, (*UPS*), Australian Embassy,
Islamabad).

23. Although Dost reported that his talks in Islamabad had been 'fruitful' (*KT*,

4 July 1979) Pakistani officials reported that he had nothing new to offer and nothing was achieved. The author was told that Dost later tacitly admitted that he had sabotaged the Afghan diplomatic intitiative.

24. Pakistani diplomatic sources.

25. Seymour Topping, 'Zia Denies Pakistan Builds Nuclear Bomb and Urges US to Resume Aid', *New York Times*, 23 Sept. 1979, p. 14. One Pakistani view of Amin is illustrated by the following report from the Indian journalist Anthony Mascarenhas of the London *Sunday Times*: '"No one could believe anything Amin said", a Pakistani diplomat explained, "He was the most treacherous of a very bad lot. Trusting him was just not on."' (*The Age* (Melbourne), 5 Jan. 1981).

26. For Taraki's statement see *KT*, 28 July 1979. Amin's repudiation of any territorial claim was reported *KT*, 4 Aug. 1979. Amin's statement, when he assumed the Presidency that 'History has clearly shown that wherever any ruler of Afghanistan wanted to make a secret deal over the national issue of the people of Pashtun and Baluch, he has been eliminated disgracefully', (*KT*, 18 Sept. 1979) seems to confirm that Taraki was prepared to take a softer line on this issue than Amin, and has been used to effect by Amin's opponents in Pakistan. It also raises the question of what passed between Taraki and Zia during their meeting in Havana a few days earlier. Those in Pakistan official circles who regarded Amin as more reasonable on the Pashtunistan issue argue that his 17 September statement quoted above was made in order to cover himself and further discredit Taraki. Kuldip Nayar however claims that the former Indian Foreign Minister, Vajpayee, told him that in September 1978 Amin had proposed to Vajpayee: 'Let us have a secret pact; you take one part of Pakistan and we take the other part.' See Kuldip Nayar, *Report on Afghanistan* (Allied Publishers, New Delhi, 1981), p. 40. This appears an incredible statement for one Foreign Minister to make to another, even if Amin were speaking flippantly. Two things should perhaps be borne in mind: the timing of Nayar's revelation, coming just after the Brezhnev visit to Delhi in December 1980, during which a former Indian Prime Minister, Moraji Desai had chosen to assert that on an earlier occasion Brezhnev had suggested to him that India 'teach Pakistan a lesson' with respect to Pakistan's support of the Afghan counter-revolution (*Times of India*, 6 Dec. 1980), seems designed to embarrass Mrs. Ghandhi's government; and the fact that both the previous Indian government (including Desai and Vajpayee) which was anti-communist, and the present one which reflects the Indian leftist preference for Parcham over Khalq, have an interest in discrediting Amin.

27. *KT*, 28 Aug. 1979.

28. *Nawa-i-Waqt*, 21 Aug. 1979, *UPS*.

29. Conversations with the author, December 1980.

30. *New York Times*, 23 July 1979; *Bangkok Post*, 24 July 1979; *Amnesty International, Violations of Human Rights and Fundamental Freedoms in the Democratic Republic of Afghanistan: An Amnesty International Report* (London, September 1979).

31. *KT*, 7 July 1979.

32. *KT*, 18 July 1979.

33. The exploiters of Afghanistan had lost their privileges and means of exploitation, he went on, and so 'the spongers . . . in other parts of the world are shedding tears for the illegal rights of the toppled spongers of our country'. (*KT*, 6 Sept. 1979). For a somewhat distorted version of Amin's statement, see Michael Kaufman, 'Afghanistan Regime Keeps Control with Core of Loyalists', *New York Times*, 9 Sept. 1979. p. 3.

34. *KT*, 26 Sept. 1979; Kabul radio in English, 26 Sept. 1979, BBC, *SWB*, FE/6232/C/3, 29 Sept. 1979.

35. See for example, Michael Kaufman, 'Afghan Driver Says he Saw Soldiers

Blind and Strangle Children', *New York Times*, 11 Sept. 1979, p. 12 and an
unattributed report, 'Afghans Talk About Torture and Killings by Regime', ibid.,
16 Sept. 1979, p. 13.

36. US Department of State, *Country Reports on Human Rights for 1979* (US
Government Printing Office, Washington, 1980), pp. 707-12.

37. That such was his view is suggested by Selig Harrison's report that Amin
indicated to him, in 1978 that he knew how to handle the Russians and that they
needed him more than he needed them. Selig Harrison, 'Did Moscow Fear an
Afghan Tito?', *New York Times*, 13 January 1980, p. E.23. See also Nayar,
Report on Afghanistan, p. 42.

38. *Observer* (London), 13 Jan. 1980.

39. Information on the attitude of the Soviet Embassy in Kabul was obtained
from diplomatic sources.

40. *New York Times*, 21 Nov. 1979, p. 1.

41. The report is based on statements made by Amin's mistress (unnamed) and
nephew Zalmai, both of whom escaped to London. (Anthony Mascarenhas,
'Invasion Born out of Error', *The Age*, 5 Jan. 1981). This report is borne out by
Amin's exchange with the correspondent of *Al Sharq al Awast*, Adel Said
Bishtawi, on 12 December 1979:

> **Bishtawi** Do you foresee the establishment of military bases by the Soviet
> Union in Afghanistan?
> **Amin** Not at all. No Soviet military bases will be built in Afghanistan
> because we do not need them. (Text of interview, *KT*, 17 Dec. 1979.)

It is perhaps worth noting that the *Bangkok Post*, 13 Jan. 1980, reported that this
interview took place on 26 December: 'While the skies over Kabul shook with the
roar of Russian military transport planes, President Hafizullah Amin gave a relaxed
interview to an Arab journalist.' *Bangkok Post* reported another comment by
Amin in the same interview welcoming Soviet aid in the defence of the revolution,
but omitted the important reference to the Soviet bases.

42. S.P. Sinha, *Der Spiegel*, 28 Jan. 1981.

43. Information from diplomatic sources.

44. *KT*, 6 Dec. 1979.

45. Kuldip Nayar, report of interview with General Zia, 'Will Soviet Troops
Withdraw?', *Indian Express*, 13 Feb. 1980.

46. Conversations with the author. Mascarenhas (*The Age*, 5 Jan. 1980), also
reported that Pakistani officials were urging the US to take the situation seriously.

47. Richard Burt, 'Soviet Buildup Seen at Afghan Frontier', *New York Times*,
22 Dec. 1979, pp. 1, 3.

48. Richard Burt, 'US Voices Concern Repeatedly to Moscow over Afghan
Buildup', *New York Times*, 23 Dec. 1979, p. 10.

49. This was an address to doctors and officials of the Public Health Ministry,
the text of which was published in *KT*, 22 Dec. 1979. He reportedly attended a
meeting of the Council of Ministers on 24 December (*KT*, 25 Dec. 1979), but this
cannot be defined as a 'public appearance'. The *KT*, 26 Dec. 1979, the last issue
to appear before the invasion, carried a photograph of Amin meeting kindergarten
children, though no date was given for the function and the general assumption
that it took place the previous day is not necessarily correct. The same issue of
the newspaper carried a photograph of Amin at what purports to be a Politburo
meeting. Apart from the fact that publication of a photograph of the Politburo in
session was utterly unprecedented, this photograph clearly included several
individuals who were obviously not Afghans. Its authenticity is therefore suspect.
Kuldip Nayar (*Report on Afghanistan*, p. 5) notes these photographs, and the fact

that Amin 'looked as if he was under strain' (although he gets the date wrong, giving it as *KT*, 27 Dec. 1979), but merely concludes, with obvious satisfaction that 'The strong man of Afghanistan was beginning to break down.' Observers in Kabul said that Amin was appearing on television throughout, even after the radio report ostensibly from Kabul but actually from the Soviet Union announcing his overthrow and execution.

50. See for example S.P. Sinha, *Der Spiegel*, 14 July 1980, whose account, ostensibly from Afghan officers, claims that Amin was shot by the Russians while an Afghan 'eyewitness' cited by the *Bangkok Post*, 13 Jan. 1980, blames Watanjar. The *Observer*, 17 Feb. 1980, cites Russian sources in Moscow as claiming that Amin was not executed as Babrak Karmal asserts, but was accidentally killed (they do not say by whom) and that Lieutenant-General Paputin, the KGB officer assigned to protect Amin failed to do so and committed suicide as a result.

51. 'At the critical stage of the revolution the DRA leadership appealed to the Soviet Union for urgent political, economic and military aid. The request was met.' I. Shchedrov, 'The USSR and Afghanistan: The Firm Foundation of Friendship and Co-operation', *International Affairs* (Moscow), Jan. 1981, p. 16.

12 '... AND THE PEOPLE REMAIN'[1]

History is written by the victors and in Afghanistan at the present time the victor is Babrak Karmal. Hafizullah Amin can therefore expect little justice from his old enemy in the evaluation of his role in revolutionary Afghanistan. But a vindication of Amin's political judgement and of his policies is to be found in the adoption of so many of the latter, with so little modification by his successor.

Despite the announcement in January 1980 that the Revolution had entered a 'New Phase', there were very few significant policy changes. There was some reorganisation of the government structure. Babrak Karmal set up his National Fatherland Front, theoretically designed to bring other political groups into alliance with the PDPA. The 53 member Revolutionary Council included several non-party members, and there were three non-party men in the Council of Ministers, one of whom, Mohammad Khan Jalalar, the Commerce Minister, served as Minister and Deputy Minister for Finance under both Daoud and Zahir Shah.[2]

The national flag, introduced by Taraki and Amin, red with a gold emblem, was changed for one in the tradition of earlier Afghan flags, red, green and black. The red flag, with a modified emblem was retained as the PDPA flag, thereby emphasising the difference between Party and State.[3]

These were however only symbolic gestures. Power remained firmly in the hands of the party. The seven member Presidium of the Revolutionary Council were all party Members and Babrak Karmal himself held the offices of President of the Revolutionary Council, Prime Minister and Secretary-General of the party, as did Amin.

Most of the policies for which Babrak Karmal took credit were initiated by his predecessor. For example, he made much of his respect for Islam and all statements and decrees began 'In the Name of God, The Compassionate, The Merciful'. So too did Amin's first major policy statement on 17 September, 1979. After he became President, Amin had the ulema declare him a true Muslim, thereby making obedience to him a religious obligation, a step towards the acknowledgement of the importance of Islam that Babrak Karmal shrank from taking although he too had the ulema endorse his government.

In mid-April 1980 (Saur 1, 1359) the new regime introduced, with much fanfare, a kind of interim constitution, which it called the Fundamental Principles of the Democratic Republic of Afghanistan.[4] It was probably no coincidence that the 58 member Constitutional Commission set up by Amin the previous October was scheduled to present the finished document in April 1980, in time for the second anniversary of the Revolution. The Fundamental Principles follow the broad guidelines Amin laid down, with the exception of passing references to the national democratic revolution and the Fatherland Front, and it is likely that the work of the Constitutional Commission provided the basis for the document produced in April 1980. Provision for a Loya Jirga or Supreme Council, the traditional Afghan consultative body, was anticipated by Amin in October, 1979,[5] and proposals for the establishment of local jirgas or councils were foreshadowed by Taraki as early as May 1979.

Although the new regime criticised the implementation of the first phase of the Land Reform completed in June 1979, there was no attempt to modify it, and the policy announced on the second phase, involving provision of rural credit, establishment of co-operatives and agricultural extension did not differ in any significant respect from that of Taraki or Amin. Nor were any of the other reforms repudiated or significantly modified.

There was little deviation from Amin's defence policies. The mopping up operation in Paktya and the major offensives in the Kunar region and Badakhshan were the next logical steps after his successful Paktya offensive in October-November 1979. Amin had already begun retaining conscripts in the army at the end of their term, and establishing local volunteer defence organisations. The encouragement of local militias by Babrak Karmal and the extension of conscription was a continuation of this policy.

Even his foreign policy, designed to reach an accommodation with Afghanistan's hostile neighbours, Iran and Pakistan, was eventually adopted by Babrak Karmal.

While his political judgement has been vindicated, at least tacitly, the two most damaging allegations levelled against Amin, that he was guilty of extreme brutality verging on auto-genocide and that he betrayed the revolution to Western imperialism are so far unsupported by any evidence. Murder will out and mass murder quicker than most, yet in nearly two years Babrak Karmal has been able to produce nothing more concrete or precise than the claim that 'tens of thousands' died under Amin. No names. No dates. No documents. No graves. No bodies. Just a phrase: 'tens of thousands' dead.

He has been no more successful in providing proof that Amin was a traitor to the revolution. The statement issued by the Ministry of Interior in January 1980 claiming to have discovered documents proving that Amin had agreed to the partition of Afghanistan and the inclusion of Gulbuddin Hekmatyar of the Hizb-i-Islami in the government is utterly ludicrous.[6] Small wonder that the 'documents' have never been published. If further proof of Amin's innocence of treason is necessary, it must surely be found in the attacks made on him by US sources which equal those of Babrak Karmal in their savagery. They are expressions of extreme frustration and disappointment: Amin was no Sadat to be bought or manipulated. Whatever it was that the Americans wanted from him, they did not get it. He remained a loyal and committed socialist to the end.

That such a man should be dead, and with him any hope Afghanistan might have had of making the difficult transition from medieval tribal-feudalism to the construction of a socialist society on its own terms and with its independence and territorial integrity intact is tragedy enough. That his vision of the new Afghanistan and his enormous contribution towards building it should also be deliberately and cruelly distorted is intolerable.

Yet while Babrak Karmal remains in power little else can be expected. Karmal enjoys scant support in the PDPA which at least twice in the past rejected his bid for leadership. The manner of his coming to power, on the back of a Soviet tank, could scarcely have improved his standing in the party or the country. Those members of the Khalq faction who survived the purge which followed the murder of Amin and his closest associates have little choice but to accept the present situation and wait for better days. They have inherited what remains of the organisation built by Amin along with his power base in the rural area and the armed forces, but it is of little use to them in the face of an occupation force of between 80,000 and 100,000 Soviet troops.

There are some among the Parchamites, led by Sultan Ali Kishtmand, who have pressed Babrak Karmal to persuade the USSR to set a date for the withdrawal of its forces. Only Babrak Karmal and the small group around him, who know that their survival depends on the Soviet presence, are prepared to condone that presence indefinitely. Much then depends on how long the USSR is prepared to continue to act as Babrak Karmal's protector. Moscow probably soon realised its blunder, but having committed itself to Karmal in a way that it never did to Taraki and certainly not to Amin, its response has been to persevere rather than admit a mistake and cut its losses.

One day the Afghan Party and people will have to come to terms with the facts, the distortions and the rape of their revolution. When they eventually do so it is very likely that Hafizullah Amin will emerge he ultimate victor.

Notes

1. The life of governments is shorter than the life of people and the life of individuals is shorter than the life of a society.

    The individuals die and the people remain, and if some of us die the people remain, thus for building of the state, death is the continuation of life. If someone dies in the building of his country, he remains alive and his life is prolonged, because his pride will remain. We should want all for our country and people.

    If we do not work for the prosperity of the country, for the defence of the country, for our dignity and pride then our life will have no purpose. If we die then in that case nobody will remember us with pride and neither will we die with dignity and honour. If we die for the sake of the country, independence and in service to the people, then our life will be long and our name remain immortal. The name of the country which remains, and the name of the people which will remain, the coming generations will feel proud of it. They will be happy in this and will take pride in us . . .

Hafizullah Amin, speech to the elders and representatives of Mamakhail of Mohmand Tribes, 10 July 1979, text in *Kabul Times*, 16 July 1979.

2. *Kabul New Times (KNT)*, 12 Jan. 1980.
3. *KNT*, 20-21 April 1980.
4. Text, ibid.
5. Amin interview with French television, 29 Oct. 1979, *Kabul Times*, 4 Nov. 1979.
6. *KNT*, 22 Jan. 1980. Babrak Karmal press conference, 23 Jan. 1980, *KNT*, 27 Jan. 1980.

SELECT BIBLIOGRAPHY

Official Documents

Afghanistan

Government of Afghanistan, Ministry of Agriculture and Irrigation Programme on Agricultural Credit and Co-operatives in Afghanistan (PACCA Project), A.P. Barnabas, *Farmer Characteristics in the Koh i-Daman Pilot Area* (Food and Agriculture Organisation of the United Nations (FAO/TF)), Technical Report No.4, April 1970

Royal Government of Afghanistan, Ministry of Mines and Industry German Economic Advisory Group, *Industry Survey 1966/67-1969/70*, Kabul, September 1971

Government of Afghanistan, Ministry of Agriculture and Irrigation Programme on Agricultural Credit and Co-operatives in Afghanistan (PACCA Project), *Farmer Characteristics in the Baghlan Pilot Area* (Food and Agriculture Organisation of the United Nations (FAO/TF)), Technical Report No.8, Kabul, 1972

Government of Afghanistan and the Government of the United States Agency for International Development, *National Demographic and Family Guidance Survey of the Settled Population of Afghanistan* 1975

Republic of Afghanistan, Ministry of Planning, *First Seven Year Economic and Social Development Plan, 1355-1361 (March 1976-March 1983)*, Kabul, 1355 (1976)

Democratic Republic of Afghanistan, *Basic Lines of Revolutionary Duties of the Government of Democratic Republic of Afghanistan* 9 May 1978 (Government Printing Press, Kabul, 1978)

Political Department of the People's Democratic Party of Afghanistan in the Armed Forces of Afghanistan, *On The Saur Revolution* (Government Printing Press, Kabul, 22 May 1978)

Democratic Republic of Afghanistan, Ministry of Planning Affairs, Central Statistics Office, *Estimate of the Population of Afghanistan in 1357 and Projection of the Population for the Years 1358-1362* (CSO Printing Office, Kabul, Sonbullah 1357 (August-September 1978))

Democratic Republic of Afghanistan, Ministry of Planning, Central Statistics Office, *Statistical Information of Afghanistan 1975-1978* (Afghan Education Press, Kabul, December 1978)

216

Democratic Republic of Afghanistan, Ministry of Information and Culture, *Comrade Hafizullah Amin's Short Biography* (Publications Department, Afghanistan Publicity Bureau, Government Publishing House, Kabul, September 1979)

Aims and Objects of the Democratic Khalq Party, unofficial English translation, Kabul, 1979

Democratic Republic of Afghanistan, Information Department, Ministry of Foreign Affairs, *Undeclared War: Armed Intervention and Other Forms of Interference in the Internal Affairs of the Democratic Republic of Afghanistan* (Kabul, 1980)

Other

US Department of State, *Country Reports on Human Rights For 1979* (US Government Printing Office, Washington, 1980)
— *Kidnapping of US Ambassador Dubs*, Summary of report of investigation prepared by US State Department, *Vikrant* (Delhi) May 1980

US International Communication Agency, *The Global Significance of the Occupation of Afghanistan by the USSR*, 1980

World Food Programme Inter-Governmental Committee, Twenty-Fifth Session, Rome, 22-26 April 1974, *Community Development in Paktia (quasi-emergency), Terminal Report* (WFP/IGC:25/11 Add. B.5, February 1974)
— *Community Development (quasi-emergency), Terminal Report* (WFP/IGC:25/11 Add. B.6, February 1974)

Books and Periodicals

Adamec, Ludwig W. *First Supplement to the Who's Who of Afghanistan: Democratic Republic of Afghanistan* (Akademische Druck -u. Verlagsanstalt Graz, Austria, 1979)

Ahmed, Akbar S. *Social and Economic Change in the Tribal Areas* (Oxford University Press, Karachi, 1977)

Akhramovich, R.T. *Outline History of Afghanistan After the Second World War* ('Nauka' Publishing House, Moscow, 1966)

Allen, N. 'The Modernisation of Rural Afghanistan: a Case Study' in Louis Dupree and Linette Albert (eds.), *Afghanistan in the 1970s* (Praeger, New York, 1974)

Amnesty International, *Violations of Human Rights and Fundamental Freedoms in the Democratic Republic of Afghanistan: An Amnesty International Report* (London, September 1979)

Anderson, Jon W. 'There are No *Khans* Anymore: Economic Develop
    ment and Social Change in Tribal Afghanistan', *Middle East Journa*
    vol.23, no.2 (Spring 1978)

Atayee, M. Ibrahim *A Dictionary of the Terminology of Pashtun's Trib*
    Customary Law and Usages (International Centre for Pashto Studie
    Academy of Sciences of Afghanistan, Kabul, 1979)

Ayoob, Mohammad (ed.) *The Politics of Islamic Reassertion* (Croor
    Helm, London, 1981)

Baloch, Hani 'How Pakistan Destabilised Afghanistan', *Link* (23 Marc)
    1980)

Bellew, H.W. *The Races of Afghanistan* (Calcutta, 1908, reprinted b
    Sheikh Mubarak Ali, Lahore, 1976)

Brunner, Christopher J. 'New Afghan Laws Regarding Agriculture', *A*
Analysis of Several Recent Afghan Laws (Afghanistan Council, Asi
    Society, Occasional Paper no.12, New York, October 1977)

Dawlaty, Khairullah *et al. Wheat Farming in Afghanistan, Cost o*
    Production and Returns (Technical Bulletin no.17, Faculty of Agri
    culture, University of Kabul, Afghanistan, June 1970)

Dupree, Louis *Afghanistan* (Princeton University Press, Princeton, 1980)
— *Afghanistan 1966* (American Universities Field Staff Reports, Sout
    Asia Series (AUFSR/SAS vol.X, no.4 (Afghanistan), July 1966)
— *Aq Kupruq: A Town in North Afghanistan, Part 1: The People an*
    Their Cultural Patterns (AUFSR/SAS, vol.X, no.9 (Afghanistan)
    Nov. 1966)
— *Aq Kupruq: A Town in North Afghanistan, Part II: The Politica*
    Structure and Commercial Patterns (AUFSR/SAS, vol.X, no.1(
    (Afghanistan), Dec. 1966)
— *Afghanistan: 1968, Part III: Problems of a Free Press* (AUFSR/SAS
    vol.XII, no.6 (Afghanistan) August 1968)
— *The 1969 Student Demonstrations in Kabul* (AUFSR/SAS, vol.XIV
    no.5 (Afghanistan), May 1970)
— *Afghanistan Continues its Experiment in Democracy: the Thirteentl*
    Parliament is Elected (AUFSR/SAS, vol.XV, no.3 (Afghanistan) Jul)
    1971)
— *Nuristan: 'The Land of Light' Seen Darkly* (AUFSR/SAS, vol.XV
    no.6 (Nuristan) Dec. 1971)
— *A Note on Afghanistan: 1974* (AUFSR/A, vol.XVIII, no.8 (Afghan
    istan) September 1974)
— *Red Flag Over the Hindu Kush Part II: The Accidental Coup, o*
    Taraki in Blunderland (AUFSR/A, no.45, 1979)
— 'Afghanistan Under the Khalq', *Problems of Communism* (July

August 1979)
— *Red Flag Over the Hindu Kush Part V: Repressions, or Security Through Terror. Purges I-IV* (AUFSR/A, no.28, 1980)
— *Red Flag Over the Hindu Kush Part VI: Repressions, or Security Through Terror. Purges IV-VI* (AUFSR/A, no.29, 1980)
'ry, Maxwell J. *The Afghan Economy: Money, Finance and the Critical Constraints to Economic Development* (E.B. Brill, Leiden, 1974)
;arrity, Patrick J. 'The Soviet Military Stake in Afghanistan: 1956-1979', *Royal United Services Institute Journal* (September 1980)
;raham, R. *Iran: the Illusion of Power* (Croom Helm, London, 1978)
;regorian, Vartan *The Emergence of Modern Afghanistan: Politics of Reform and Modernisation, 1880-1946* (Stanford University Press, Stanford, California, 1969)
Halliday, Fred 'Revolution in Afghanistan', *New Left Review*, no.112 (November-December 1978)
— 'War and Revolution in Afghanistan', *New Left Review*, no.119 (January-February 1980)
Hunter, E. *The Past Present: A Year in Afghanistan* (Hodder and Stoughton, London, 1959)
Jones, Schuyler *Men of Influence in Nuristan* (Seminar Press, London, 1974)
Kakar, M. Hassan *The Pacification of the Hazaras of Afghanistan*, (Afghanistan Council, Asia Society, Occasional Paper no.4, New York, 1973)
Khan, Azmat Hayat 'Afghan Groups Based in Peshawar' *Central Asia* (Summer 1980)
Knabe, E. 'Afghan Women: Does Their Role Change?' in Louis Dupree and Linette Albert (eds.), *Afghanistan in the 1970s* (Praeger, New York, 1974)
Kohlschuetter, Andreas 'The Day of the Kabul Rising (& after)', *Encounter* (Aug-Sept. 1980)
Male, Beverley 'Afghanistan: Rebels Without Policies', *The Bulletin* (Sydney), 17 Feb. 1981
Mironov, L. and G. Polyakov 'Afghanistan: the Beginning of a New Life', *International Affairs* (Moscow), no.3 (1979)
Missen, Francois *Le Syndrome de Kaboul* (Edisud, Aix-en-Provence, 1980)
Nayar, Kuldip *Report on Afghanistan* (Allied Publishers, New Delhi, 1980)
Newell, Richard S. *The Politics of Afghanistan* (Cornell University Press, Ithaca, 1972)

— 'Revolution and Revolt in Afghanistan', *The World Today*, vol.35
    no.11 (November 1979)

Petrusenko, V. 'The CIA and Imperialist Propaganda', *Internationa*
    Affairs (Moscow), no.4 (1980)

Poullada, Leon B. *Reform and Rebellion in Afghanistan, 1919-192*
    (Cornell University Press, Ithaca, 1973)

Schedrov, I. 'The USSR and Afghanistan: The Firm Foundation o
    Friendship and Cooperation', *International Affairs* (Moscow), no.
    (1981)

Selbourne, David 'Conversation in Kabul', *New Society* 31 Jan. 198(

Sinha, P.B. 'The Afghan Revolution and After', *Foreign Affairs Report.*
    Indian Council of World Affairs, New Delhi, vol.XXVIII, no.7 (July
    1979)

— 'Rise and Fall of Hafizullah Amin', *Strategic Analyses*, vol.III, no.1(
    (Jan. 1980)

Smith, Harvey H. *et al. Area Handbook for Afghanistan* 4th edn (U!
    Government Printing Office, Washington, 1973)

Spain, J. *The Way of the Pathans* (Oxford University Press, Karachi
    1972)

Uberoi, J.P. Singh 'District Administration in the Northern Highland!
    of Afghanistan', *Sociological Bulletin*, vol.XVII, no.1 (March 1968`

Vaidik, V.P. 'India and Afghanistan', *International Studies*, vol. 17, nos
    3-4 (n.d.)

Table 1   221

Table 1: Afghanistan 1977: Some Social Indicators

1. Population: 15 million.   Urban: 14%
                      Rural/nomadic: 86%

2. Education
   (i) Total number of schools (village, primary, secondary and vocational high schools):   3,728
   (ii) Number of schools for girls: 273
   (iii) Percentage of children aged 6 to 14 attending school:
   - a) all Afghanistan   24%
   - b) rural Afghanistan   20%
   - c) girls in rural Afghanistan   3-4%

3. Public Health
   (i) People per doctor:
   - a) all Afghanistan   16,000
   - b) Kabul city (55% of total)   3,697
   - c) Ghazni province   49,333
   - d) Ghor province (Hazarajat)   59,333
   (ii) People per hospital bed:
   - a) all Afghanistan   4,980
   - b) Kabul city (45% of total)   1,987
   - c) Parwan province (near Kabul)   30,100
   - d) Uruzgan province (Hazarajat)   48,000
   (iii) Infant mortality: 185 per thousand (Compared with 133 for Egypt, 30 for USSR and 24 for the USA)

4. Motor Transport
   (i) Asphalt, concrete or paved roads: 7,729 kilometres.
   (ii) Total number of motor vehicles (including motor cycles):   60,517
   (iii) Trucks: government owned   2,385
                privately owned   15,289
                     Total   17,674

5. Telephones
   (i) Total for Afghanistan: 20,851
   (ii) Telephones in Kabul city: 12,582

Source: The above figures are estimates compiled from Democratic Republic of Afghanistan, Ministry of Planning, Central Statistics Office, *Statistical Information of Afghanistan 1975-1978* (Afghan Education Press, Kabul, December 1978); and Government of Afghanistan and Government of the United States Agency for International Development, *National Demographic and Family Guidance Survey of the Settled Population of Afghanistan* (1975).

Table 2: Distribution of Land in Afghanistan, 1978

Area of land	Percentage of landowners	Percentage of arable land
1-20 jeribs[a]	83	35
20-50 jeribs	12	20
50-100,000 jeribs	5	45

Note: a. One jerib is approximately half an acre.
Source: Saleh Mohammad Zeary, *Kabul Times*, 19 July 1978.

Table 3: Literacy in Afghanistan

Percentage of population illiterate:	Male	Female	Total
Urban	63.8	84.3	73.2
Rural	83.8	98.4	90.5
Total	80.8	96.3	87.8

Source: Based on information contained in Government of Afghanistan and Government of the United States Agency for International Development, *National Demographic and Family Guidance Survey of the Settled Population of Afghanistan* (1975).

INDEX

Abdur Rahman, Amir 70, 78-9, 84, 90, 97, 173

Afghanistan: administration 40, 58, 77, 81-5 *passim*, 94-9, 111, 113, 118; administrative reform 100, 115-16; agrarian reform 99-100, 109-13, 117-18, 213; agriculture 71, 73-6, 89, 117-18, 161; armed forces 52-63 *passim*, 85, 108, 127, 130, 135, 160-3, 166, 181, 191, 202; class system 37, 52, 72-8, 90, 107, 118-23, *see also* Afghanistan, feudalism; counter-revolution 116, 118-23, 129, 168, 171-4 *passim*, 179-80, 182, 195-7; education 21-2, 24, 28, 83, and integration of religious establishment 97-8, PDPA reforms 114, *see also* Afghanistan, literacy; Amin, Hafizullah; economic planning 92-3, 99-100, 160, 163, 193, 195; feudalism 70, 75-6, 85, 90, 95, 99, 107-8, 111; foreign aid 28, 92, *see also* USA; USSR, industry 90-4; irrigation and water supply 71-2, 74, 92, 112; jirga system 70, 80-1, 213; judiciary 97-8, 114-15, 194; labour: agricultural 75, 77, 85, 161, industrial 37, 94; land tenure 69-82 *passim*, 99-100, 109-12; literacy 113, *see also* NACAI; merchant capital 86-90; per capita income 68, 73, 76; political prisoners 16-17, 137; population 68, 78, 84, 100; religion: religious establishment 88, 97-8, 108, 114, 119-23, 171-2, 192, Shi'is 68, 160, 162, 171, 173, 176, 179, Sunnis 68, 162, 173; security police: AGSA 128, 165, 185, KAM 191-2; taxation: customs duty 86-90 *passim*, company and income tax 87, land tax 69, 81, 87, 99; trade 68, 86-9; transport and communications 78-9, 86-7, 91-3; tribal structure 70, 80-5 *passim*, 95-9 *passim*, 108, 111, 118, 176-7, 192

Agha, Sher 20

Agricultural Development Bank 112

Akbar, Mir Ali 135

Alemyar, Mohammad Siddiq 19n1, 165, 194-5

Amani High School 23

Amanullah Khan (King of Afghanistan) 20, 23, 78, 87-91 *passim*, 98-9

Amin, Abdullah 21-2, 65, 182

Amin, Abdur Rahman 22, 62, 65, 134, 191

Amin, Assadullah 22, 176, 195, 208n14

Amin, Habibullah 21

Amin, Hafizullah, family and early life 20-2, 26-9 *passim*, 38-9; as a teacher 27, 29, 39-40; *see also* Amin, Abdullah; Amin, Abdur Rahman; Amin, Assadullah; Amin, Habibullah; Amin, Khwazak and Yaqub, Major

Amin, Hafizullah, political career (entries in chronological order) 14-18; at Kabul University 26; power base among teachers and students 30; absence from PDPA founding congress 37-8; President of Union of Afghan Students in US 37; defeated in 1965 election 39; alternate member of PDPA Central Committee 38; work among civil servants 40; full member of Central Committee 46; election to parliament 1969 48; rise in PDPA 53-4; base within armed forces 56-64 *passim*, 157, 159, 166; plan to seize power 1976 58-60; excluded from Politburo after PDPA reunification 1977 57, 156; April 1978 Revolution 56, 61-5; Deputy Prime Minister 128; Foreign Minister 131-2, 139n3; role in exile of Parchamite leaders 135; appointed to Politburo, Secretary to Central Committee Secretariat 134;

223

ATE DUE